★THE QUEER SOUTH★
LGBTQ WRITERS ON THE AMERICAN SOUTH

DOUGLAS RAY
EDITOR

SIBLING RIVALRY PRESS
LITTLE ROCK, ARKANSAS
WWW.SIBLINGRIVALRYPRESS.COM

The Queer South

Copyright © 2014 by Douglas Ray

Cover art, "Backwoods Happening" by Hollie Chastain. Used by permission. Please support this artist at www.holliechastain.com.

All rights reserved. No part of this book may be reproduced or republished without written consent from the publisher, except by reviewers who may quote brief excerpts in connection with a review in a newspaper, magazine, or electronic publication; nor may any part of this book be reproduced, stored in a retrieval system, or transmitted in any form, or by any means be recorded without written consent of the publisher.

Sibling Rivalry Press, LLC
PO Box 26147
Little Rock, AR 72221

info@siblingrivalrypress.com

www.siblingrivalrypress.com

ISBN: 978-1-937420-80-2

Library of Congress Control Number: 2014944841

First Sibling Rivalry Press Edition, September 2014

CONTENTS

13   DOUGLAS RAY
       Introduction

21   DOROTHY ALLISON
       This Is Our World

31   SHANE ALLISON
       Predominately Black High School

33   JOHN ANDREWS
       Things Come Back
       To Hell With Love
       The Heart is a Shotgun House
       The Boy Becomes a Stag

39   DERRICK AUSTIN
       Vigil
       After Fat Tuesday
       Canaan
       Breakwater

44   JEFFERY BERG
       Monument Avenue
       Azalea Pink

48   RICHARD BLANCO
       Making a Man Out of Me
       Abuelo in a Western
       Love as if Love
       Maybe
       Thicker Than Country

57   PERRY BRASS
       An Indelible Mark

62   DUSTIN BROOKSHIRE
       Signs

64   JERICHO BROWN
         Big, Fine
         Fairy Tale
         The Ten Commandments
         On Daniel Minter's *High John the Conqueror*
         Another Angel

69   JOEY CONNELLY
         Debris

70   WILLIAM CORDEIRO
         Lullaby
         Wing Night
         Ocean City

75   C. CLEO CREECH
         Mecca

76   JAMES CROTEAU
         Lord, I Am Not Worthy
         Camp Revelation

78   J.K. DANIELS
         Street, Streak
         As the Prodigal Daughter
         What Have You Gone and Done?

81   NICK DEPHTEREOS
         Gay Sex Slaves in Savannah

84   DAVID EYE
         Second Baptism

85   JASON K. FRIEDMAN
         First Love, or Sex and the City

91   D. GILSON
         Riding In Cars With Brothers

94 ELLEN GOLDSTEIN
After the Wedding
Estates

96 MIRIAM BIRD GREENBERG
Elegy

98 ELIZABETH GROSS
Staring Contest
Talking in the Dark

100 JOHNATHAN HARPER
Southern Gothic

102 SCOTT HIGHTOWER
Alexandra's Ragtime Band
Boys Gym
Rural Discipline

105 MATTHEW HITTINGER
The Light, the Idea of Light, Repeats Itself at South Beach

109 DARREL ALEJANDRO HOLNES
Tú
Baptism

114 REX LEONOWICZ
tributaries

116 SASSAFRAS LOWREY
Jacksonville

124 TYLER LYNN
Boxes

131 BO McGUIRE
Evelyn and Willis
Evelyn and Dot
Evelyn and Me
Dot Eating Greens at Top O' the River

138 RANGI McNEIL
    Paterfamilias
    Family Reunion
    Samson
    What I Tell Myself (Concerning Death) When Next I
        Have My Full Attention

142 KELLY McQUAIN
    Brave
    Spirit Animal Chant

147 M. MACK
    Havelock Spots Inverts at the County Fair (Their genders are
        classified as other.)
    Later, at the County Fair

149 ED MADDEN
    Among men
    Wrestling / Fable with shag carpet and bean bag chairs
    Heaven

153 JEFF MANN
    Blue Ridge Heating and Air
    Dear Pastor Dickweed,

156 RANDALL MANN
    Complaint, Poolside
    The Shortened History of Florida
    South
    Social Life
    The End of Last Summer

162 MARY MERIAM
    The Sum of Fall

164 STEPHEN S. MILLS
    Even Drag Queens Are Christian in the South

165 CAMERON MITCHELL
    Pornography for the Gods

174   **FOSTER NOONE**
Fostering

178   **JOSEPH OSMUNDSON**
This is not My Story to Tell

190   **EDDIE OUTLAW**
Coming Out to Jimmy Swaggart in a Pantsuit

197   **SETH PENNINGTON**
Death-Raised

198   **EVAN J. PETERSON**
Heck House

209   **KENNETH POBO**
Deep Into Georgia
This Guy I'm Married To
The Factory, Knoxville

212   **BRAD RICHARD**
Carl
Alex (Flamingo's Café, New Orleans, 1983)

214   **HANNAH RIDDLE**
Georgetta, Alabama

215   **LAURENCE ROSS**
A Partial Guide to Camp: How To Get Dry Again

220   **LIANA ROUX**
Brookgreen Gardens, South Carolina

222   **KEVIN SESSUMS**
Skeeter Davis, Noël Coward, and Eudora Welty

233   **DEL SHORES**
The Story Teller: from *Del Shores: My Sordid Life*

237 ERIN ELIZABETH SMITH
Singing Blue
Considering the Variants

240 WILL STOCKTON
Pat Conroy, Godlike
Revolution
Best Little Boy in the World

243 DAN STONE
Emancipation

244 CHRISTINE STROUD
Accidental Passing
Farmville High

247 BILLIE TADROS
interstate:
intercourse:
interact:
interstices:

252 TC TOLBERT
Speaking in Tongues: How we cannot see the fire by which we've been touched

257 DAN VERA
Balinesia in Virginia
Gay Mythology: How the rivers first flowed
Lucifer

260 ANNIE VIRGINIA
At DOMA's Deathbed

262 VALERIE WETLAUFER
Southern Comfort

264 C.T. WHITLEY
Finding My Southern Roots

275 SCOTT WIGGERMAN
Postcard from West Texas

276 CRISTAN WILLIAMS
Alpha Male

279 L. LAMAR WILSON
Times Like These: Marianna, Florida
Resurrection Sunday
Substantia Nigra

288 CONTRIBUTOR BIOGRAPHIES

299 ACKNOWLEDGMENTS

301 PUBLICATION CREDITS

302 ABOUT THE EDITOR

303 ABOUT THE PRESS

INTRODUCTION
★ THE QUEER SOUTH ★

> *I'm saying this is the South, and we're proud of our crazy people. We don't hide them up in the attic. We bring 'em right down to the living room and show 'em off. See, no one in the South ever asks if you have crazy people in your family. They just ask what side they're on.*
>
> — Julia Sugarbaker, from *Designing Women*

> *What is it? something you live and breathe in like air? a kind of vacuum filled with wraithlike and indomitable anger and pride and glory ... ?*
>
> — Shreve asking Quentin about the South in Faulkner's *Absalom, Absalom!*

1.

Sure, "the" is wrong; "queer" subjects by nature resist being completely defined. "The" (definite article) is overreaching where "a" (indefinite article) is probably better. Queer subjects are slippery and always in flux. And, right at the start, let's come to terms with terms. I use "queer" as an umbrella term to encompass, amongst others, gay, lesbian, bisexual, transgender, intersex, genderqueer, queer, and questioning positionalities. I love Eve Sedgwick's definition of queer in her essay "Queer and Now," "'[Q]ueer' can refer to: the open mesh of possibilities, gaps, overlaps, dissonances and resonances, lapses and excesses of meaning when the constituent elements of anyone's gender, of anyone's sexuality aren't made (or *can't* be made) to signify monolithically." I suppose a region cannot be sexed or gendered, but if we apply this definition of queer to the South's character, I think it fits the dissonances that are so prevalent in dear (?) Dixie. The American South, to me, is similar to what South Africa's constitution says of that "rainbow nation": South Africa is "united in [its] diversity." We think of diversity as that which highlights individuals as different, but when difference is the rule, difference (strangely) becomes the bond. That's been my experience for my entire life lived in the South.

This project came about from a need I noticed as I was teaching a class on Southern Literature and Culture to a group of seniors at a boarding school in Alabama. When I conceived of "units," there were the obvious ones: food, music, religion, Old South vs. New South, the major canonical Southern writers (Agrarians, O'Connor, Welty, Faulkner, Allison, etc.). I wanted to do a unit on "the queer South," as the topic offered me an opportunity to speak about both my academic interests and personal experiences. I thought, "Surely there's an anthology out there that I could use." I didn't want anything purely academic, nor was I looking for a few pieces of short fiction. What I found was a "queer" gap in the publishing landscape. And one that this queer could fill.

The role of "the anthologist" is one that is a constant negotiation of choices, trade-offs, and limitations; that's a pretty awkward position when the idea of "queerness" is all about possibilities and limitlessness. So, I'll concede that this work of love is an imperfect one. Though imperfect, I feel as though (and I hope you do too) this is a worthy step, a hopeful gesture towards providing a voice for queer folks in the South and a characterization of the South as a queer space.

2.

I grew up in Jackson, Mississippi, the son of an independent school teacher and an Ole Miss football player turned pharmaceutical rep. My family is something of Southern Baptist royalty—my great-great grandfather was pastor of the largest Southern Baptist Church in Mississippi for 40+ years, and that was the church where I was baptized, sang in choirs, learned that Hebrews 11 was "the Hall of Faith," that the Bible was "inerrant," that interpretation had one speed: literal, and that "homosexuality" was an "abomination." In that tradition, I learned the cadence of the Psalms, the power of words, the importance of community, the power of convictions and articulate speaking, the ability of music to manipulate emotion, and the importance that narrative and fear play in shaping who we are and who we think we can and should be. I learned, too, that what I know and what I feel can be at odds. In the church, opposites were easily woven together.

I haven't been a fixture in the pews of Baptist churches for over 10 years, but I've watched various characters from my church past come out on social media and have realized that others were queer when I've encountered them as adults. I always wonder what it would be like to compare notes of how they wrestled with (or didn't) their own identities and the teachings of the church—like Jacob wrestling (an obviously fraught battle) with the angel. I suppose my own trauma was complicating my own sense of truth, destabilizing that which was absolute to something that was constructed and slippery. I wanted to believe what I had proclaimed so many times in hymns: "On Christ the Solid Rock I stand / All other ground is sinking sand / All other ground is sinking sand" or "All to Thee, I give my all to thee" or "Here's my heart, Lord, take and seal it / Seal it for thy courts above" or "The Great High Priest whose name is Love / Who ever lives and pardons me." I wanted to abandon myself for and in the truth. I wanted to be fundamentally right and forever saved. Instead, I realized that I was fundamentally queer, that the business of reading embraces a crayon box way bigger than just black and white, that 50 shades of gray is just a paltry start.

3.

I graduated high school in 2004, was deeply closeted and dating a wonderful girl (my desperate hope not to be queer). Partially for fear that my parents would find out that I was gay and reject me, I got a real estate license at 18 in order to have a way to make money, and I accepted an offer to stay in state for college because the scholarship package was such that I would make money each semester. The thought of going to a ritzy, private college to study classics and English, coming out and being rejected (and cut off) by my parents was too much. Gay, alone, and in-deep-deep debt: that was not an option for me. I planned for the worst and created my own elaborate cushion.

This is the fear that can consume in an environment that doesn't seem queer positive or queer inclusive. I should say that my parents are kind, decent, and loving people. They've done everything in their power to give me everything I've needed and wanted. And they've done so. Perhaps my elaborate fears were also based in my wish for them to be protected from the stigma of having "the gay son." It's a subject worthy of conversation in fashionable Northeast Jackson.

Now, 10 years later, I teach at a high school in Birmingham, Alabama. One of the courses I teach is called Queer Literature and Theory. There's a Gay Straight Alliance, and students come out to little or no fanfare each year. I've chaperoned dances where students brought same-sex dates, and they danced together just as awkwardly as the straight couples. The gays will come out, and they'll still not recognize the comma splices in their own sentences. The baby gays are still thrilled to learn about Harvey Milk, Bayard Rustin, and *Paris is Burning*. It doesn't get old for me. Things still aren't smooth sailing for queer kids in the South—far from it. But seeing real people, young people make steps towards authenticity (and be affirmed in doing so) is a total job perk.

4.

Afternoons after school (grades, say, 4-6), I'd come home to a snack of popcorn and *Designing Women*, which reran on Lifetime: Television for Women and Budding / Bloomed Gays. It ran along with such excellent game shows as *Supermarket Sweep* (the big prize being a pair of Geo Trackers) and *Shop 'Til You Drop*. You could say that my middle school TV choices were a clear indication that I would be a lousy Boy Scout or straight man.

"The Ladies" of *Designing Women* were the best priestesses of Southern queerness—camp, sincerity, grace, hair, tirades, shoulder pads, drawls. The issues they tackled were as big as their Emmy-winning hair. While many of my peers were awestruck by Michael Jordan's prowess on the basketball court, I was enamored with Julia Sugarbaker's ability to say, deftly in bless-your-heart fashion, "Fuck off." And, to add to Julia's passion and convictions, I had Suzanne, whose over-the-top, campy Southern Beauty Queen routine episode in and episode out made this queer heart weep for joy. Suzanne, too, was the first person I remember saying "homosexual," and she did so memorably: "home-ah-seck-shal."

When I first saw the episode "Killing All the Right People," which dealt with AIDS as The Ladies designed the funeral for a young gay friend, I realized that there was peril associated with being gay—rejection, hatred, and health threats. This was all before I saw myself as a sexual subject, but my taxonomy of queerness was being formed. My education as a Southern queer was under way.

Throughout those afternoons watching The Ladies, I saw them stick up for women, gays, people with AIDS, fat people, Southerners, victims of domestic violence, and more. They were advocates and unabashedly so.

5.

As I was finishing up graduate school, in the years when *Designing Women* was finally being released on DVD, I was reminded of what's at stake being queer in the South. Two queer people, both dear to me in different ways, committed suicide in my home state (also theirs) of Mississippi. One was 23, the other 20. While the world was saying again and again that "it gets better" for LGBTQ youth, the message was difficult to take to heart in a place that seemed to reject the idea of tolerance, much less acceptance.

I knew from both of these people how difficult high school had been for them—bullying, intimidation, the lack of feeling safe in school. I remember my own struggle to mask or defeat my own queerness at that age for fear of rejection. The questions came to mind: what if things had been different? What if we had all felt safe at such a vulnerable time?

6.

The voices in this anthology are queer subjects who get to take charge of their narratives affected by the South. While queer people have often been objectified in the South by the church, by politicians, and by their families, this anthology gives queer folks control over their ideas, their own words, their own humanity. Experiences are as diverse as the individuals themselves; there's no typical master narrative for Southern Queers. To try and interpret these poems and essays in such a way to represent Southern queerness monolithically would be both an impossibility and an ethical disaster. I'll let them sing themselves.

What I hope you'll walk away with is a more complicated view of the South and the experience of queer people in the region. I hope you'll view the South as a place of possibilities, rather than a lost cause. I hope you'll realize that the legacy of Southern queer writers—from Tennessee Williams, Carson McCullers, Reynolds Price, Dorothy Allison, Truman Capote—continues in these pages.

Yes, Ms. Sugarbaker, I'll parade out these crazies, these darling queers.

7.

As I mentioned earlier, putting together an absolutely inclusive anthology is impossible. Choices have to be made—difficult ones—and those choices make what aspires to be inclusive exclusive. I acknowledge that this anthology, like any anthology, is problematic in its exclusivity. Over a period of about eight months, I received submissions of essays and poems from over 200 people. Now, in this final form, 63 writers have their work showcased; there are 63 different perspectives of what queerness looks like, feels like in the American South.

I ask my students regularly to consider how their positionalities bias their individual epistemology. And I wondered that myself as I had to make curatorial and editorial decisions in forming this book. The choices I made are undoubtedly influenced (perhaps "biased" is more appropriate) by my very privileged positionality as a white, cisgender, middle-class, formally-educated, Millennial, gay male. Perhaps my relatively conservative or traditional aesthetics have unduly silenced more experimental, more generically "queer" modes of writing. I hope that's not the case, and I was conscious of my own aesthetic biases in assembling this book. My goal was to form a book that communicated both clearly and queerly so that its audience, no matter how one may identify, could be inspired to, as Eudora Welty says, "part the veil of indifference to each other's presence, each other's wonder, each other's human plight."

8.

When Shreve and Quentin are having that very queer conversation in Massachusetts about the South, Shreve says, "Now I want you to tell me just one thing more. Why do you hate the South?" To end his masterpiece that explores the nature of history and our relationship to it, Faulkner shows us Quentin:

> "I dont hate it," Quentin said, quickly, at once, immediately; "I dont hate it," he said. *I dont hate it* he thought, panting in the cold air, the iron New England dark: *I dont. I dont! I dont hate it! I dont hate it!*

He's wrestling with the region that so infuses and informs who he is. He's impulsive with his initial answer—almost defensive. Then panic settles in, as he pants the difficult cold. It's as if he is confessing his faith, though through negative identification. Faulkner offers no closure for Quentin here, but we know Quentin's fate: there's a plaque commemorating his suicide on the Anderson Memorial Bridge over the Charles River in Cambridge, Massachusetts, with Quentin's dates alongside "drowned in the odour of honeysuckle." There's no denying the tragedies here in this anthology as well; it is far too common for Southerners to sweep difficult topics under the rug for the easier, more polite conversation. But just as Quentin's declaration of "not hating" isn't an easy statement to decode, neither is the vast array of characterizations of the South that follows.

9.

My father, when he wasn't working, was always fishing—an outdoorsman, surely, and most of all an angler. Though I had little to no interest in fishing (I preferred the smells of department stores to live bait; cashmere to camouflage; loafers to muddy boots), I picked up the vocabulary of fishing. I remember hearing about this reckless, fearless way of catfishing called grappling, a word with address also in wrestling, of course. To grapple, one wades into the murky waters where catfish have their hiding places in order to catch the fish with one's hands. The risks are plenty: skin loss, injury to arms and hands—the consequences of blindly reaching into the unknown. Here, you'll see grappling of the wrestling and catfishing variety, as these writers probe the past, reach for mystery, and examine their relationship to queerness in a queer space.

Douglas Ray
Birmingham, Alabama

DOROTHY
★ ALLISON ★

This Is Our World

The first painting I ever saw up close was at a Baptist church when I was seven years old. It was a few weeks before my mama was to be baptized. From it, I took the notion that art should surprise and astonish, and hopefully make you think something you had not thought until you saw it. The painting was a mural of Jesus at the Jordan River done on the wall behind the baptismal font. The font itself was a remarkable creation—a swimming pool with one glass side set into the wall above and behind the pulpit so that ordinarily you could not tell the font was there, seeing only the painting of Jesus. When the tank was flooded with water, little lights along the bottom came on, and anyone who stepped down the steps seemed to be walking past Jesus himself and descending into the Jordan River. Watching baptisms in that tank was like watching movies at the drive-in, my cousins had told me. From the moment the deacon walked us around the church, I knew what my cousin had meant. I could not take my eyes off the painting or the glass-fronted tank. It looked every moment as if Jesus were about to come alive, as if he were about to step out onto the water of the river. I think the way I stared at the painting made the deacon nervous.

The deacon boasted to my mama that there was nothing like that baptismal font in the whole state of South Carolina. It had been designed, he told her, by a nephew of the minister—a boy who had gone on to build a shopping center out in New Mexico. My mama was not sure that someone who built shopping centers was the kind of person who should have been designing baptismal fonts, and she was even more uncertain about the steep steps by Jesus' left hip. She asked the man to let her practice going up and down, but he warned her it would be different once the water poured in.

"It's quite safe though," he told her. "The water will hold you up. You won't fall."

I kept my attention on the painting of Jesus. He was much larger than I was, a little bit more than life-size, but the thick layer of shellac applied to protect the image acted like a magnifying glass, making him seem larger still. It was Jesus himself that fascinated me, though. He was all rouged and pale and pouty as Elvis Presley. This was not my idea of the son of God, but I liked it. I liked it a lot.

"Jesus looks like a girl," I told mama.

She looked up at the painted face. A little blush appeared on her cheekbones, and she looked as if she would have smiled if the deacon were not frowning so determinedly. "It's just the eyelashes," she said. The deacon nodded. They climbed back up the stairs. I stepped over close to Jesus and put my hand on the painted robe. The painting was sweaty and cool, slightly oily under my fingers.

"I liked that Jesus," I told my mama as we walked out of the church. "I wish we had something like that." To her credit, Mama did not laugh.

"If you want a picture of Jesus," she said, "we'll get you one. They have them in nice frames at Sears." I sighed. That was not what I had in mind. What I wanted was a life-size, sweaty painting, one in which Jesus looked as hopeful as a young girl—something otherworldly and peculiar, but kind of wonderful at the same time. After that, every time we went to church I asked to go up to see the painting, but the baptismal font was locked tight when not in use.

The Sunday Mama was to be baptized, I watched the minister step down into that pool past the Son of God. The preacher's gown was tailored with little weights carefully sewn into the hem to keep it from rising up in the water. The water pushed up at the fabric while the weights tugged it down. Once the minister was all the way down into the tank, the robe floated up a bit so that it seemed to have a shirred ruffle all along the bottom. That was almost enough to pull my eyes away from the face of Jesus, but not quite. With the lights on in the bottom of the tank, the eyes of the painting seemed to move and shine. I tried to point it out to my sisters, but they were uninterested. All they wanted to see was Mama.

Mama was to be baptized last, after three little boys, and their gowns had not had any weights attached. The white robes floated up around their necks so that their skinny boy bodies and white cotton underwear were perfectly visible to the congregation. The water that came up above the hips of the minister lapped their shoulders, and the shortest of the boys seemed panicky at the prospect of gulping water, no matter how holy. He paddled furiously to keep above the water's surface. The water started to rock violently at his struggles, sweeping the other boys off their feet. All of them pumped their knees to stay upright and the minister, realizing how the scene must appear to the congregation below, speeded up the baptismal process, praying over and dunking the boys at high speed.

Around me the congregation shifted in their seats. My little sister slid forward off the pew, and I quickly grabbed her around the waist and barely stopped myself from laughing out loud. A titter from the back of the church indicated that other people were having the same difficulty keeping from laughing. Other people shifted irritably and glared at the noisemakers. It was clear that no matter the provocation, we were to pretend nothing funny was happening. The minister frowned more fiercely and prayed louder. My mom's friend Louise, sitting at our left, whispered a soft "Look at that" and we all looked up in awe. One of the hastily blessed boys had dog-paddled over to the glass and was staring out at us, eyes wide and his hands pressed flat to the glass. He looked as if he hoped someone would rescue him. It was too much for me. I began to giggle helplessly, and not a few of the people around me joined in. Impatiently the minister hooked the boy's robe, pulled him back, and pushed him toward the stairs.

My mama, just visible on the staircase, hesitated briefly as the sodden boy climbed up past her. Then she set her lips tightly together, and reached down and pressed her robe to her thighs. She came down the steps slowly, holding down the skirt as she did so, giving one stern glance to the two boys climbing past her up the steps, and then turning her face deliberately up to the painting of Jesus. Every move she made communicated resolution and faith, and the congregation stilled in respect. She was baptized looking up stubbornly, both hands holding down that cotton robe while below, I fought so hard not to giggle, tears spilled down my face.

Over the pool, the face of Jesus watched solemnly with his pink, painted cheeks and thick, dark lashes. For all the absurdity of the event, his face seemed to me startlingly compassionate and wise. That face understood fidgety boys and stubborn women. It made me want the painting even more, and to this day I remember it with longing. It had the weight of art, that face. It had what I am sure art is supposed to have—the power to provoke, the authority of a heartfelt vision.

I imagine the artist who painted the baptismal font in that Baptist church so long ago was a man who did not think himself much of an artist. I have seen paintings like his many times since, so perhaps he worked from a model. Maybe he traced that face off another he had seen in some other church. For a while, I tried to imagine him a character out of a Flannery O'Connor short story, a man who traveled around the South in the fifties painting Jesus wherever he was needed, giving the Son of God the long lashes and pink cheeks of a young girl. He would be the kind of man who would see nothing blasphemous in painting eyes that followed the congregation as they moved up to the pulpit to receive a blessing and back to the pews to sit chastened and still for the benediction. Perhaps he had no sense of humor, or perhaps he had one too refined for intimidation. In my version of the story, he would have a case of whiskey in his van, right behind the gallon containers of shellac and buried notebooks of his own sketches. Sometimes, he would read thick journals of art criticism while sitting up late in cheap hotel rooms and then get roaring drunk and curse his fate.

"What I do is wallpaper," he would complain. "Just wallpaper." But the work he so despised would grow more and more famous as time passed. After his death, one of those journals would publish a careful consideration of his murals, calling him a gifted primitive. Dealers would offer little churches large sums to take down his walls and sell them as installations to collectors. Maybe some of the churches would refuse to sell, but grow uncomfortable with the secular popularity of the paintings. Still, somewhere there would be a little girl like the girl I had been, a girl who would dream of putting her hand on the cool, sweaty painting while the Son of God blinked down at her in genuine sympathy. Is it a sin, she would wonder, to put together the sacred and the absurd? I would not answer her question, of course. I would leave it, like the art, to make everyone a little nervous and unsure.

I love black-and-white photographs, and I always have. I have cut photographs out of magazines to paste in books of my own, bought albums at yard sales, and kept collections that had one or two images I wanted near me always. Those pictures tell me stories—my own and others, scary stories sometimes, but more often simply everyday stories, what happened in that place at that time to those people. The pictures I collect leave me to puzzle out what I think about it later. Sometimes, I imagine my own life as a series of snapshots taken by some omniscient artist who is just keeping track—not interfering or saying anything, just capturing the moment for me to look back at it again later. The eye of God, as expressed in a Dorothea Lange or Wright Morris. This is the way it is, the photograph says, and I nod my head in appreciation. The power of art is in that nod of appreciation, though sometimes I puzzle nothing out, and the nod is more a shrug. No, I do not understand this one, but I see it. I take it in. I will think about it. If I sit with this image long enough, this story, I have the hope of understanding something I did not understand before. And that, too, is art, the best art.

My friend Jackie used to call my photographs sentimental. I had pinned them up all over the walls of my apartment, and Jackie liked a few of them but thought on the whole they were better suited to being tucked away in a book. On her walls, she had half a dozen bright prints in bottle-cap metal frames, most of them bought from Puerto Rican artists at street sales when she was working as a taxi driver and always had cash in her pockets. I thought her prints garish and told her so when she made fun of my photographs.

"They remind me of my mama," she told me. I had only seen one photograph of Jackie's mother, a wide-faced Italian matron from Queens with thick, black eyebrows and a perpetual squint.

"She liked bright colors?" I asked.

Jackie nodded. "And stuff you could buy on the street. She was always buying stuff off tables on the street, saying that was the best stuff. Best prices. Cheap skirts that lost their dye after a couple of washes, shoes with cardboard insoles, those funky little icons, weeping saints and long-faced Madonnas. She liked stuff to be really colorful. She painted all the ceilings in our apartment red and white. Red-red and white-white. Like blood on bone."

I looked up at my ceiling. The high tin ceiling was uniformly bloody when I moved in, with paint put on so thick, I could chip it off in lumps. I had climbed on stacks of boxes to paint it all cream white and pale blue.

"The Virgin's colors," Jackie told me. "You should put gold roses on the door posts."

"I'm no artist," I told her.

"I am," Jackie laughed. She took out a pencil and sketched a leafy vine above two of my framed photographs. She was good. It looked as if the frames were pinned to the vine. "I'll do it all," she said, looking at me to see if I was upset.

"Do it," I told her.

Jackie drew lilies and potato vines up the hall while I made tea and admired the details. Around the front door she put the Virgin's roses and curious little circles with crosses entwined in the middle. "It's beautiful," I told her.

"A blessing," she told me. "Like a bit of magic. My momma magic." Her face was so serious, I brought back a dish of salt and water, and we blessed the entrance. "Now the devil will pass you by," she promised me.

I laughed, but almost believed.

For a few months last spring I kept seeing an ad in all the magazines that showed a small child high in the air dropping toward the upraised arms of a waiting figure below. The image was grainy and distant. I could not tell if the child was laughing or crying. The copy at the bottom of the page read: "Your father always caught you."

"Look at this," I insisted the first time I saw the ad. "Will you look at this?"

A friend of mine took the magazine, looked at the ad, and then up into my shocked and horrified face.

"They don't mean it that way," she said.

I looked at the ad again. They didn't mean it that way? They meant it innocently? I shuddered. It was supposed to make you feel safe, maybe make you buy insurance or something. It did not make me feel safe. I dreamed about the picture, and it was not a good dream.

I wonder how many other people see that ad the way I do. I wonder how many other people look at the constant images of happy families and make wry faces at most of them. It's as if all the illustrators have television sitcom imaginations. I do not believe in those families. I believe in the exhausted mothers, frightened children, numb and stubborn men. I believe in hard-pressed families, the child huddled in fear with his face hidden, the father and mother confronting each other with their emotions hidden, dispassionate passionate faces, and the unsettling sense of risk in the baby held close to that man's chest. These images make sense to me. They are about the world I know, the stories I tell. When they are accompanied by wry titles or copy that is slightly absurd or unexpected, I grin and know that I will puzzle it out later, sometimes a lot later.

I think that using art to provoke uncertainty is what great writing and inspired images do most brilliantly. Art should provoke more questions than answers and, most of all, should make us think about what we rarely want to think about at all. Sitting down to write a novel, I refuse to consider if my work is seen as difficult or inappropriate or provocative. I choose my subjects to force the congregation to look at what they try so stubbornly to pretend is not happening at all, deliberately combining the horribly serious with the absurd or funny, because I know that if I am to reach my audience I must first seduce their attention and draw them into the world of my imagination. I know that I have to lay out my stories, my difficult people, each story layering on top of the one before it with care and craft, until my audience sees something they had not expected. Frailty—stubborn, human frailty—that is what I work to showcase. The wonder and astonishment of the despised and ignored, that is what I hope to find in art and in the books I write—my secret self, my vulnerable and embattled heart, the child I was and the woman I have become, not Jesus at the Jordan but a woman with only her stubborn memories and passionate convictions to redeem her.

"You write such mean stories," a friend once told me. "Raped girls, brutal fathers, faithless mothers, and untrustworthy lovers—meaner than the world really is, don't you think?"

I just looked at her. Meaner than the world really is? No. I thought about showing her the box under my desk where I keep my clippings. Newspaper stories and black-and-white images—the woman who drowned her children, the man who shot first the babies in her arms and then his wife, the teenage boys who led the three-year-old away along the train track, the homeless family recovering from frostbite with their eyes glazed and indifferent while the doctor scowled over their shoulders. The world is meaner than we admit, larger and more astonishing. Strength appears in the most desperate figures, tragedy when we have no reason to expect it. Yes, some of my stories are fearful, but not as cruel as what I see in the world. I believe in redemption, just as I believe in the nobility of the despised, the dignity of the outcast, the intrinsic honor among misfits, pariahs, and queers. Artists—those of us who stand outside the city gates and look back at a society that tries to ignore us—we have an angle of vision denied to whole sectors of the sheltered and indifferent population within. It is our curse and our prize, and for everyone who will tell us our work is mean or fearful or unreal, there is another who will embrace us and say with tears in their eyes how wonderful it is to finally feel as if someone else has seen their truth and shown it in some part as it should be known.

"My story," they say. "You told my story. That is me, mine, us." And it is.

We are not the same. We are a nation of nations. Regions, social classes, economic circumstances, ethical systems, and political convictions—all separate us even as we pretend they do not. Art makes that plain. Those of us who have read the same books, eaten the same kinds of food as children, watched the same television shows, and listened to the same music, we believe ourselves part of the same nation—and we are continually startled to discover that our versions of reality do not match. If we were more the same, would we not see the same thing when we look at a painting? But what is it we see when we look at a work of art? What is it we fear will be revealed? The artist waits for us to say. It does not matter that each of us sees something slightly different. Most of us, confronted with the artist's creation, hesitate, stammer, or politely deflect the question of what it means to us. Even those of us from the same background, same region, same general economic and social class, come to "art" uncertain, suspicious, not wanting to embarrass ourselves by revealing what the work provokes in us. In fact, sometimes we are not sure. If we were to reveal what we see in each painting, sculpture, installation, or little book, we would run the risk of exposing our secret selves, what we know and what we fear we do not know, and of course incidentally what it is we truly fear. Art is the Rorschach test for all of us, the projective hologram of our secret lives. Our emotional and intellectual lives are laid bare. Do you like hologram roses? Big, bold, brightly painted canvases? Representational art? Little boxes with tiny figures posed precisely? Do you dare say what it is you like?

For those of us born into poor and working-class families, these are not simple questions. For those of us who grew up hiding what our home life was like, the fear is omnipresent—particularly when that home life was scarred by physical and emotional violence. We know if we say anything about what we see in a work of art we will reveal more about ourselves than the artist. What do you see in this painting, in that one? I see a little girl, terrified, holding together the torn remnants of her clothing. I see a child, looking back at the mother for help and finding none. I see a mother, bruised and exhausted, unable to look up for help, unable to believe anyone in the world will help her. I see a man with his fists raised, hating himself but making those fists tighter all the time. I see a little girl, uncertain and angry, looking down at her own body with hatred and contempt. I see that all the time, even when no one else sees what I see. I know I am not supposed to mention what it is I see. Perhaps no one else is seeing what I see. If they are, I am pretty sure there is some cryptic covenant that requires that we will not say what we see. Even when looking at an image of a terrified child, we know that to mention why that child might be so frightened would be a breach of social etiquette. The world requires that such children not be mentioned, even when so many of us are looking directly at her.

There seems to be a tacit agreement about what it is not polite to mention, what it is not appropriate to portray. For some of us, that polite behavior is set so deeply we truly do not see what seems outside that tacit agreement. We have lost the imagination for what our real lives have been or continue to be, what happens when we go home and close the door on the outside world. Since so many would like us to never mention anything unsettling anyway, the impulse to be quiet, the impulse to deny and pretend, becomes very strong. But the artist knows all about that impulse. The artist knows that it must be resisted. Art is not meant to be polite, secret, coded, or timid. Art is the sphere in which that impulse to hide and lie is the most dangerous.

In art, transgression is holy, revelation a sacrament, and pursuing one's personal truth the only sure validation.

Does it matter if our art is canonized, if we become rich and successful, lauded and admired? Does it make any difference if our pictures become popular, our books made into movies, our creations win awards? What if we are the ones who wind up going from town to town with our notebooks, our dusty boxes of prints or Xeroxed sheets of music, never acknowledged, never paid for our work? As artists, we know how easily we could become a Flannery O'Connor character, reading those journals of criticism and burying our faces in our hands, staggering under the weight of what we see that the world does not. As artists, we also know that neither worldly praise nor critical disdain will ultimately prove the worth of our work.

Some nights I think of that sweating, girlish Jesus above my mother's determined features, those hands outspread to cast benediction on those giggling uncertain boys, me in the congregation struck full of wonder and love and helpless laughter. If no one else ever wept at that image, I did. I wished the artist who painted that image knew how powerfully it touched me, that after all these years his art still lives inside me. If I can wish for anything for my art, that is what I want—to live in some child forever—and if I can demand anything of other artists, it is that they attempt as much.

SHANE ALLISON

Predominately Black High School

Travis Asbell getting fucked by Scott Barber
Scott Barber getting fucked by Claude Booker
Claude Booker getting fucked by Michael Brack
Michael Brack getting fucked by Ryan Bruce
Ryan Bruce getting fucked by John Brice
John Brice getting fucked by Lee Conner
Lee Conner getting fucked by Aaron Carroll
Aaron Carroll getting fucked by Jason Casseaux
Jason Casseaux getting fucked by David Chaffin
David Chaffin getting fucked by Michael Chapple
Michael Chapple getting fucked by Jared Casseaux
Jared Casseaux getting fucked by Carlton Crawford
Carlton Crawford getting fucked by Josh Cummings
Josh Cummings getting fucked by Fred Davis
Fred Davis getting fucked by Shawn Davis
Shawn Davis getting fucked by Xavier Dempsey
Xavier Dempsey getting fucked by Dwayne Estelle
Dwayne Estelle getting fucked by James Fuse
James Fuse getting fucked by Chris Garye
Chris Garye getting fucked by Darren Gibson
Darren Gibson getting fucked by Shawn Gregg
Shawn Gregg getting fucked by Brian Gurr
Brian Gurr getting fucked by Michael Hardy
Michael Hardy getting fucked by Grady Harper
Grady Harper getting fucked by Michael Harris
Michael Harris getting fucked by Moise Harris
Moise Harris getting fucked by Andy Harrison
Andy Harrison getting fucked by Eric Hatcher
Eric Hatcher getting fucked by Richard Herring
Richard Herring getting fucked by Brandon Houston
Brandon Houston getting fucked by David Howl
David Howl getting fucked by Danny James

★THE QUEER SOUTH★

Danny James getting fucked by Travis Jones
Travis Jones getting fucked by Scott Joyner
Scott Joyner getting fucked by John Keillor
John Keillor getting fucked by Brian Kelly
Brian Kelly getting fucked by Brent Labounty
Brent Labounty getting fucked by Richard Langly
Richard Langly getting fucked by Abe Lerner
Abe Lerner getting fucked by Richard Lollie
Richard Lollie getting fucked by Brian Miller
Brian Miller getting fucked by William Miller
William Miller getting fucked by Ed Mock
Ed Mock getting fucked by David Moore
David Moore getting fucked by Fred Nichols
Fred Nichols getting fucked by Shawn O' Shields
Shawn O' Shields getting fucked by Willie Parker
Willie Parker getting fucked by Brian Reed
Brian Reed getting fucked by Cleaveland Richardson
Cleaveland Richardson getting fucked by Anthony Whitehead
Anthony Whitehead getting fucked by Leroy Williams
Leroy Williams getting fucked by Titus Williams
Titus Williams getting fucked by Russell Wilson

JOHN ANDREWS

Things Come Back

The Ivory Billed Woodpecker reappeared
without a marching band.

Swamps on the Cache River
return lost things.

I stole his t-shirt
from the dresser,

to bury my face in his scent.
Every night I'm a hound dog.

In the woods around Brinkley,
where a hunter spotted his lost bird,

there must be a hay-haired
boy in his underwear.

To Hell With Love

he was a stag

so deep in rut
none of the trees

could keep on
their bark

I still don't know
his name

just loved
falling down

the oak staircase
his chest

at the foot
of my bed

like all the trees
in winter

took off
his clothes

too soon

The Heart is a Shotgun House

*

no hall

three rooms
rubbing up against
each other

a house without
a backdoor

in the living room
smell every spice

the pots
boiling over

the wind
through the bedroom
window

*

we made moonshine
in the bath

put all the bottles
on the front lawn

to bathe them
in moonlight

left the tap
running

kissed

on the porch

*

I caught him eating
leftover spiced apples
in the midnight kitchen

after sleeping
with a shotgun

you'll pull the trigger

aim for anything
in the dark

The Boy Becomes a Stag

*

some nights he would wear
a pair of antlers

do a little dance

over the bed
his ass

hanging out
of his underwear

*

tins on string

someone's mother said
keep the
deer from eating

all the beets

*

but the deer had spread

trash across the lawn

the pie plates

danced all over

*

last time he was a man
he leapt from bed

all I remember

before dawn

the flash of white
tail off

through the dark

DERRICK AUSTIN

Vigil

Having abstained from flesh but thinking little
else—chasing flesh, piercing flesh, and tiring
of flesh—I sat on Florida's pale, familiar shore.
Then I was dazzled, like Eve on her first morning
cleaved from darkness, by the mane of the sun
and the mane of the man, Walt Whitman.
He asked if I would join him (and I would not)
as he shed the baggy shirt and jaunty hat,
but I watched him jack-knife into hissing foam,
muscle through surf. The sea couldn't have been
warm enough to touch, yet the sun transfigured
the water and the man: black to blue to red,
like lit propane, the sea flickered, flamed,
and Walt rejoiced, neither ached nor burned.

I imagined myself with him: the world tilted
when I tossed myself in. I didn't believe
in total immersion until then, sunlight leafing
the surface, the sky abstracted silver and blue.
Even in the Florida of my mind I could not swim.
Bruised, I was thrown out. Then he stood over me,
face bright like a lantern, and had me drink
the warm sea-drops like tea wrung from the fine,
white leaves of his beard, taste the sea grass,
salt, and sea glass of his soles' travels as he
gifted me the circuits of his breath. He is father
and lover, the best in me I have yet to claim.
I could never touch him, flesh to flesh, instead
we listen to what the waves intone, *this mere breath*—

wind, sea smoke, circling tide, and grey-eyed
Walt Whitman traveling further up this shore.

After Fat Tuesday

Revelers peel labels from bottles
the way some men undo buttons,
slow and insistent and tender.
They could be drinking tears.
Rain falls, slight at first, then
like the heaviest beads
from floats that passed them over.

Canaan
after the BP Oil Spill

See the figs and citrus groves, beehives
like noisy bangles. A couple gathers
oranges sweeter than the word *orange*.
Egrets preen on the riverbank.

You would bask here forever.
Move toward them. So little divides you,
those quiet birds, and buckets of fruit
from the water. If only the river forgot

the land: pickups, houses, picnic tables
hurricanes cover and carry away.
From the other bank look back
through haze brooding over the river,

ambiguous as oil burning off the coast,
at windward trees bent east, where you are going.

Breakwater

In the photograph, my grandfather stands
    in sepia water off Mont Saint-Michel,
barely older than I, having chased wine

and women enchanted by black soldiers
    fresh from the Italian Campaign.
He points at his brother beyond the frame

(killed a year later by cops who mistook him
    for "another black man")
watching lambs whose salty meat is prized

in Normandy, whole racks for christenings.
    You could taste the tide, he says.
Which means what exactly? That he could taste

the salt of stones and locals' tears
    seeking St. Michael's blessing, before
the water's shift, its sudden gallop?

As a kid, he taught me the tide's faces
    on morning fishing trips,
the Gulf eroding the bricked-up present,

gray light opening over emerald waters
    like the camera flash that froze him
in France—one of the few things fixed

in his afflicted mind. When the nurse
    carries in his meal, she takes me
in the hall, asks if his memory's holding.

I shake my head. When it started to go he said,
    most days it's like hearing Marvin Gaye
being shot, the same news over and over,

and I never know if I'm Marvin or his father.
        I take him to the park for an afternoon.
He skips rocks on the river's opaque surface.

Once there was nothing here but water—
        an argument with no winner; a row
of sandbags to reproach the building waves—

where the North Star line rusts on tracks,
        where his wheelchair idles beside me.
The Gulf will wash and sweep us into silence

where grief cuts like breakwaters.
        I don't claim to understand anything—
whether all this will turn into salt or waves

of light containing what we've lost or forgotten,
        where Technicolor flowers spring
and spray the air with oils. For now

the dark river laps the white, bristling heads
        of clover where my grandfather stands
by a peacock when its green-gold tail flashes.

JEFFERY
BERG

Monument Avenue

In a bathroom window, a light goes out.
I leave my apartment for 7-11 to buy cookies and milk.
Queasy—a wasted evening

watching the TV movie about the creation
of "Charlie's Angels." In the alley
behind my complex, a torn canvas

painted orange. I spy the artist
through his window eating a bologna sandwich
in the glint of the 11 o'clock news.

Another murder.
Snow on Wednesday.
War. It's still dark

at Ann's. A year ago, we jogged nights
panting past the monuments, glanced
inside houses of grand pianos,

Colonial fireplaces, modern art
in gold, gaudy frames. Barred windows.
She told me where she first

snorted crystal—in the basement
of renovated apartments—cobwebbed rooms
of locked suitcases, a baby doll dress.

Now, frosted streaks in unruly hair,
days without eating, trimmer
than Farrah Fawcett, Ann smokes

in the bathroom, slams the door,
while her dog slobbers in the bathtub.
She rummages the closet for a pair of shoes

paid with a stolen credit card.
Cameras caught her in Target.
She faces a court date soon

in a courtroom of low ceilings,
wood paneling like the room
where Aaron Spelling sued Fawcett-Majors

for ditching the Angels to spend hours
with her beefy husband, Lee, serving him
mashed potatoes and brown liquor in bed.

Before *Charlie's Angels* and fire hydrants,
the 7-11, the Laundrateria, Fan-tastic Thrift,
Sammy's Video (a video store with no videos,

just cartons of cigarettes), Café Diem
with inflatable palm trees
on checkered cloth tables. Before the unveiling

of Arthur Ashe, dead in '90s bronze,
midair tennis racket unfortunately weak
against the Confederate muskets. Before

Robert E. Lee's horse's hooves pointed
toward the direction of Pizza Hut, the landscape
was awash in tobacco, crowds

on wood bleachers, mimicking
the Confederate flag with the colors
of their hats, waiting for the loosening

of ropes: a massive black cloak
rumpling off stony-eyed
Stonewall Jackson. He faces Ann's apartment

where the dog craps under the bed.
Power out.
Bill four months late. I try to imagine

those before us: little girls
in dresses, 4th of July sparklers
in their blistered grip, the humming of "Dixie"—

a low night moan. I cry soft
at the muddy image, the false music. There are no notes
left here. Just the wet, white dusting

on somber statues lit by street lamps.
In an alley, I eat cookies, I give
a plastic 7-11 bag to the snowy wind

to scuttle the streets
in remembrance of me. I remember
Spelling worried about ratings,

Farrah, please stay.
The Angels are so important
for all of us

in our living rooms, trying
to make ends meet.

Azaela Pink

Pink azalea shrub out my window,
sometimes at night you shake
with a bluish blur: the ghost
of the man who built this house—
cancer in his throat.

Last night I dreamt I was a speck
in a studio audience watching the drag queen
acidic and sharp-witted
in a hot pink sequined sheath
lip sync to Aretha's "I Say A Little Prayer."

I woke to sweat, to your pink
blazing, to my contention with my
slow-wit, my fears, my man's body.
What to do with me? You've endured these
bumblebees, my warbling along to records,
Carolina heatwaves, green-skied hurricanes.

A sudden fog out of you—
cigarette smoke of the ghost.
Perhaps a lover will come along
to draw the blinds to, to tell me
lover is passé terminology.

Perhaps it will just be
another year of an open window
to my electronic message dithering.
Harbored in my sight, you stay in my heart,

azalea pink, azalea browned
in your late-summer withering.

RICHARD
BLANCO

Making a Man Out of Me

I'm six or seven years old, riding back home with my grandfather and my Cuban grandmother from my *tía* Onelia's house. Her son Juan Alberto is effeminate, "*un afeminado*," my grandmother says with disgust. "*¿Por qué?* He's so handsome. Where did she go wrong with dat *niño?*" she continues, and then turns to me in the back seat: "Better to having a granddaughter who's a whore than a grandson who is *un pato* faggot like you. Understand?" she says with scorn in her voice. I nod my head *yes*, but I don't understand: I don't know what a faggot means, really; don't even know about sex yet. All I know is she's talking about *me, me*; and whatever I am, is bad, very bad. Twenty-something years later, I sit in my therapist's office, telling him that same story. With his guidance through the months that follow, I discover the extent of my grandmother's verbal and psychological abuse, which I had swept under my subconscious rug. Through the years and to this day I continue unraveling how that abuse affected my personality, my relationships, and my writing. I write, not in the light of Oscar Wilde, Walt Whitman, or Elizabeth Bishop, but in the shadow of my grandmother—a homophobic woman with only a sixth-grade education—who has exerted (and still exerts) the most influence on my development as a writer.

I am seven, I think. My grandmother tells me I eat wrong: "Don't use a straw, ever. *Los Hombres* don't drink soda with a straw. Now throw dat away and sit up." I look wrong: "*Dios mío*, you nosin but bones. Dat's why the boys at school push you around. Even a girl could beat you up. Now finish your steak, or else." My friends are all wrong: "I no taking you to dat Enrique's house neber again. He's a *Mamacita's* boy. I don't want you playing with him. I don't care what you say, those GI Joes he has are dolls. Do you want to play with dolls; is dat what you want *señorita?*" I play wrong: "I told your mother not to get you those crayons for Christmas. You should be playing outside like *un hombre*, not coloring in your girly books like dat *maricón* Juan Alberto." I speak wrong: "*Hay Santo*, you sound like *una niña* on the phone. When is your voice going to change?" And I walk wrong too: "Stop clacking your sandals and jiggling like a sissy. Straighten up *por Dios*—we're in public." I am wrong ("I'll make a man out of you yet ..."), afraid to do or say anything ("... you'll see ..."), scared to want or ask anything ("... even if it kills me ..."), ashamed to be alive.

At thirty-one, I sit at a candlelit table across from the man who will be my husband. I tell him about my grandmother and the coping mechanisms I developed; how they naturally led me to writing; mechanisms that became part of my very creative process. Becoming withdrawn and introverted, I grew to become an observer of the world, instead of a participant. In order to survive emotionally I learned to read my environment very carefully and then craft *appropriate* responses that would (hopefully) prevent abuse and ridicule from my grandmother. I explain to my husband-to-be that I am still that quiet, repressed boy whenever I am in a room full of people, trying to be as invisible as possible, but taking in every detail, sensory as well as emotional, that will eventually surface in a poem. My work is often described as vivid and lush; relatives often marvel at my recollection in my poems of family events and details. Qualities I attribute directly to the skills spawned from my coping with my abuse. But beyond that, I've come to understand why writing and me became such a great fit. It allowed me to participate in the world, to feel alive, while remaining an invulnerable observer, safe in my room, at my desk, in my imagination where no one, especially my grandmother, could hurt me.

I'm eight, definitely. I remember because my grandmother is horrified that I'm already *eight* and haven't learned to ride a bike yet. "*Qué barbaridad*, no wonder ..." she tells me, leaving me to fill in the blanks with her words: No wonder: I'm a sissy, effeminate, a weakling. I'm used to her words for me. "I'll teach you," she barks, "Put your sneakers on." We walk my bike to the empty parking lot at St. Jude's Church where I pedal and fall; pedal and fall; pedal and finally glide in perfect balance, leaving her behind clapping and cheering me on: "¡*Andale! Finally! ¡Andale!*" On the way back home, I ride my bike beside her as she praises me, "*Qué bien*. You did great! ¡*Qué macho!*" and kisses my forehead. That night she makes chicken *fricasé*—my favorite—with extra drumsticks and olives just for me. For a moment I can almost believe she loves me, that she'll never call me a faggot again, that she'll let me play with my *sissy* Legos and watercolors. But that very night she shoos my cat Ferby off my lap: "Stop dat. You looking like *una niña* sitting there petting dat thing. Why don't you like dogs?" Apparently, I have the wrong pet, too.

Twenty-eight years later, I get a cat at the suggestion of another therapist, who says it would be good for me; I should indulge myself. I name him Buddha—a leopard-spotted stray who follows me everywhere around the house. He kneads my arms and stomach; he licks my eyebrows. Though he's an animal, his "love" feels unconditional, unlike my grandmother, who only loved me if I didn't strike out at little league games; if I didn't swing my arms as I walked; if I sat still and behaved like the straight little boy she wanted to turn me into. At an early age I came to believe that all love was conditional like my grandmother's. Consequently, I shut down my emotional communication with others, because in my mind no one could be trusted. I became afraid to love, because no one could truly love a faggot like me: not my father or mother, not my brother—or my lovers. But writing allowed me to connect emotionally with others, albeit as a substitute for the real thing. In a poem I could love from a safe distance, love virtually; *say* what I couldn't ordinarily say, make myself vulnerable.

I'm nine, maybe ten, sitting on the family room sofa, sneaking a look through the Sears catalog, again: pages and pages of men without shirts, men in tight briefs, men in boots. Wanting to touch them, I run my fingers across their smooth chests, their hairy chests, their arms, their crotches, pretending. It feels good. It feels terrible. I want to touch myself, but I can't because that's what my grandmother means by faggot, I know that by then. She knows I know and that I'm up to no good when she bursts into the room. Before I can stuff the catalog back into the magazine rack, she tears it from my hand, tosses it across the room, and yells: "Stop being such a *mariconcito*. You wanting me to put you in ballet classes? Is dat what you want? What's wrong with you? Go playing outside like a normal boy." Instead I dash to my bedroom. In tears I tear out a page from my composition book and write: *I, Ricardo De Jesus Blanco, swear to never do what I did today, ever, ever again, or else. As God is my witness.* I sign and date it; seal it an envelope and place it under my mattress.

Thirty-two, maybe thirty-three years later, I'm remembering I couldn't even bring myself to write down exactly what it was *I did* on that day, afraid my grandmother might read it and find me out; that I would out myself through what I wrote. A fear I carried well into my thirties, through my first and second books of poetry, never daring to come out on the page. Those love poems I *did* dare to write, I wrote in second person, a gender-neutral "you;" and used only initials in my dedications: for M.K., for C.A.B., for C.S.B. All my beloved and almost beloved—Michael, Carlos, Craig—reduced to anonymous letters, acronyms for my sexuality that my grandmother would (hopefully) never figure out. I remained safely locked inside the literary closet. Though lately I've come to think it was a cultural-closet I was hiding in. Since I couldn't even begin to entertain writing about my sexual identity, I focused my work on issues of cultural identity and negotiation as a Cuban American instead. Not that these weren't important and honest concerns of mine (and continue to be); but in part it was my living in the shadow of my grandmother's abuse that kept me from investigating and identifying with gay writers, much less writing about my sexuality or my grandmother's abuse. I simply was not *one of them*, in my mind, but I was of course.

I'm twenty-six visiting Cuba for the first time. We are having lunch at *tía* Mima's house, when I learn that her son Gilberto set himself on fire at eight years old, and died. I feel an instant kinship with this child, this boy I never met. In a flash, I remember what I meant/felt when I wrote *or else*: that desperate feeling of wanting to end my life, too; that deep, entrenched sadness that was my childhood. A sadness I have carried since then, according to yet another therapist who diagnosed me with dysthymia—a low-grade, but persistent mild depression. At forty-one I realize I've been sad all my life and have always written from that psychological point of view. I am inspired by the melancholy I see mirrored in others, in the world, and the ways we survive it. I strive to capture sadness and transform it through language into something meaningful, beautiful. Although throughout most of my writing career I had never consciously written for or about the gay community, thematically I feel I've unconsciously been a very gay writer all along in this sense: trying to make lemonade out of lemons, castles out of mud, beauty out of pain.

Would I have become a poet regardless of my grandmother's abuse? Probably, but not the same kind of poet, nor would I have produced the same kind of work, I think. Nevertheless, in the end her ultimate legacy was to unintentionally instill in me an understanding of the complexities of human behavior and emotions. I could have easily concluded that my grandmother was a mean, evil bitch and left it at that. But through her I instead realized there are few absolutes when it comes to human relationships. People, myself included, are not always *good* or always *bad*. They can't always say what they mean; and don't always mean what they say. My grandmother loved me as best she could, the way she herself was loved, perhaps. Her trying to *make me a man* was an odd, crude expression of that love, but it inadvertently made me the writer I am today. And for that I feel oddly thankful I realized fourteen years ago: I'm standing alone at her bedside at Coral Gables Hospital: She's drugged up. The tubes down her throat don't let her speak; she can't say terrible things to me anymore. Watching her, I flash back through all the sound bites of her verbal abuse, and start scribbling down a few lines for a poem I tentatively title, "Her Voices." The first poem I will ever write for her, about her, and my sexuality. My first *out* poem. I'm twelve, I'm thirty-eight, I'm seventeen, I'm thirty-one, I am a man when she wakes up, opens her eyes wide for a moment, looks at me and squeezes my hand, then slips away, quietly, silently, without a word—and I let her go.

Abuelo in a Western

A stranger steps into our Florida room,
glaring at Abuelo and me on the couch.
He shoots a man in the gut, then spits.
A real hombre, Abuelo says. The stranger

speaks mostly with his eyes, his gun,
shoots another man, punches another.
He never misses or loses, unlike Abuelo,
who misses his farm, his only brother,
and *his* Cuba, all lost to the revolution.

The stranger meets a woman, pins her
against a barrel. She pushes back but
then kisses him—he leaves her crying.
He can have any women he wants

but doesn't need a woman, like Abuelo,
who still holds my grandmother's hand
down the supermarket aisle, dances slow
on New Year's Eve with her. The stranger
doesn't have a wife, a home. He doesn't

watch TV like me and Abuelo, who lets me
rest my head on his lap while he scratches
my back, goose bumps daze my body limp.
He carries me to bed, kisses my forehead,

and leaves me in the dark, goes back
to the stranger, the hall echoing with more
bottles breaking, chairs smashing, women
screaming, shots that won't let me sleep—
Abuelo is nothing like that stranger, is he?

Love as if Love

Before I dared kiss a man, I kissed
Elizabeth. Before I was a man, I was
twenty-three and she was thirty-five,
a woman old enough to know songs
I didn't—and that we wouldn't last
beyond the six weeks spent drinking
sweet German wine off our lips,
candles burning and music lifting
off the black vinyl, easing the taboo
between us, barefoot and sprawled
on blankets over her studio floor.

She played The Mamas & The Papas,
Holiday, and Carole King, closed my eyes
with her fingers until the notes broke
in my palms and the room filled up
with the flicker of monarchs. She sang
her life to me in lyrics about running
like a river, about rain, fire. She sang
until I wasn't afraid of her loose hair,
the scent of lilacs creased in her neck,
her small bones in the space between
her breasts, until I dared undress her.

Before I ever took a man, I gave in
to Elizabeth by the tiny green lights
of her stereo glowing like fireflies,
the turntable a shiny black moon
spinning with the songs I still hear
on the radio—driving and singing
straight into clouds moving farther
and farther away, but never quite
vanishing, like those nights falling
asleep with her rooted in my arms,
loving her as if I could love her.

Maybe
for Craig

Maybe it was the billboards promising
paradise, maybe those fifty-nine miles
with your hand in mine, maybe my sexy
roadster, the top down, maybe the wind
fingering your hair, sun on your thighs
and bare chest, maybe it was just the ride
over the sea split in two by the highway
to Key Largo, or the idea of Key Largo.
Maybe I was finally in the right place
at the right time with the right person.
Maybe there'd finally be a house, a dog
named Chu, a lawn to mow, neighbors,
dinner parties, and you forever obsessed
with crossword puzzles and Carl Young,
reading in the dark by the moonlight,
at my bedside every night. Maybe. Maybe
it was the clouds paused at the horizon,
the blinding fields of golden sawgrass,
the mangrove islands tangled, inseparable
as we might be. Maybe I should've said
something, promised you something,
asked you to stay a while, maybe.

Thicker Than Country

A Cuban like me living in Maine? Well,
what the hell, Mark loves his native snow
and I don't mind it, really. I love icicles,
even though I still decorate the house
with seashells and starfish. Sometimes
I want to raise chickens and pigs, wonder
if I could grow even a small mango tree
in my three-season porch. But mostly,
I'm happy with hemlocks and birches
towering over the house, their shadows
like sundials, the cool breeze blowing
even in the summer. Sometimes I miss
the melody of Spanish, a little, and I play
Celia Cruz, dance alone in the basement.
Sometimes I miss the taste of white rice
with *picadillo*—so I cook, but it's never
as good as my mother's. I don't miss her
or the smell of her Cuban bread as much
as I should. Most days I wonder why, but
when Mark comes home like an astronaut
dressed in his ski clothes, or I spy him
planting petunias in the spring, his face
smudged with this earth, or barbequing
in the summer when he asks me if I want
a *hamberg* or a *cheezeberg* as he calls them—
still making me laugh after twelve years—
I understand why the mountains here
are enough, white with snow or green
with palms, mountains are mountains,
but love is thicker than any country.

PERRY
★BRASS★

An Indelible Mark

The South leaves an indelible mark on you. I grew up in Savannah, Georgia, in the 1950s and early 1960s, and moved to New York in August of 1966, a month before my 19th birthday. I was working then in advertising, first in a small art studio, and then in a large agency's art department. The first impression New Yorkers always had about me was that, being blue-eyed and softly spoken, I had to be a Southern WASP, one of those genteel Southerners whose roots go way back on the land and who still subscribed to a code of chivalry New Yorkers find initially quaint and charming and eventually annoying. I was in a fact a Southern Jew, and in that I was also very much out of stereotype since I had grown up in a kind of poverty unseen among most Southern Jews.

My father, after a series of business setbacks, died of colon-rectal cancer at the age of 42, when I was 11, pushing my mother, sister, and me into a state of complete indigence. Since this was a time in the South when bodily functions of any sort were never mentioned in polite company, and certainly never to children, I was not told that he had died of cancer—a forbidden topic of conversation anyway—and certainly would not have been told that the origin of his cancer was an area of the body (the colon leading to the rectum), that was meant only for the bathroom, something normally you should have to pass through three doors to find.

I was not told this bit of information until after my mother's funeral, when I was 38 and one of her brothers let it out the bag. I also learned that colon-rectal cancer is one of the most inheritable of all forms of cancer; still it wasn't something you could talk to children about, no matter how old they were. I was also informed that my mother Helen, after several lengthy hospitalizations, had been formally diagnosed (when I was 14) as a paranoid schizophrenic, but neither I nor my sister was ever allowed to know this as well. What I learned once again from these late revelations is that in every Southern family there's a closet stuffed with secrets. The secrets may be sexual, psychiatric, or even monetary, but they will remain in the closet until something catastrophic, like a death, forces them out.

This secrecy stems from the ingrained Southern attitude that most things pertaining to the body, your self, or your bank account, are best left alone—an attitude that always had racial overtones to it, in that eminently decent, upright, hardworking white people always wanted things left alone, since over time they would prove (like it or not) *best* that way. And black people were not in a position to question it.

Strangely enough, growing up Southern, Jewish, and very much queer (certainly quietly sissified), questioning things had become a part of my own secret wardrobe since I was a child. I was abetted in this by my father Louis, and the strange, contradictory, and even romantic way he lived his life. He was born in 1916 in Charleston, South Carolina, an only child of two prosperous Lithuanian Jews, and even though very spoiled, had been brought up as a little Southern gentleman in dark velvet shorts and white silk shirts. Both of my paternal grandparents died before I was five, but Louis liked to talk about them. His mother was a cosmopolitan woman who spoke French, Yiddish, Russian, and of course English. A marvelous cook, she presided over a genteel Jewish home that in the presence of black servants mixed kosher laws with Southern politeness. My father's nickname was "Bebe," Yiddish for baby; he was headstrong, quick-tempered, and almost shockingly rebellious: he hated working for other people and loved taking time out to be on his own. He had that distinct presence, masculine, strong-smelling, and handsome that many Southern men of his generation had. I remember his smell. Camel cigarettes, sharp, salty perspiration, and a dash of the Mennen deodorant just coming in. Like a lot of Jewish men, he went off to fight in World War Two, and when he came back I had a feeling he was very changed; he couldn't just be a nice Jewish boy anymore. Energetic, affable, talkative, he brought back with him a lot of gentile Army buddies, and regularly went out drinking with them. Although he admired *yiddishkeit* (Jewish culture), he was crazy about guns, hunting and fishing, and frequently met with his buddies to kill and eat flesh Jews would object to—like squirrel, rabbit, or deer. These ventures horrified my mother. She couldn't understand why *Bebe* couldn't be a regular enough Jew, while he told me how important it was to accept people for what they were, but still question their actions if they weren't good.

He put this into practice by making me feel always accepted by him, even though we had little in common. I hated killing anything, found fishing boring, and loved art and puppets. Strangely, my mother hated that I loved puppets. She referred to them as "Perry's dolls" in front of other people, humiliating me. My father though, who adored fantasy, adventure, and the very Southern art of story telling, made me a puppet stage and helped me make hand puppets and marionettes. I was scared of his guns and bloodshed of any sort, but we bonded over this so that the most beautiful parts of my childhood were spent working on puppets together. He would say about these times, "Let's make an adventure out of this. Just the two of us."

The genuine intimacy of this seemed very Southern to me—that it was important to like people genuinely, and not simply use them. But, if you didn't like them, not to be hypocritical about it. I have a feeling this attitude destroyed him in business, and it might have led to why he died in complete poverty, in what would be a "shameful" circumstance (as anything involving money in the South at that time was), which colored my entire growing up. The good thing, though (and I learned that every bad thing had to have one), was that I learned to question everything, even if I kept any answers I got to myself. I questioned why black people were routinely treated like subhumans (something that embarrassed many Southern Jews, since the Nazis had treated Jews the same way); I questioned that there were things boys should do and girls should do and that they should never meet; and I questioned why I felt so alone, so isolated as a kid from the other youngsters in the housing project where we went to live after Bebe died; even if I couldn't put a name on why.

But I knew there was something there. What I wanted was someone to share that thing with me. Someone to reach into that loneliness, and attach himself to me—and I knew it had to be a boy, even if I could barely speak it—passionately, romantically, as you could only do in Savannah, Georgia. Because the city, and I knew this, was so romantic in itself.

What made it so? It was that sense of the past being all around you, and being real. That was the thing that held Southerners together: we knew it. It was terrible. This strange, twisted legacy of the landscape itself, dream-drenched stretches of salt marshes, fields and farms, the clay soil, ancient oak trees and old houses, Civil War sites, and of course the trail of race, class, and speech. When I first got to New York, I missed it all so much it was painful. Even after all the hell I'd gone through, in a trial-by-fire adolescence marked by a suicide attempt at 15, I missed being in Savannah in the rain at night; and the slow hot days, and Southern boys and the way they talked and smelled. I was truly head-spun with New York; there were lots of gay Jewish men I could meet—in Savannah that would have been impossible. And New York, amazingly, was very good to me; I still retained a coastal Georgia accent, and the reserved Southern manners generations of Southern gay boys have learned to use seductively up North. But there was something missing in Yankees: they moved and talked too fast, and they could dispense with you way too easily.

For a while I went back to the South yearly to visit my mother. By this time there was at least one gay bar in Savannah, existing between raids by the cops who found every way to close them down. I would come back and smell the air and listen to the way people talked, always telling stories without even telling them. But by then I found myself in that strange no-man's land between being too much of a New Yorker to fit in to the South again, while still too much of a Southerner to feel really at home in the North. The South was moving quickly. It was now full of dope-smoking hippies and gay communes and alternative "lifestyles" that would have been massacred when I was growing up. A colder, Yankee corporate brain was also moving in, puncturing the landscape with faceless new office towers. It was getting harder for Southerners to find the "real South," that connection with a past you could not shake: now the past was being marketed as a tourist attraction instead of something you simply lived with. By 1980 when I met my husband Hugh, who grew up in the genteel white suburbs of Birmingham, Alabama, there was little of the Old South left, except for the constantly pervasive, now fairly polite, racism of Alabama. We went back once a year to visit his conservative doctor father and his mother who still lived in the fantasy of the rural South she had grown up in, where everyone knew their place and no one wanted anything *ever* to change.

Both of his parents are dead now, and things have changed even more. The Birmingham Civil Rights Institute recently had a show of large-scale photographs of Southern lesbian couples and their families. Hugh and I walked through it extremely impressed, but also noticed that other people, black and white, walking through kept a tight-lipped composure, like they were not ready for this thing, even in the context of Civil Rights in Birmingham, still an area of controversy. Almost 40 years earlier, Hugh had been arrested in a raid on a gay bar in Birmingham—a very sudden and horrifying way for him to come out to his parents. Now we were looking at blow-ups of Southern lesbian couples—not men, but lesbians. Maybe women in a queer role were easier for Birmingham to deal with than men. Still, I asked him, "Did you ever think this day would come?"

"No," he said. "But I'm glad it did. It was about time."

DUSTIN
BROOKSHIRE

Signs

My mother dreams of dark running water.
She calls. It was the death dream.
I follow the speed limit.
I walk faster than normal through crosswalks.
I am even more careful when showering,
a fall now seems more probable.
When I was a child she told me
the secret of this dream—
someone would die
but she didn't know who.
The dream came when my grandmother
was admitted to the hospital,
when a family friend
was supposed to be winning
her battle with cancer.
And, the time it came
when she couldn't think
of anyone sick, my father's favorite
employee was hit by a car.
I told you, she whispered.
I prayed to God—begged Him
not to pass this curse to me.
I had no desire to ache in my soul
with limited knowledge.
As a teenager I thought it all
a world of coincidence—
that there aren't signs placed
to tell us what will come.
But, yesterday,
I was in a Knoxville bar
with Julie, trying to let go
and when I looked up

I saw we were sitting under
a poster of Dolly Parton.
I knew this was a sign.
The night was going to be good.
Everything on our trip would be okay.
This sign was meant just for me.
Honestly. How much different am I from my mother?

JERICHO BROWN

Big, Fine

Long ago, we used two words
For the worth of a house, a car,
A woman—all the same to men
Who claimed them: things
To be entered, each to experience
Wear and tear with time. But
Greater than the love for these
Possessions was the love one man
Offered another saying, *You lucky.*
You got you a big, fine _____.
Good thing men don't have that
Problem now. Surely, we wouldn't
Dare wait on other men to tell us
We exist or grant existence
To those who cry *mine* like infants
Grabbing at what must be
Beautiful since someone else saw it.

Fairy Tale

Say the shame I see inching like steam
Along the streets will never seep
Beneath the doors of this bedroom,
And if it does, if we dare to breathe,
Tell me that though the world ends us,
Lover, it cannot end our love
Of narrative. Don't you have a story
For me? You tell one with fingers
Over my lips to keep me
From sighing when—before the queen
Is kidnapped—the prince bows
To the enemy, handing over the horn
Of his favorite unicorn like those men
Brought, bought, and whipped until
They accepted their master's names.

The Ten Commandments

But I could be covetous. I could be a thief.
Could want and work for. Could wire and
Deceive. I thought to fool the moon into
A doubt. I did some doubting. Lord,
Forgive me. In New Orleans that winter,
I waited for a woman to find me shirtless
On her back porch. Why? She meant it
Rhetorically and hit me with open hands.
How many times can a woman say why
With her hands in the moonlight? I counted
Ten like light breaking hard on my head,
Ten rhetorical whys and half a moon. Half
Nude, I let her light into me. I could be last
On a list of lovers Joe Adams would see,
And first to find his wife slapping the spit
Out of me. I could be sick and sullen. I could
Sulk and sigh. I could be a novel character
By E. Lynn Harris, but even he'd allow me
Some dignity. He loved black people too
Much to write about a wife whipping her rival
On a night people in Louisiana call cold.
He'd have Joe Adams run out back and pull
Her off of me. He wouldn't think I deserved it.

On Daniel Minter's *High John the Conqueror*
acrylic, 50x60 cm

The sun inflicts its whitest light, heat
High enough to warp the pavement,
So John gives up on the new road north
And cuts through red clay at first sight
Of shade, barbed wire broken, miles
Of green to be cleared or cleaned growing
In rows like welts behind him. God's
Not on his side. John won't work
A whole day and can't keep cancer
Out his mouth. Oh, he's got the shoulders
For it, the stride, arms and hands
The size of a laboring man's, but one
Itch for smoke in his throat and John
Heads for hell. Nothing about Georgia
Can slow him down. King of all
That slithers, here he chokes a snake.
I catch his yellow eye and remember
My own pack of menthols, days I'd drag
And puff lies in front of my wife who
Waited while I wished for man after man,
Black in two dimensions, to run my way,
Dear John, a region painted against me.

Another Angel

I found myself bound to Him and bound to His
Bidding. He left water without color and land
With no motion to mention but kept me going

Like a toy wound tighter than His one odd eye
When I failed to deliver a message on time.
He built bugs and beasts; I understood my

Sexlessness. He invented men and women;
I knew I had no father. He never told me
What I was, what He could be. So what—

Two boys in Oil City, Louisiana, complain
About their bodies, featherless, modeled after
The reflection He passes in streams. They got

Sick playing barefoot in mud, and they hate
Their symptoms. I am that kind of pain put
To purpose but unloved, bound to the Lord who

Looks at those brothers, never noticing his own,
Bound like their strange sister told to bathe them
Once, filthy and feverish, they finally come home.

JOEY
CONNELLY

Debris

Shame was so present then,
that summer of setting, cutting,

hanging the tobacco.
Sunburns, dirty fingernails, the sweat

all primed me for different activities.
The humid silence of barn rafters

was not enough to quiet my body,
demanding what it should not.

The turned earth gave way;
crickets clung to us briefly.

Still I knew I would always and never be more than flesh.

WILLIAM CORDEIRO

Lullaby

Mother hung the wash while daddy drank.
It rained and rained. The sheets got soaked.
The dog gnawed off its mangy fur. The world began
to shrink with each denial, annihilating thought.
Mother did the dishes, though we never ate.

Daddy didn't give a fuck. My parents fought (it rained
and rained) like cats and dogs. I thank my folks for ending
up some dud. I sulked though childhood and never
said one word. Mother spanked me for not telling her
I saw the tom make babies with the bitch next door.

I couldn't sleep. I slept it off. The neighbor
wore a mask with big blank eyes and a rubber
piggy snout. He cured each rib; he burned a god-
damn barbeque. The children hid amid the smoke.
The children smoked and gave each other hickeys.

We tortured one another with a teasing expertise.
We played deadbeats. We licked each other good.
No joke, we lapped up every trick. I wet the bed, but
never fell asleep. Nightfall—leap years. Daddy drank
until one day he washed away with rain. I wanted to

grow up so I could disappear. In middle school I hid
inside the bathroom to read Immanuel Kant. Who am I
kidding? I hid inside my thoughts; I read a manual
of how to, fiddling with things that one can't do, so I could
wank. I took my lumps, went limp. Things got hairy. I can,

I can't jump from my old tree-house. Jesus, mother died.
I often told her to each time I told her off. It rained down

on my head with blows; I got—whether high or low—
nailed until I hit the studs. Up from down (downers, uppers),
I couldn't tell how many holes were beat into my head;

my head beat holes into the walls. All told, I got fucked
up—got to liking blows, was blown wherever I was taken.
Each broken home upon our block was soon broke in.
Oh, daddy said I didn't cut it, but I did. I jumped a box
car and then followed tracks. That's when I found a better

way to skin those doggone cats. I bottomed out the dreamy glory-
holes. It seemed like yesterday would never come. I didn't change.
Nothing did. My clothes fell off they stank so bad. I thought
to think, and then I's thunked again. My dad turned up skunk dead
drunk when we got broke. That's bunk, the bed where every bone

of mine was banged. I'm hardened now: no one can touch
the gauges of my rings. How many missing persons I've been
mistaken for. I took things quick. People said I had a glow;
I had some spunk. I punched right in. Soon enough I flopped
around the wayward halfway places and got my kisser clocked.

The way I told it, I never spoke. Money speaks. I made it rain.
So I cleaned up; I cleaned my plate. Mother's on the porch
with cats, calling me, come in. I say my peace, my last regrets.
I'm hanging round the gallows tree, our family branch. Blood-

lines of kin are just another line I's given. My palm got read, red-
handed. I fell in line. Assembled in the factory, it was all an act.
Went down a dead-end street the realtor called a cul-de-sac,
that sack of shit. But still, I shat my pants. I brought the house
down, blowing smoke. You'll never smoke me out. You hit

up any of my flames? They'd want to tie you up and cross you
to the wrong side of the tracks. Burned out, I stole away. I stole
my mother's diary, as if that's all she wrote, so many empty pages
in a bind. Well, there's no looking back. Wrote off, into the sun-
set, settled in my ways. I'm not looking anymore at all. I'm going

blind. Like water under bridges burned, my daddy's one good piece of straight advice, before the smithereens, before my mother passed and out and out and out I came, to voice any feeling's a sign of being weak. I still live at home. I hear the gate clink shut. But I'm beating it on down the road. I tried to wake, but my eyes were opened wide.

Wing Night

Piles of wing night debris—all bones and Buffalo
smeared empties, pyramids of crumpled napkins
stained with sweat-rings, faux kissprints—but no

one's number. We pretend to care about the score
of ballgames scrolling at the bottom of a fuzzy box,
forgetting which team is ours. A busy waitress laps

up residue, too dragged to offer back a smile,
wringing out the rag and swinging it back over.
Each would-be lover spills, drunk-dialing, out.

This late into a wasted night it sometimes gets pretty
hard to understand, standing under lights now turned
up high, old trick to say it's past last call. I try to bump

my slumping wingman forward. "Hi, dude,"—a chaser
swigged, his blurry face leans in and on me, mumbling.
Both blackout, I lay him on my pickup truck's flatbed.

Ocean City

Sun-candied, one boy stands near a square's stopped traffic
light beside his board, limp lumps of sin & sand all damp &

dimpled on his wet white shorts. He wears little else but flip-
flops & coy shades tilted up, crass mirrors, fingering at taffy.

More waves crash in, in a haze of salt, grime, & tanning lotions;
a riddling chatter as pinball cradles pop while sludge from spills

off-shore rush up with swells, careening crushed lush froth
on castles, which hit the bucket near bronzed, brazen high

school bodies sprawled, worshipping the fresh, fleshed air
of summer as banners buzz above the shore. Two tattooed

teenyboppers in bikini tops keep texting. The gulls pair off.
Buoys bob & jounce. Time gets wasted back at a time share.

C. CLEO
★ CREECH ★

Mecca

Southerners learn early who's clan, who's tribe,
the right people, who's good people,
who's from the right side of the tracks.
We hear the dropped hints,
pick up the crumbs of
hand-covered conversation
about "those" and "them" and the others,
the ones who don't belong, don't fit in.
The ones talked about in whispers.
Our sense of ill-fitting skin
making us wonder, if they're talking about us.
We listen carefully out of the corner of our ears
for tidbits about these outcasts,
knowing only that it's important,
somehow pertains to us, before we even know why.
Knowing at some point, we will be leaving for parts unknown,
that this place of birth, is not our home, not our people.
Through no choice of our own,
we will wander through the wilderness alone.
We will suffer mirages and thirst,
until we find our meccas, our true tribes.
We will follow the interstates to the promised lands.
One day we will stand in midnight churches of shirtless men,
feeling the spirit and speaking in tongues,
dancing to the gospel of our tribe.
We will march in parades of the like-minded,
argue the meaning of culture and community,
and we will know we have found our way home.

JAMES CROTEAU

Lord, I Am Not Worthy

A Mississippi delta mother
born of Italian immigrants
meets a New England Yankee
set free from seminary, out
comes a boy who learns
he's not a boy, at eleven,
on the dry mud field
of the only Catholic Church
for a flat hundred miles.

Here transpires the Passion,
Good Friday 1959, Joel
an older farm boy Jesus,
garmented on the cross,
towel wrapping sacred
loins, the revelation
of terrycloth devotion.

So what could then be done? Pray
to the Virgin Mary, memorize
the Latin, *Ecce Agnus Dei,*
don the white sheet
chasuble, gather the faithful
family dog, consecrate cookies,
and plead *Domine, non sum dignus.*

Camp Revelation

The south Mississippi summer moon
through a single window, my recollection
dimly lit like the inside of Cabin 6.

Night vision bound to our bunk bed,
stacked, wooded things, rusted springs,
musty, narrow, just enough memory

to light a name through fifty years: Matt
above, me below, humid insect sounds,
a slow metallic creak, a sweaty scent

of nearness, just beneath the bottom
of the bunk, his bare shadowed
shoulder, arm extended, handing me

a new-fledged thought that cracked
the shell that sealed my world:
There is another boy like me.

J.K. DANIELS

Street, Streak

She was the deer trail, before it was a foot path or wheel-
rutted then widened and paved passing among the cinder

block houses, among scrub palms, flooded swales: she lay
on me, her thigh between my thighs—both of us younger

than even I believe—on an uncovered mattress on a garage
floor. The interstate plowed through, dredged up clods of

damp sand: she said of the unsettled nest of Cottonmouths,
what if they slipped under your parents' door: you could stay with me

forever. I went home, then, crying. The dirt ended; the asphalt
began: I walked past the monkey chained to the plywood

platform with links enough to reach the lowest branch
of the one shade tree and behind him the groves and beyond

that bikers—a gang, someone said, squatting in an abandoned
farmhouse, when the house burned, someone said, a state trooper

led the dousing, held the torch. From Orange Avenue to the King's
Highway, she led to you above me, and me waiting to be driven away.

As the Prodigal Daughter

My mother played "Greensleeves," her fingernails clicking on the ivory keys. Alas, my love, my gosling, my silly goose. She took me to the pond to feed her swans, all guile and aggression, their tail feathers lurid, she said, in the original sense, a ghastly pale yellow.

*

In her cedar chest, my inheritance: a rabbit fur glove, lurid in the original sense, ghastly pale yellow, her wedding dress, a red leather Bible, gilt-edged.

*

My mother met me at the gate, early one morning, to cast me off. Yes, I was drunk and lurid, in the later sense, glaring, glowing. The gleam of sex. The stink and steam of it. A lass, my love. Sunlit mist above the brackish pond.

*

The amber husk of a bee clings to the cemetery's one tree. In my arms, an ivory urn, gold-handled. Behind the columbaria, the bank of ash, a snakeskin sloughed, no, a condom snagged, in the grass. A body, Mother, cannot be uncast.

What Have You Gone and Done?

I leaned against the smelted grate, she kneeled
      on the concrete:
            we unsoldered the iron gate
                     of mate and merge, her mouth
    on the verge of my median, that short
                    weave. She drove,
  I rode
     the trolley home.

  Not trolley, streetcar.

        I can't say
           I didn't because I did.
                I won't say
     what will be will be
         after three cheap drinks
          under the green awnings of Que Sera—

Not median, neutral ground.

What's done is done. This
          is my stop: neutral
  ground, avenue, eight blocks
    of cracked sidewalk,
 an iron gate, unlocked.

This is where I get off.

NICK
★DEPHTEREOS★

Gay Sex Slaves in Savannah

Savannah, Georgia, is an odd town, lovely to look at, just right for a little romance. Cobbled streets, old Victorian homes, swirling latticework, and gothic towers, all hidden under a veil of Spanish moss. Straight couples holding hands walking down Broughton Street isn't an unusual sight. Middle-aged tourists with maps and fanny packs, white-haired locals out to dinner, and art students, tastefully disheveled and tattooed, amble down the city's main drag clasping hands in an endless parade of affection. Two men holding hands, however, is almost unheard of.

My boyfriend, Joseph, and I go downtown about as often as anyone else living in Savannah. As college students, it's hard to resist the temptation of $5.25 Mexican on Wednesday nights, or $3.00 frozen yogurt. (We've learned, however, not to indulge in both delicacies on the same night out. A spicy bean burrito followed by a chocolate sundae with all the fixin's has a habit of cutting a date short in favor of a toilet faster than you can say frozen chimichanga.) Joseph and I have never been ashamed of holding hands in public. With so many visitors, students, and transients, we've always felt it's easier to get away with being gay in Savannah than, say, Jackson, Mississippi. And yet, it's hard to live in a place for three-and-a-half years and still think, *is it okay to be myself here?*

Holding hands on Broughton Street after dinner, Joseph and I often get a scoff or roll of the eyes from some pot-bellied, pink-faced tourist in khaki shorts and sneakers unused to gays being let out in public. Worse still are the young mothers, visiting from a small town in the Middle South perhaps, that look us up and down and squeeze their child's hand a little tighter as if uttering a silent prayer, *please, God, don't let my baby turn out like that.*

One night after dinner, walking to our favorite frozen yogurt café, Joseph and I passed by a McDonald's, a recent addition to the downtown scene. After renovating an old storefront, McDonald's, like Gap, Banana Republic, and Starbucks, managed to squeeze itself onto Broughton Street and get a piece of Savannah's tourist action. Since opening, the McDonald's has become one of the most popular hangouts for the city's homeless—it is, after all, about the only place downtown that offers sandwiches and coffees for a dollar.

Hand in hand, Joseph and I walked past two men lying in the street outside McDonald's, between them an upturned ball cap filled with a few coins. They called out to passersby for donations. They were only looking for a hot meal, they promised. They were good Christians, they assured us. Their mousy, sandy hair stuck to their red foreheads, shiny with sweat, and their white work pants, stained with black grime and grease, were cut off at the knee exposing their burnt, bare legs. They looked to be in their mid-twenties, not much older than us.

"Ooooooh, *faggots*! Go suck each other's *dicks*," called out one of them as we walked by, evidently more enticed at drawing attention to us than his own need for money. Though the suggestion didn't sound half bad, I didn't want to spoil the night fighting with a bum. I said nothing, but glared angrily. As we crossed the street, I could still see him, legs outstretched on the sidewalk, slouched back against the window of McDonald's, miming a blowjob with his hand and mouth. It looked like he'd had some experience.

As Joseph and I finished our frozen yogurts at a table outside the café, we saw the other, silent vagrant hurrying across the crosswalk headed for us.

"I think he's coming over to talk to us," Joseph said, avoiding eye-contact with the man we both knew would soon be at our table. "What if he's coming over to tell us homosexuality is an unnatural sin and we're going straight to Hell?" It was likely.

I spooned through my puddle of yogurt, fishing out the chocolate pieces. "I'll look him straight in the eye and tell him, 'I'm going to finish this Kit-Kat, remove my jacket, and make you rue the day you ever decided to become homeless.'" As it happened, I did not have the opportunity to say this.

"Hey, y'all, I just wanted to come over here and say a few things." As the hitherto silent bum began his speech, Joseph and I looked at each other, preparing ourselves for a streetside condemnation. "Yeah, I just wanted to say I think it's really great y'all have the courage to walk down the street holdin' hands like that."

This was unexpected.

"Yeah, my name's Tiger an' I live downtown." Tiger brushed his hair out of his face and wiped his hands agitatedly across his dirty shorts. "But that guy that called y'all faggots isn't a friend of mine. He's just my business associate."

Still Joseph and I were silent.

"Jus' wanna let y'all know that I myself am bisexual. Or gay, actually. Well, I'm whatever you want me to be."

I wadded up my napkin and tossed it into the empty yogurt cup.

"Now, I don't want y'all to associate me with that guy over there," Tiger pointed across the street to his associate, still slumped against the McDonald's window.

I smiled, not having much to say, wondering when he'd make a plea for spare change.

"An' basically, what I'm tryin' to say here is," Tiger moved in closer, looking side to side, dropping his voice to a low, intimate tone, "is if you ever need a sex slave, I'll be outside McDonald's. Jus' come an' find me."

I looked over at Joseph, incredulous, and still Tiger persisted.

"You can tie me up, handcuff me, put a gag in my mouth, whatever you're into. I'll be your complete sex toy." Tiger held his hands together as though they were shackled, exposing tracks of dirt and filth encased beneath his nails.

Smiling, thanking Tiger for his offer, Joseph and I got up to leave. Tiger made a dramatic, Renaissance bow with a flourish of his hand. "Remember, it's Tiger. I'll be at McDonald's. You know what for," he said with a crusty wink.

Joseph and I still walk down Broughton Street hand in hand, but we've made some concessions. Oddly, we choose to avoid McDonald's not for fear of being called faggots, but to avoid offers for wild, unrestrained gay sex.

DAVID EYE

Second Baptism

Cicadas in the trees, shrieking Heat! since morning,
have cross-faded to crickets. Frogs and toads chirp,

thrum, more insistent with the coming darkness.
Two boys, 16 and 20, clothes puddled in dew-wet grass,

sprint off the dock and leap to the moon just cresting
the pines across the pond. Pale light coats their skin

as over and over they launch, plunging through silver
into the black water. They pull their feet from edge-muck

with every round, slap mudprints onto weathered planks.

Quiet now, they cling to a float, chins on crossed forearms,
bodies and legs dangling, like a giant man-o'-war. The pond

licks at shoulders, armpits. Crickets trill, and one hand slips
off, grazing the younger boy's chest, lower. His stomach

thrills, his jaw trembles, limbs slide and entwine. One hand
each goes as far as its reach, the other hanging on to the raft.

The younger boy lets go, slides down the other's torso, luminous
in the teeming water, and takes in something new.

The only sound the pounding in his ears. Until he has to
breathe, and when he emerges, anointed in moonlight,

the older boy laughs at his eagerness. The younger too, at his luck,
in his relief. They kiss then. On their lips, the pond, the moon.

JASON K. ★FRIEDMAN★

First Love, or Sex and the City

1.

My parents didn't seem to object to my being gay. They just didn't want me to be gay in Savannah, a category, it might seem, like driving while black except limited geographically and therefore less onerous. And even being gay in Savannah didn't seem to trim their wick much; it was the sex they objected to. When our reputation was imperiled, they referred to our hometown as the City of Savannah. What they meant, I believed, was that as long as I practiced my unspeakable acts beyond the city limits, then they would have no cause for complaint.

The only problem was that I was living in Savannah and had just met a guy.

It was the summer after my sophomore year of college, and I was waiting tables at the Pirates' House, known for its conjoined historic buildings and kitschy décor. Two guys—one tall and fair, the other short and dark—sat at the table nearest the gated entrance to the steps leading down to the tunnel, which supposedly ran to the river and was used to shanghai sailors. On the landing just before the steps turned out of view, a dummy pirate lay with his head bent unnaturally. At the top of the steps, you pressed a button, and he spoke: *Ahoy, ye mateys!* The guys left me a nice tip along with a scrap of paper with a phone number on it. I assumed it belonged to the little dark one—the fair one had hardly looked at me all evening, while the dark one had asked various questions. His queries were so idiotic that I assumed he was flirting with me. I responded cheekily—*Yeah, a pirate really died in the tunnel*—but he didn't seem to mind.

I wasn't interested. But the next night, horny and bored, I called anyway. I still knew nothing about men: it was the guy who'd ignored me, the fair one, who left me the number. Martin and I had sex in his hotel room while the dark one, nicknamed Coca-Cola because he was built like the glass, pretended to sleep in the next bed. They were best friends—they lived in Tampa but were visiting for the weekend. At one point, I managed to fall partway off the bed. I blindly sent up a hand and ended up tickling Martin in an unexpected and unexpectedly sensitive place. A spontaneous act, but in his view the gesture of a grand courtesan; he was impressed. It was the second time I had ever had sex. I sneaked back into my parents' house just before daybreak.

Two weeks later, Martin came back. When he left, I was in love. He had a hairy little paunch and thin legs and frosted receding hair, and I thought he was beautiful. I wrote him a sugary letter and left it on the breakfront, in the front hall, to be mailed.

2.

Watching *All My Children* was a family enthusiasm, though we rarely did it together. When I was growing up, my folks got to see the show at lunch, when it came on; my brother, sister, and I watched the day's episode on videotape when we got home from school. We heated up a box of Chun King mini-chicken egg rolls—I liked to dunk mine in soy sauce and ketchup—and enjoyed them while catching up on the exploits of Erica Kane, Phoebe Tyler Wallingford, and the rest.

In college, I had stopped following the show, but my mother kept me *au courant* by phone. The summer I met Martin I usually wandered downstairs each day in time to watch with my parents. They ate lunch while I sat groggy and bleary-eyed, gulping down tea.

A drug lord who orders a hit on her own grown daughter; new mothers who go crazy when their babies are kidnapped or die or even when they survive; a baby-stealing nurse; an evil twin sister; long-lost daughters who return to embitter their mothers' lives.... Having been exposed to so much televisual female pathology, I should have been on to my own mother. Instead, I fell for that hoariest of plot twists—the purloined letter.

3.

I walked into the house one afternoon and found Dad in the den. "Sit down," he said. He was in his easy chair, and I took a seat on the fixed-reed sofa, under the three-part Japanese silkscreen. The TV was off, which was unusual, and all you could hear was a low electric hum. "I don't want you taking my wife away from me," he said. "Excuse me?" I replied. "I said, 'I don't want you taking my wife away from me.'" "What are you talking about?" I asked. "You know what I'm talking about." The letter! It never made it to Martin. Over the years, my mother had rummaged through the bag of a girlfriend of my brother's, looking for birth control; she'd hidden my wallet and keys to teach me not to lose my wallet and keys; I'd forgotten that whatever was left on the breakfront was fair game to her. "Now I know it's fun," my father began. He did? "But we have a reputation to uphold in the City of Savannah. What you do when you're away at school is your own business, but when you're home, we expect you to play by our rules."

I crossed my arms and looked out at the backyard, the clumps of grass that never quite coalesced into a yard, the azalea bushes growing over the fence. Then a moaning began from upstairs. "This thing is killing your mother," Dad said. I ran up to find Mom zonked out on the bed, a bottle of pills open on the bedside table. "I'm calling an ambulance," I said, reaching for the phone. "No, don't," she said. "But if you took all those pills!" I said. "I didn't take that many," she replied. She sounded very tired and spoke so slowly, as if every word were a stone that had to be hauled up from a pit. I looked at the bottle—it was aspirin, regular strength, and the bottle was still half-full. I knew she took these things six at a time at the first sign of a headache. "I just wanted to talk to you," she said.

Tears were burning my eyes, streaming down my face. But at the same time a meta-narrative was revealing itself: the one where my parents plotted in the den, and my mother climbed the stairs and took her place, spreading her hair tragically across the pillows. I grasped her upper arms, as if I were pinning her to the bed. "Promise me," she said, "you'll never do it again." I withdrew my arms and folded them across my chest. "Okay," she said, immediately ready to compromise, "then promise me you won't do it when you're in the City of Savannah." "Promise me you won't do this again," I said. "I promise," she replied. And then she said my name.

4.

Martin came back two weeks later, alone. I went to his hotel, let him fuck me, and drove back home through the yellowing light of dawn, a world awakening to all its possibilities. I crept inside the house. Mom jumped out from behind the door and began hitting me with a hairbrush—on the back, between my shoulder blades, the way cops do with clubs on TV. It hurt, but I kept quiet and ran up the stairs. As soon as I reached the landing, the door to their room opened, and Dad came out, a cuckoo emerging from a clock. He was wearing a nightshirt and looked stunned. "What's happening? What's going on?" he asked. Every upstairs light was on. In the mirror at the top of the stairs, Mom was Medusa-headed, her hair crazed, fury in her eyes. "Your son's been out all night long sucking men," she explained. This is what she said—*sucking men*. "What? What?" Dad asked, with a distasteful look. "Why don't you buy your son a dress!" she cried. "Do you want us to buy you a dress?" she yelled in my direction.

In the mirror, I saw the hairbrush rise above her head. I ran to my room and locked the door, slumping down against it the way Glenn Close would in *Fatal Attraction*. My mother's botched line didn't make me laugh, but it did pull me out of the scene a bit—if not to enjoy the absurdity of it, then at least to feel a little less sorry for myself.

5.

Dushka and her younger brother, George, and I were going to Tampa. She was my Yugoslavian classmate and best friend, and she was as boy-crazy as I was. Sometimes she came to the restaurant at closing time and ordered a flaming dessert. I wheeled out the cart, poured butter and booze into a pan, set it on fire, and she cheered. Then we went dancing. She had been in on my thing with Martin from the start. Things had gotten difficult for me in Savannah, and now she was enabling my romantic weekend with him. She gave me the perfect cover—a semi-family trip.

Early Saturday morning, Dushka and George pulled up in their folks' Oldsmobile station wagon. I opened our front door. Mom seized me by the arm and whispered fiercely in my ear, "I want you to fuck her. And I want you to like it." This was the first, and practically the last, curse word I ever heard pass her lips. Her breath bored into my earhole, agonizing something deep inside my head.

Dushka dropped me off at Martin's apartment complex, and I didn't see her brother or her until it was time to drive home. Martin took me to his hangouts, which all had pools with bars around them. I was always swimming over for a cup of bourbon and ginger ale while he watched, nursing a bottle of light beer. Coca-Cola was around and a few of Martin's other friends, all of them Spanish speakers. Martin was a white guy from upstate New York, now teaching high school Spanish in Florida, and he had so immersed himself in the Spanish language that he spoke English with a foreign accent. He taught me words in bed. *Te amo*, I whispered to him, cantilevered over me. *Te adoro*, he replied when he finally collapsed.

When I got back, Mom wanted to know only if I had had a good time.

6.

I moved through the city differently, now that I was in love. My parents' house on the suburban southside, the beach 20 miles east, the historic district to the north—until I met Martin, I had only traveled two sides of this triangle, going out to the beach each day and returning to my parents' house to clean up for work. But when Martin was in town, we met at the beach and took the expressway from the islands directly to his hotel in the historic district. We made the most of our days, since I didn't dare get back to my parents' house too late. I hadn't told Martin about their flip-out, but he seemed to understand.

Savannah had pretty much shrunk to the restaurant, where Martin waited patiently for my shift to end, and his hotel, which we walked to afterward. We no longer even went to the bars much. The southside was where I slept and waited to see Martin again. But what the city had lost in size, it gained in intensity. Tourists rode around in tricked-out hearses and horse-drawn carriages, chasing after moonlight and mystery and magnolias, legends and ghosts, all the fake mystique the Chamber of Commerce could manufacture and retail. But Martin and I had come by our magical city honestly. The restaurant, the hotel, and every cobblestone and building in between were burnished by our romance.

7.

One afternoon, a week or so before I headed back to school, I was lying on my bed reading when my mother came in and asked if I had a special friend. It was raining, the world outside the window a green blur, and Martin wasn't in town.

"No," I said, not looking up from my book.

She stood there quietly, just inside the door, then repeated the question.

This time when I said no I looked at her, for emphasis.

She didn't seem to be laying a trap. And I could see I was in no immediate physical danger; both her hands were free. But there was no way I was going to tell her a thing.

Later I would understand that her poor weapons—hairbrush, dress, pills—made for better tools. They were my mother's ways of coping with the stress of working a tough blue-collar job while trying to raise three kids. You can see it in the pictures my dad liked to take before they left the house for an occasional evening out. Raccoon-eyed and white-faced under cotton candy black hair, buxom in a low-cut gown, she's as glamorous as Erica Kane herself. My mother never smiles in these shots, but she seems at rest, confident in this one triumph. Even aspirin, in those days before Paxil, must have helped, at least to face her everyday trials. But nothing in her kit steeled her for having a queer son.

One day I would understand. But for now, the brush, the dress, the pills stood between us. She had put them between us, and her sudden interest in my love life wasn't going to take them away.

"Because if you did have a special friend," my mother went on, relentless, "I would hope you'd want to tell me about him."

But I just turned back to my book—the sound of the rain swallowing up her silence as she stood by the door, continuing to wait even after the possibility of a response had passed.

D.
GILSON

Riding In Cars With Brothers

> *If you would win the hard identity*
> *Of brothers—a long race for men to run*
>
> – Allen Tate, from "Sonnets of the Blood"

On October 3, 2004, the EA Sports 500 took place at the Talladega Superspeedway. That humid Sunday, 172,138 ticketed attendees filled the stands of the largest track used by the National Association for Stock Car Auto Racing, NASCAR, though the number is conservative given the tens of thousands who pack the miles of abandoned farmland which surround the track, tailgating and camping and raising cane. It is not unlike a Dixie Woodstock, and the lore goes that on race day, Talladega becomes the most populated city in Alabama. On October 3, 2004, I was a college freshman—young and awkward and uncomfortably queer—sitting on the searing metal of stadium seating as stock car drivers looped 188 laps around the 2.66 mile track, often in excess of 200 miles per hour. Such speed is a dizziness that blurs, or perhaps revises, memory.

    I had traveled from Missouri to Alabama as a concession. My mother guilted—a coercion I learned of much later—my father and brother, Randy, into taking me for my birthday. I did not want to go, really, and they probably would have preferred going without me. But these men asked so earnestly. Nineteen and weird and on the verge—like every nineteen year old, it seems—of some great self-revelation, I wasn't in the position to turn down the attention. Our trip itself? Unmemorable but for flashes. Ten hours in Randy's Chevy Lumina listening to an endless loop of Johnny Cash, Elvis Presley, and Alabama. *Song, song of the South. Sweet potato pie and I shut my mouth. Gone, gone with the wind. There ain't nobody looking back again.* During the race itself, reading *Catcher in the Rye* and Dad spilling beer onto the paperback. Drinking my first beer with Dad and Randy, neither of whom drink in front of Mom. Going to a local mall for dinner at Applebee's. Finding a cruisy bathroom at the mall. Finding a boy at one of the urinals. Finding his cock as he finds mine, and we masturbate into the pool of piss and pink disinfectant disc. My brother finding me in the bathroom just as the boy and I are cumming and never speaking of this. Later, after many more beers at the house we had rented for the weekend, skinny dipping in the cedar lined hot tub with my brother and feeling his hand brush my knee. Then again. His eyes closed because he is married and straight and also my brother and we are drunk.

In St. John's Gospel, Jesus claims, "My Father's house has many rooms." In the Gospel no one has written of my family—*my Father's house has many rooms. Rooms in which camps segregate.* A house divided against itself can, it turns out, stand, however shakily. In my Father's house there are many rooms, and I am usually in the sewing room with Mom and my sister Jennifer, drinking Diet Coke, watching HGTV, and *Carrying on like we ain't got a care in the world,* Mom says. The river of a family's genetics rarely flows evenly. It eddies and meanders, dams and trickles. Jennifer and I, for instance, are both extroverts like our mother. Our big, strange laughs, guffaws, sound like birds in pain. We are both teachers, both hold graduate degrees, and are both finicky eaters (she, a vegetarian, me, a vegan). Physically, however, I look most like Randy. We are both slim, but not waifs, with the pale skin of our Welsh blood mixed with darker Hopi Indian. Our facial hair borders on red and our smiles are crooked, turning higher on the left side of our faces than the right. And because we were drunk in a hot tub and we are brothers and he is Randy and our memory revises, the last thing I remember of that night is accidentally tickling his thigh, leaning in to kiss my brother and his smile, like my own, making the kiss lopsidedly sweet and strange and familiar.

No man in my family should drink. We are, in this way, very Southern indeed: taken by muggy nights to points of excess. My father, now sober, is an alcoholic and my mother will not stand for this in her house. My other brothers—Marty, dead now, and Mike, rarely coherent—have spent so much time in and out of emergency rooms, rehab, and prison, it seems a moot point to drone on about them. Randy and I know our limits and rarely pass them. But on a night in a hot tub after your brother has watched you cum in a public bathroom with another boy beside you, you will both want to drink.

And when you kiss—and whatever follows this—you will want to both remember that the world was one of possibility then, but not want to remember the particulars. You will both be thankful for the line of demarcation a blackout provides. A before and an after, a known and an unknown.

Why, I wonder now, did I desire—and sometimes desire still?—my own brother, the one I most closely resemble, though we are so vastly different. He, a father, a builder of palatial, custom homes for the wealthy. Me, a writer, an almost doctor of American literature. Is this an exercise in queer narcissism? When I visit home during Christmas my first year of graduate school, Randy asks—a question he has never asked me before or since—"What have you been reading?" I'd been reading Freud, who has much to say on the subject of desire and the ego, of course. Is ours, this relationship between Randy and I, silently volatile, an example of, as Freud describes, "very intense feelings of rivalry giving rise to aggressive desires, which, after they have been surmounted, are succeeded by love for the object that was formerly hated or by an identification with it?"

I know we sat alone and sweating in a hot tub in the middle of Alabama, where we were, briefly, just brothers at a NASCAR race. But I don't remember, or cannot remember, what happens until the next day. When, hungover but drinking again under the hot Sunday sun, we watched Jeff Gordon wreck somewhere around the 150th lap, a wreck that would ultimately cost him the race. I remember later trying to make this a metaphor for what had happened and not happened the night before as we drove home through the lowlands of western Tennessee. I remember how strange it was that Cole Porter was on the radio. How he sang, "Read and let read, write and let write. Love and let love, bite and let bite." How strange it is now that I think of Talladega, and Randy, and my sudden, quick waning love for NASCAR. My queer love for NASCAR, much like my love for the South it represents, and my brother ... how I think about all this at a hip coffeeshop in Washington, DC—a city that, like myself, has a complicated relationship with its Southern roots. This shop serves coffee in excess of $5 a cup alongside vegan pie. Today, I order the sweet potato, and wistfully, shut my mouth.

ELLEN
GOLDSTEIN

After the Wedding

The moon is a dark searchlight,
casting unfamiliar shadows, me in a dress,
a man sitting next to my place at the table.
Once I shaped a deer out of the darkness,

a couple caught between flesh and dirt.
Once I walked through these fields with Steph,
picking dandelion greens

for her mother, rolling down the hill
south of the barn, pushing into each other's
warmth, her breasts, for the first time,
soft against my arm. Once

the older folks have gone to bed, their toasts
linger in the mosses along the reservoir,
messages we repeat, like fraying
blankets, an acre of moonlight.

Steph's new girlfriend talks to my partner.
She looks nothing like me.
Once I go back in, I take
his hand. We have no idea
what we are capable of.

Estates

Sometimes I miss those days spent scraping dirt
across the graves, where clots of clay broke open
in my hand, swarming with roots. There were sounds
among the hours, a clattering of stones
and crows, no hum of the train easing
between track and wire. I find myself
shaking off dim rooms, sour sofas
swept with too many words. For years
you held onto the cold promise
of bridges, but never answered to
the river. Red clay stains my skin like a debt.
Crows press provocations against the sky, they ask
How many lives have you left behind?

THE QUEER SOUTH

MIRIAM BIRD
GREENBERG

Elegy

Early on in the city
on weekends claimed by fog
I came back to your farmstead,
your emptied creek-side shanty house
from my laboratory wage work,
pockets full of micropipettes
and stolen white gloves as if to outfit a regiment
of ghost butlers
in an imagined antebellum manor
neither of us, if offered, would inhabit—
but still I saw the manor's cut crystal
glinting in night-frost on the fescue
beneath persimmon trees
where great horned owls left bones
to bleach. These nights
lately—with the fine rain singing
through ragweed, through mulberry
we'd kept for feeding ducks, the silkworm farm
we planned to someday have—
I swim the wild wheat that shines
like a lake on far back acres. I unstring
my jewelry, tarnishing from the work week
even still—
in the city of sooted brick and grimy air—from my neck
and wrists, spread the legs
of the wooden-runged ladder and hang
it in arcs inside the bower of the fig tree's
ribcage, hay rick, displayed
like ceremonial specimens
pinned to felt-lined glass cases
by the fig's knobby twigs. But deprived of ceremony
I find nothing

in my hands but unmoored symbols: one week
I caught june bugs in a jar every night
to feed the ducks, or once burnt
so methodically old letters from lovers
and the First National Bank alike,
as if a prayer summoning spirits
could ever come from cynics' lips. The layers
of history cat's-cradling between us, an elegy
which, unwillingly—
as algae on creek stones
loosed downstream rejoins indistinct matter—
we forget.

ELIZABETH GROSS

Staring Contest

It takes the kind of mirror
some boy's flat chest
can be, when fully naked

to show the monster back.
It has some questions
about gender. It asks

the three brave hairs
standing out from the valley
of his sternum. (So rare—

like the hairs of very young
elephants. Did you read that Bishop
letter—Moore plucks an elephant

to fix her bracelet? Elizabeth
the circus distraction.) Oh, can we eat
ice cream inside the orgasm?

Should we take separate cars?

Talking in the dark

Night-blooming jasmine
steals air from air until
it makes a solid shape.

I can't breathe underneath
this scent shimmering like heat.
Flowers pant out reek

like dogs, tongues out
for all the air, for what
they can get. Blinking

white from the choke
of the chain link fence.
They say it's sweet

but I hold my breath
head down, bull-like
run past every vine.

THE QUEER SOUTH

JOHNATHAN
HARPER

Southern Gothic

When the rain comes, the only voice
to call me in is my own. I know I'm alone now.
My feet churn red mud,

I slog through the clay earth—slog through
my southern blood, groping for traction. I think
God made my crooked face from this clay.

The pines' branches bow but each wooded
intersection maps a cross. The jagged architecture
of magnolia leaves slice water as it falls, framed

silhouettes are locked in spider moss.
The silhouette of his smile, the taste of him
still on the tip of my tongue—a word, his name

forgotten. At the creek the cicadas
had split the air with their song after waiting
seventeen years to open themselves.

I waited seventeen to open myself
to that moment. He cupped my cheek,
kissed me and whispered *Let's do this again.*

I found the ring he lost in the thick of it,
took it from the muddy bank and placed
it into the palm of his hand, smooth and cool

as a rain drop. The rain drops collecting
in my brow now. He departed quick
as a voice lost on storm wind.

The trees' arches close in. The crows,
watching in rows on the buttresses, don't speak.
I'm dumb enough to keep my silence, too.

SCOTT
HIGHTOWER

Alexandra's Ragtime Band

It's my business to stop what's wrong.

— Alexandra, from *The Little Foxes*

At Malmaison, just outside of Paris, the staircases,
while wide and elegant, are simple and utilitarian;

no way are they a spectacle. But here, in
the Gidden's family house, Regina pauses

before the round mirror in the high-toned room
adjoining the entry with its carpeted luxurious

sweep of stairs. "Better learn how," up
and down them, Ben's and Oscar's

fraternal soundtracks. The wallpaper encages;
meissen prances about a dresser-top and shelves.

Regina's hair glows. Imperiously, she turns
around to tell us what we "can" talk about:

"Zannie is going alone to Baltimore." Raise
a glass to the Hubbards & Giddens to "the little

foxes that spoil our vineyards;" to bacon
and coffee, medicine, and money. Without love

and affection, neither Capitalism nor Socialism
can deliver justice. Without love and affection,

puffy-faced Fascism wakes up, cavorts
in its unfettered violence, greed, and meanness.

Boys Gym

The first minutes of gym we have
to hurry to our coach who stands
on the glossy blond gym floor.
His left hand and hairy arm
curl around a clipboard;
a corner of his cruel
mouth clenches a whistle.

Come spring, he and his assistant
have us pile into the back
of a couple of pick-ups. They drive us
down a caliche road and put us out.

As he sets his watch. Coach, both
a married man and a father,
mumbles things derogatory—
but meant to be motivational—
about "candy asses," "pansies,"
"pantie waists." It will be years
before several of my best buds
confesses, each in confidence,
to having clandestinely
"hooked up" with him.

As he and his assistant drive back
to school, we run the country road.
I know the names of the ranches:
the Kirby's, the Kincheloes', the Owens's,
the Old Adams Place. (Nobody
calls them that anymore but me;
And when I do, only old people
know what I'm talking about.)

We sweat and stretch out our strides.
The brittle road crunches beneath our feet.
It is a pleasure to push until our muscles
burn, all the while, our lungs bellowing air;
a small pack of boys, ephebes, our small
town's unsullied brood, proud bantams.

Rural Discipline

Our fathers trained us
to rig a horseshoe on a cane
before going up
into the branches.

That way a thrasher
doesn't spoil the crown
but can reach the prized
and husky nuts:

that yellow smear
that stains naked flesh
a stubborn brown.
Later, I leaned over

glosses. In spareness,
with lithe Chinaberry switches,
they had escaped breaking

the ancient "Rule of Thumb."

MATTHEW
★HITTINGER★

The Light, the Idea of Light, Repeats Itself at South Beach

    The sun rises twice : once over the earth's
        rim as it spins, turns
its face; once from the clouds, the ray shafts cast
        like search lights. The high

    up wisps catch fire, the tail, peach-edged greets
        beach and sea, broken
white line, broken black line, stroked and folded
        into marigold

    rhymes, echo and sketch the receding V
        side stretch side spread no
longer V but the entire sea though
        not like that at all.

    How many times has a hand tried and failed
        to capture this scene?
What I missed : oil tanker slides along
        the bar like a rule

    or level : this side foam, this cloud mirrored,
        divided, the sea
doubling what it sees, the sky unmoved
        by its seam; couple

    beach-huddled face the rise side by side, first
        shadow opposite
the last shadow cast on the art deco
        stucco; those night boat

    lights at off shore intervals close enough
        to count their party
tiers; that mysterious phosphorescence
        riddling the waves

  that approached then backed away. What was missed
    was hours ago,
and hours before those hours a beach
    memory : the men

  who stood as sentinels on sand dunes near
    Provincetown, forearms
crossed, eyes behind mirrored shades so I saw
    only my own face

  its awe at intertwined limbs behind stone
    calves down between grass
and shore drifts the old men sitting naked
    and facing the sea

  as I sit naked and face the sea, read
    "scientists pin-point
the origin of deja vu." Is this
    deja vu? It is

  section 1E removed not just from this
    but each *Miami*
Herald down the hall. The Tropical Life
    spotlight on 1A,

  "A Turning Point—Miami-Dade Battle
    Thirty Years Ago"
but no page no photo to turn to see
    Anita. Forget

  the sun, the paper, the days of summers
    past no matter how
much they rhyme. Repeats, like my scuba friend
    who dives and dredges

  Bluehead Wrasse, do not put me at ease :
    the female turns male,
alone and yet surrounded—the circle
    beholds their transformed

  elder, but with awe? or could they simply
     not perform, mate no
matter how long the voyeurs wait? To change
    sex at will. Surface

having seen it, having claimed to see it
    but not knowing how
to describe what you see—try. Try again.
    The sun burns higher,

the shadows go shallow, the paper once
    through cannot be gone
through the same way just as the surface once
    broken cannot be

broken the same way in the same spot twice
    so what started ten
years ago does not end but continues :
    the sun still the same

(but not) the ocean still (but not) island
    to the south island
to the north their shorelines the same (but not)
    the lost coast and Port

Royal sunk cut off from the land then cays
    reclaimed, waterfronts—
the Palisadoes and Battery Park—
    the whole idea

in that light that grew and shrunk, like peeny
    wallies in the tree
canopy glowing there out in the sea
    not the reflected

moon off some sand bar or reef but a light
    its slight phosphors its
essence comes and goes as if some jelly
    like brain found itself

THE QUEER SOUTH

   caught between itself and its desire
        to fully surface
to not fall back, to glow and not grow dim,
      to strike and to sting.

DARREL ALEJANDRO
HOLNES

Tú

In the music video it looks like Shakira is dying.

I want to die for you
      though we've just met,

give you my bones to help you stand taller
and my feet for you to walk on when yours are worn.

      This is what she sings, love
worth dying for.

Seven years ago I loved her video

and now hear its song wailing in my head
as I struggle to hear what you're saying,

a good omen at Café Adobe,
      the setting of our first date.

Make love to me on this table for two.
I don't need my flesh if I have you.

So take my body as you need,
      breaking into the garden,

a wall to keep our home countries
out on the other side,

your sins washed in my old
blood and complexion.

Listen to my swan song gospel,
the unusual yodel in my throat,

a ballad as I nail my limbs to
this restaurant table:

Eres tu amor, mis ganas de reír, el adiós que no sabré decir, porque nunca podré vivir sin ti.

But for this feast to nourish your body we must first pray
or at least say we believe in something.

I don't believe in this Texas nation

but can in your naked grace. Come
make me a man   of faith.

And leave your body too, if you'd like.

In my country I dreamed of leaving
my body all the time,

the scar below my right eye,
flesh broken by soldiers

trying to scare my mother
into telling them my father's whereabouts;

my sun kiss undertone torn open to reveal
an ancestor's sinless shame

mejorando la raza
brightening our brown.

But I don't want to be whiter, just free,

sweetly delivered into dark matter,
and its boundlessness.

Redemption in shedding
incarcerating flesh.

Redemption in being reborn
in love, risen

in translation.

Baptism

A little boy is sent out toward the horizon
in an infinity pool with no life vest.
This is how I was required to swim

during my first lessons with my father, struggling upstream
to what seemed like the edge of the world at five years old. I failed
the swim test twice again years later in sixth grade

for the Boy Scout badge, once in the pool
diving from the top plank into the deep end,
and a second time trying to flip a submerged

capsized canoe from underneath it. My father,
el capitán, wondered if I'd ever grow
a pair and swim back on my own to the ledge

each time someone dove in and rescued me.
But somehow I managed to still make it
to the rank of Life Scout.

At seventeen in America they called me FOB,
fresh off the boat, though I flew here first class
the first time, on my own.

In the dorms, Tametrice renamed me Ricky Ricardo
until I dropped the accent and convinced her
I wasn't anything close to Cuban.

I hear Latinos are good swimmers, frat brother James
said with a smirk waiting for me to get
Black-man-angry so he could laugh at that too.

Summer heat in Texas was unbearable at times,
but I kept cool by going muddin' and bayou
bathing with Cowboy Brian, and other new friends.

Buffalo Bayou was my favorite;
the San Jacinto River feeds it;
a river named after the same saint

after which my father was also named, as if my head
under its waters would save me from drowning
myself by making me as man as from where I came.

But could such baptism move my body
onto a future path of past men? Water currents
pulled me in opposite directions.

The sun's light bouncing off the river's surface
nearly blinded this floating swan, but
upon reopening his eyes he discovered he had wings.

REX LEONOWICZ

tributaries

I.

minnows tugged at my ankles.
my solitary smile as i looked to the
gesturing glass surface of water,
happy for a creature's kiss, the first
impact of a shoal of mouths; happy
for mica drying shine onto my skin.

II.

i held the swannanoa
water in my palm. a cup
of everything, little pool
of river where bodies
would run into each other.

III.

a day on the river, you had said
our meeting had meant an end
to waiting, a calm. relief, a bridge
built between cities that couldn't
touch before.

IV.

you loved where i was going.
you could see my path, the gifts

i would give. you walked behind
for a moment, i stood by a stone
in the cold mud. i thought
of current and drift. you
caught up, cupped my hip
bones, *let's go*.

V.

you didn't think we could
take it outside of north carolina,
we had to keep our story anchored
in the blue ridge valley. the soft
touch of river stones would hold it,
though the waters would splinter,
you were sure

we would go, we would be fine
as the silt in the sieve of my hands.

SASSAFRAS
LOWREY

Jacksonville

She runs her grown-out, broken-off acrylic fingers across the Kool-Aid sticky shelter table edge as though it were the ivory keys of the finest church organ. Under breath, humming the hymns she sang as a Southern altar boy, she stops and says in the deep Mississippi drawl she slips into when she isn't thinking about hiding it, "Miss, did you know your fingers have more memory than any other part of your body?"

What do my fingers remember? A time when I'd have fought anyone that called me Miss, I was young and queer, finding safety and sex in playing with masculinity. I remember most the feel of leather, the smooth warmth of the cuff hy'd wrapped around my wrist, the burn of metal on the car, the masochistic dare to see which of us could keep their hands there longer. My fingers remember wrapping around my first cock, the one hy bought me at the novelty store out on the freeway, the way he taught me to bind my chest flat with the Walmart back brace. How dangerous and beautiful it felt to touch hym in the front seat of hys momma's car that we'd borrow for late night drives into South Georgia.

I moved to Jacksonville, Florida, less than a month after I turned 18. I'd been kicked out and was homeless, and the windowless basement where I stayed in Portland was nothing compared to the lusty promises hy whispered through hurried pay-phone conversations. We'd met at a queer youth conference in DC; hy was older, in experience more than years.

Dean and hys wife Star had saved up for months to drive up to DC. They'd even pulled enough together to stay at a hotel. On the drive up through the Carolinas, she said it was o.k. for hym to fuck other people. They'd never really been much for monogamy, and Star knew Dean's eyes were always wandering up seamed thighs of big femmes. Star was the first femme I ever met. She was fierce, brazenly fat, covered in tattoos, and quoted Bikini Kill. Much to my own dismay, a decade later I look a lot like her. Star wore a bikini to swim in the hotel pool and sang "Rebel Grrrrl" as she cannonballed into the deep end, daring vacationing families to stop her. Dean met me, scared little puppy dog of a baby butch who had traveled alone from the west coast to be at the conference. Star called me a Yankee. Dean told me I could hang out with them for the weekend. We ditched hys wife. Star said it was o.k., but hy should have known it wasn't really; the boundaries got all mixed and busted. I should have known hy'd do the same to me.

Before me, Dean had never even thought about being with another butch. It just wasn't done that way down South is what hy told me. I was hunting for a tough butch like Dean, all denim, leather, and crisp, white t-shirts. Sitting on the ugly floral comforter, Dean wrapped hys arms around me, t-shirts and ace bandages meeting. We attended conference sessions about passing and coalition building, sharing glances across crowded rooms. At the end of the weekend Dean took one of the leather cuffs from hys wrist and put it around mine. Pressing me against the ice machine in a hotel hallway alcove, hy whispered, "You're mine." Hy looked away as my eyes filled with tears. "We'll make this work won't we?" I barely dared to ask. "You damn right," hy replied, pressing me farther into the alcove and back against the ugly wallpaper.

My flight into town was early. Dean's momma agreed to go to work before her shift so that Dean could take the car and pick me up from the airport. Hy wore hys mechanic's jumpsuit, parked, and waited crouched against the wall right by the security checkpoint. Hy told me to buy *Stone Butch Blues* and read it on the flight. Hy told me that was the best education I could get about what living in hys world would look like. I was scared transferring flights in the Dallas airport. Dean and I kissed hard as soon as I passed through security, even though families were staring, and the TSA guards looked like they were getting ready to kick us out.

We spent that first day driving, so hy could show me all the important places in town. First was the street where Rhonda, hys mentor, was murdered the year before we met. She was out about being trans, and one night hy got a call that something happened. Dean raced to her house, but it was too late. All hy could do was cradle blood-soaked gravel. Next was the school softball field where hy'd busted hys knees in the dusty grass and fucked a girl for the first time behind the bleachers. Dean said hy'd had to leave high school right after that. Some closet case on the team ratted them out to keep her Southern Baptist parents looking the other way. Hy had to get a GED, but hy said it had been worth it. I was lying in the outfield dozing in the sun while Dean walked the bases when hy saw something glinting against the hot, late-afternoon sun. Reaching into the red, a thick plume billowing before third base, hys hand closed around the hard, smooth handle of a switchblade.

I hadn't known quite what to expect showing up in the South with a backpack. I blew the last of my cash on that ticket, told the slumlords someone else could take the moldy basement room, and gave the rest of my shit to some buddies. I worried that we'd be living with Dean's mother. Out West I didn't know anyone who even talked with their parents. In Portland, the goal was to stay as far away as possible. Even the thought of parents made me uncomfortable, and I wasn't sure how I would handle living with someone else's.

There wasn't much to do in Jacksonville, especially at night, particularly if you weren't interested in a fight. Back in Portland, I was used to wandering the streets like they were mine. In Jacksonville, Dean always reminded me we weren't safe outside the car. Back in Oregon, some buddies and I had been chased around by skinheads a few times, but they were easy to avoid and didn't really come looking for you. In Jacksonville, everything seemed different. Even on that first day out driving, Dean refused to stop somewhere for me to pee because we were in deep Klan territory. Dean gave me that knife hy found in the softball field, cleaned it with alcohol, and then pressed it into the palm of my hand. Dean said it was to keep me safe in case hy ever wasn't around to take care of me.

When I left Portland, I hadn't expected to be so bored. We slept most of the day and were up at night when we could take mamma's car so long as they were at the hospital where she worked by 5am to pick her up. Most nights we went to Wal-Mart. Being there was the closest to hanging out with other butches as we could get. The overnight stock crew was all dykes; I never really talked to them outside of a polite nod. Just seeing them as I walked the aisles, groceries to pet food, magazines to housewares, helped me to feel a little less alone.

Some nights Dean was real sweet, like the time hy took me to the novelty shop—closest thing to a sex shop you could get in JAX. Hy helped me to pick out my first dick. Back in the car, I unzipped and nestled the cock against my thigh. Dean said hy wanted to help me in ways no butch had helped hym when hy was newly out. I leaned over the center consul and started to kiss Dean, hard pressing hym back against the driver-side door. I tried hard to be patient with Dean, to understand how hard it was for hym to be with another butch. In Portland, there really weren't any femmes, and I thought nothing of making out with butches throwing each other up against the steel supports of bridges and the bricked walls of dark side streets. Dean tried to explain, said that hy had a reputation. Hy talked about all the femmes hy'd had and what was expected of a butch. Hy took me into Little Five Points, but wouldn't take me to hys bar yet. Hy said hy wasn't ready, said there would be drama. Then hy started disappearing some nights, taking hys mamma's car and not telling me when hy would be back.

Since getting into town, I hadn't seen Dean's ex, Star, the one we ditched in that DC hotel. I was scared of her. I picked dried mud out of the creases of my boots the night Dean suggested that maybe one night the three of us should all hang out. I thought maybe Dean had already started to see Star on those late nights hy disappeared. Dean said hy would call to see if Star could come out that night, and I went back into our little room. It was pretty empty, just an old twin mattress and a sloping dresser. There hadn't been room in it for my clothes, so I kept them stacked in the corner next to Dean's life-sized cardboard cutout of James Dean. Supposedly hy'd had it since middle school, back before hy was Dean. There was a TV that pulled in endless re-runs of *The Golden Girls* and not much else and the leather pride flag that Dean had strung up as a curtain over the little window.

I had dressed up: t-shirt and work pants, fresh from the washer, and boots, laced tight. I was surprised to see Dean take the driver's seat and watch Star climb in next to hym. The shock must have been visible on my face because Star turned to Dean and said, "Femmes don't sit in backseats." I knew better than to argue with anything anyone said about butch/femme and especially knew better than to fight with Star. The whole goal of the night was for the three of us to be together and to keep Dean in sight. I knew if I fought with Star, especially before they even started driving, that Dean would likely just leave me to another night of bad TV. I climbed into the back, carefully shifted skirts, bras, and wigs out of my way.

I watched as Star pushed a tape into the stereo and turned up the volume. The speakers were behind my head against the rear window, making it hard to hear anything other than the Bikini Kill screaming "Rebel Grrrrl," Star's signature song: "That grrrrl thinks she's the Queen of the neighborhood, I've got news for you SHE IS!"

Star and Dean kept exchanging glances and speaking in whispers. I stared out into the dark marsh that lined the interstate and said nothing; I didn't know where they were going, but tried to just relax into knowing at least I was with Dean.

I dozed off during the drive, and awoke to find myself alone in the car. It was dark, no streetlights, but the front door was open and music still blaring. As I rubbed my bleary eyes, I realized that in the glow of the headlights Star was dancing. At some point, she'd switched tapes from screaming dykes to Dolly Parton. Dean was resting on the front bumper watching as Star slowly slipped the hem of her pinup dress higher and higher up her thighs rolling her hips and singing along to the crackling cassette: "I'm begging of you please don't take my man ...."

In the headlights, I saw what looked like a ring glinting on her left hand as her dance became an unzipping, the fabric pooling at her feet. Her red bra cradled her heavy breasts; garters strained to hold the tattered thigh-highs. Squinting through the glare of the windshield at Dean, I recognized the movement of hys arm and realized that hy was so focused on Star's dancing that it hadn't even occurred to hym, or hy didn't care, that I might wake up. When the song ended, Star pulled her dress on, and she and Dean got back into the car. I pretended to sleep for another 20 minutes or so, then yawned loudly and stretched. Star said she was hungry so we pulled into a Waffle House. I smeared the runny part of my eggs across the pancakes and tried not to make eye contact with Dean, who was sipping black coffee across the table from me, next to Star.

On the drive back to Jacksonville, I was too tense to sleep. I knew how to take care of myself. I thought about that last night with parents, the months that led up to the run, the bruises. In the last few weeks before my escape, they hardly ever even let me out of their sight. I unbuckled and buckled the leather cuff in the dark. I knew things were getting bad, fast. Still, I wasn't sure if I could walk away no matter how clear it was becoming Dean wanted me to.

We got back home just as the sky was getting light. Dean said hy'd never let a femme walk herself to the door, so hy jumped into hys mamma's car and prepared to follow Star home and walk her to her door. I knew the implication was that I should go into the house and leave Dean and Star alone. We drove to Star's apartment without talking. I was surprised that Dean hadn't put up a fight about my climbing into the passenger seat and insisted on tagging along. It was probably because hys mamma was home, and hy didn't want her knowing how messy everything was.

Dean told me that Star had a hard time sleeping, especially when it was already morning, so hy was going to tuck her into bed before coming back to the car. I wondered what Star really thought of all this. I figured she had to know that I was still with Dean. Evidently she didn't care, or like me she was stuck. I thought of getting out of the car and leaving, but there wasn't anywhere to go. I only wanted to run if Dean would chase and hunt me down, bringing me back with kisses or promises. I knew Dean wouldn't follow.

Dean stumbled back to the car, tired, with hys t-shirt untucked, binder slipping and boots untied. Hy offered no explanation for how long hy'd been in Star's apartment. I had planned to stay quiet, but as we sped through downtown, by the big Southern Baptist church, I couldn't hold back: "You fucked her."

I expected denial but was met instead with cold anger. I liked the mean butches whose anger sometimes got the best of them, but something here felt different. Dean didn't deny anything. Hy didn't say anything at all, just suddenly lurched across me, opening the passenger door and tried to shove me out onto the deserted bridge. The seatbelt held. Panting, I got the door closed, the image of moving pavement burned into my memory.

When we got to Dean's home, I stripped in the bedroom before heading to the bathroom and locking the door. I was exhausted but felt too dirty to sleep. I stood in the shower until the hot water ran out. When I got back to the bedroom, Dean wasn't there. As I got dressed, I realized my knife, the one that Dean dug from the softball field as a gift, was missing. Dean's mamma was sleeping in her room. The last thing I wanted was to talk to her. I didn't know how to talk with my own parents, let alone someone else's. Mamma seemed to like

Star, and didn't really know what to think about me. She was never mean, but worried about what the neighbors and the ladies at church thought of another not-girl girl, living in her house. I slipped past her bedroom and into the empty living room. I almost expected to see Dean in the kitchen making a grilled cheese, but the light was off and the room empty. I was about to go back to the bedroom to see if Dean's keys were where hy'd tossed them on the bed when we came in, when I noticed light coming through the crack under the door to the garage.

At first I thought Dean's mamma had just left the light on when she was doing laundry. Then, I saw the knife next to the washing machine. As I stepped farther into the garage, I saw Dean smoking a cigarette leaning against the wall next to some boxes. The left leg of hys jeans were rolled up, and as I got closer I could see "RIOT GRRRL" carved vertically down hys calf in thick capital letters.

There was nothing to say. Unbuckling the leather cuff and setting it on the cracked concrete next to the knife, I realized I didn't belong to Dean anymore. "I think you better go," Dean said.

I couldn't believe I was back at the airport, setting off metal detectors with my steel-toed boots and safety pin closed ACE bandage binder. I spent the cross-country flight puking and crying in the little airplane bathroom, wiping my nose on the sleeve of a work shirt that had belonged to Dean. Portland and everyone living there looked just as I remembered, like a brown bag from the grocery store dropped in a puddle, all soggy and falling apart.

My time in the South was not all broken hearts and busted promises. There was work too, the organizing Dean and I did with the small queer youth center where adults risked safety and reputation to be out, to stand with us in that homophobic town. Living in the South is a huge part of where I learned to organize, to understand that I wasn't alone and that together we could fight parents and systems and build our own queer worlds. These were the kids I learned how to survive from. They taught me that all us queers are a family, that there was a legacy to our struggle, to leaving where we came from and building our own home. These were girls who took their names from Disney princesses, who lived in boys group homes smuggling hormones and HIV meds from their drag mammas. They danced when the AC broke, straightened our ties, and laced their fingers with mine when bottles broke at our feet. I hate that I never got to say goodbye.

A decade later, I see them reflected in the eyes of every girl I meet on New York's streets, fresh from buses, accents thick. They sleep on New York City subway trains, on the pier and in parks. The streets of the Village are filled with children whose eyes are glazed over by needles, bottles, pills, powder. Sometimes, they tell me about the trans mammas who helped them get the ticket, taught them how to turn tricks, took them in when God and everyone had abandoned them. I think of those girls I grew up with and offer up a silent prayer that they are still fighting, that they too have grown up, that have become the queer mothers helping this new generation of kids just as lost and broken as we all were.

She runs her grown-out, broken-off acrylic fingers across the Kool-Aid-sticky shelter table edge as though it were the keyboard of the finest church organ. Under breath, humming the hymns she sang as a Southern altar boy, she stops and says in the deep Mississippi drawl she slips into when she isn't thinking about hiding it, "Miss, what do your fingers remember?"

THE QUEER SOUTH

TYLER
LYNN

Boxes

During my physical transition from female to male, every time I filled out a form of some kind, I would pause at the two dreaded boxes—their black and white lines so straight and narrow, their corners at perfect 90-degree angles. Where in their two perfectly symmetrical, absolutely congruent shapes was there room for me? Should I check "female," I wondered, since I had the reproductive system of one? Should I check "male," since I had facial hair and was gaining weight in the form of muscle mass? Was I defined as female if I didn't view myself that way? Was I defined as male if I lacked a penis, something that seems completely and undeniably an integral part of manhood in our society? Those two perfect boxes were just too unforgiving.

When I was younger, I checked female because I did not dare to express or even hope for a different option. I knew what I had been taught, and that was that no matter how I felt on the inside, I was female on the outside. When I was born, the doctor declared me a fine, healthy baby girl, and that was that. The first time I felt a respite from those two small black boxes was at college, when I was asked what pronoun I prefer. If pronouns could be flexible why couldn't that extend to other areas of my life? Why didn't my own opinion of my identity matter? Why had no one taken the time, or better yet, why hadn't *I* made the time to respect it?

Official documents are a tricky business for transpeople. Before transitioning medically, you are told that you must live a year in the gender that you feel yourself to be in order to get permission from a therapist to undergo a medical transition. In theory this is a great idea. Of course one should take a trial run before committing to expensive, body-altering surgery and hormone therapy. But in practice, it is not quite so simple. Not everyone is lucky enough to pass as the opposite sex without any form of medical intervention. Fortunately I was able to do so. I was blessed with tall parents, which meant I grew to be 6'2", huge for a girl. I was also blessed with large hands and feet, broad shoulders, and a voice that could be made somewhat lower with minimal practice. As one of my friends said to me, "As far as trans people go, you won the genetic lottery." While I easily passed as male, my lack of facial hair and higher than normal voice placed me around the age of 16 and prepubescent. This look lasted until my 23rd year, the year I began to take testosterone and had a double mastectomy.

During college, even though I was living life as a male and going by male pronouns, I was in label limbo, unsure of which box to check. Throughout my childhood, there had never been a question in my mind of which box I was *supposed* to check, even though every time I did so, it felt like losing a piece of the identity I had fought so hard to silently hold on to. I would be standing at a desk applying for a library card, staring at those two boxes. The nice librarian would look up and wonder why this soft-spoken, pretty-faced young man was having so much trouble filling out a form for a library card. Did it matter what gender I was in order to check out a book? Is there a section of the library where people of only one gender are allowed? Why does our society insist on knowing people's gender in every possible situation?

By college, this "honesty" became too much of a hassle and confusion for people, and on most forms I assumed it didn't matter anyway. Unless I was willing to sit down with every secretary and receptionist and explain the difference between sex and gender, what it meant to identify as transgender, and why I felt that way, it didn't seem worth it. I hated the double-take that inevitably occurred when they looked up at me, smiled, looked down at my completed form, frowned, looked back up at me, and stared.

....

After undergoing sexual realignment at age 23, there was no longer any doubt that I was legally male. I was to be free of this liminal state between genders after one last challenge. I had to first change the gender marker on all of my official identification documents. This seemed like a daunting task, made all the more nerve wracking because I was undergoing it in the state of Georgia, which has a historically conservative stance on these types of laws.

My first stop was the Dekalb County Department of Motor Vehicles, where I arrived with every form of documentation I could think to bring. I also had letters written by each of my surgeons stating that I was now "biologically" male. When my number was called, I nervously approached the surly-looking woman behind the DMV help desk, while clasping my large and unruly sheaf of documents. "How can I help you?" she asked, looking suspiciously over the top of her glasses at me.

This was the moment of truth. I had had a whole speech planned out in my mind, explaining what exactly had been done to me, what it meant to be transgender, and what the laws on the subject were to the best of my knowledge. As she looked expectantly at me, I froze. "Umm, well, my driver's license says female right now, and I need to change it to male." She looked at me quizzically and held out her hand. I slid my license across the counter to her. She picked it up and examined it. "Well, I'll be damned, it does say female. You need to get that fixed, now don't you," she said and laughed. And that was it. Who knows what that woman thought as to the reason why I arrived with a driver's license that said "female" on it. Whatever reason she assumed was fine by me. She turned to her computer, pulled up my file, and pressed a few keys. I waited while my new license was printed out, and then she handed it over to me. I felt much lighter as I walked out the door of the DMV that day.

Next up was the Social Security office, which was located in downtown Atlanta. The ambience in this office left a lot to be desired, much like that of the DMV. Long wait times made the patrons agitated in the overcrowded waiting room, and most of the office clerks looked exhausted and overworked. As I sat waiting for my number to be called, I scanned the clerks behind the counter, picking out one woman with a friendly looking face whose desk I wanted to be called to. Luckily, 20 minutes later she called out my number. After my initial request to simply get my gender marker in the Social Security records changed, she stated that that was possible, but wondered why it was currently female. I nervously but very quietly rambled on about having had sexual reassignment surgery and about how I had read on their website that in order to change your gender marker you needed to bring a letter from a doctor. In my flustered state, I slid across the counter my now somewhat crinkled bundle of papers. She looked through them briefly and then smiled at me and said, "Hold on, let me go get my supervisor."

It turned out that neither the clerk nor her supervisor were sure of the exact protocol for changing a person's gender marker in their records. After I explained to them what they were to the best of my knowledge, we seemed to all come to the consensus that this seemed reasonable. As I talked, my fear slipped away. The two women laughed and joked with me, saying that they would never have known I was born a girl. They thought it was quite funny. Once everything was taken care of, I thanked them and got up to leave. The supervisor winked at me and said, "Honey, let me just say how cute you are. Good thing I am married."

Getting my passport changed was the easiest of them all. I went to a large postal service building in Tucker, Georgia, a suburb of Atlanta that flows so seamlessly into the urban center that you are not quite sure when you have left the city limits. When I arrived, the man behind the counter directed me to the back to fill out a passport change request form. I placed this form in an envelope along with a copy of the letter from one of my surgeons and handed it, along with my current passport, to the guy behind the counter. He took the envelope, placed it in a bin, and then punched a hole in my current passport to signify that it was no longer valid. There were no questions, no supervisors, and best of all, I did not have to come out as being a transsexual to anyone. About two weeks later, a brand new passport arrived in the mail.

Because there are countless numbers of forms in life, I still occasionally run across some record of mine that has not yet been changed. Now that my official forms of identification all say "male," I have become quite brazen in these situations. "Huh, that is weird," I say and smile when someone points out that they have me listed as "female" for such and such. They agree and laugh as well, attributing it to my gender-neutral first name and feminine sounding last name. I will occasionally rattle off my whole explanation if I feel it is warranted. I am actually somewhat thankful that I have had to go through this process of coming out to strangers in a conservative state. Even though I am also a Southerner, it was still fairly easy for me to fall into a distrust of those around me, assuming their prejudice and hatred without ever testing that bias. After having come out as a transsexual to multiple strangers in this process, I have been forced to completely change this false view that I had. I have not once experienced hate from these people. Confusion and curiosity yes, but not hate. I now feel safer and more at home in the state in which I grew up, a place that, before this, I had only hesitantly called my own.

....

I am now male for all intents and purposes. Outwardly I am legally and physically male. I blend seamlessly into polite society, flying under the radar. I have a masculine appearance and possess a generic style. I am drawn to many sports, outdoor activities, and mostly stereotypical male activities and preferences. This has suited me well over the years. My manner and interests allow people to move me quite fluidly from the female box in their mind to the male box. People think to themselves that there was a mistake, and I am simply making it right by becoming a man. They cite my love of basketball, my desire for adrenaline-pumping activities, or the fact that I don't care about celebrity gossip as reasons why I was meant to be a man.

I do this, too, a lot of the time. It's easy for me to justify my decisions based on superficial qualities I possess, but that is doing others and myself an injustice. I am glossing over the fact that what makes someone a man or a woman is much more profound than what they like to do, whom they choose to spend their time with, or how they express their feelings. I have no idea why I feel male and always have, where I feel it, or even how to describe it. All I know is that I do, and that this feeling is much deeper in my core than any personality trait that may be used to describe me or any interest I may have.

I still do not fit into that male box completely, however. After all, even though I have always felt myself to be male, I was still raised as a girl. Carl Jung believes that every individual is composed of dualities. He theorizes that every male possesses some feminine characteristics, and that every female possesses some masculine characteristics. He calls this the *anima* and *animus*. Although my brain is male, I was raised as a girl and, hence, had more time nurturing my feminine traits.

My parents' house sits on a quiet, tree-lined street within walking distance of Emory University. It has been many years since I graduated from high school, but my bedroom has remained relatively unchanged. There is a poster over my bed of the cast from the television show *CSI: Crime Scene Investigation*, in which the characters are lined up and dimly backlit with the headlights of a truck. Another poster on the opposite wall shows a cougar jumping from one jagged cliff face to another. Below the picture is the inscription: *Courage is the ability to leap beyond the familiar.* On the back of my door is a large target from the shooting range that I go to, riddled with bullet holes. Neatly laid side by side in front of my bookshelf is my set of 15 metal dumbbells of varying weights. On one of the shelves above them are trophies that I won from various sports. Mixed in with my book collection are twelve *Hardy Boys* books with frayed covers and dog-eared pages from having been read so many times.

In that same line of sight from the doorway, you can also see the top of my dresser. On it sits a lone photograph in a faded wooden frame. It is of a smiling toddler who has curly brown hair and is dressed in a blue corduroy dress with a bib of teddy bears and apples. This is a picture of me when I was a little over a year old. Next to this is a pastel blue jewelry box with cupcakes, lollipops, party hats, and hearts painted on it, also in pastels. When you lift up the lid of the box, a little fuzzy brown bear twirls around atop a small spring. There is a handle on the back of the box that can be twisted, causing a simple melody to play. My mother gave me this jewelry box when I was three years old.

When I was a child, relatives would frequently send me children's jewelry, for which I could find no use, so it quickly got stored in this box. A few pearl and flower bracelets and colored barrettes have weathered the years and are still kept in the box along with an assortment of other objects. There are multi-colored guitar picks and a few coins of foreign currency from past trips. When I was in middle school, hemp chokers became quite popular unisex necklaces, so there are also some homemade and commercially made ones in the box. Along with that are some boys' seashell chokers that I purchased during various summer beach trips with my family. Clanking around at the bottom are also some bullet casings that I kept once from the floor of a shooting range.

Recently, my mother asked if I wanted the photograph and jewelry box taken out of my room, worried that I might find them offensive to my male identity. The thought of removing either the picture or the jewelry box had never occurred to me. Because they had always been there, they had never struck me as out of place. To get rid of them would be like denying my past. Living life as a young girl while feeling myself to be a boy had been very painful and disconcerting, but it was the only childhood I knew or will ever know. Some memories of those years are sad and painful, but just as many are joyous. I would much rather have had a typical boyhood, but the fact is that I did not. The childhood I did have made me into the man I am today. A man with a mottled assortment of boys' and girls' personal objects as well as masculine and feminine personality traits. I am very proud of the man that I have become and would never want to discount whatever it was that got me here.

BO McGUIRE

Evelyn and Willis

Willis was Evelyn's Daddy, yes.
Willis' favorite word, Goddamn.
As in, *I guess your mama sent you out here, Goddamn*
woman don't think I can walk, Goddamnit
I can walk when the moon is out from under.
And Willis could walk and would spin
everything out from under. Willis traded with the coloreds. One day
Willis took Evelyn with him. They went to seine minnows.
The place where they were headed was down
on some property. And this property, good for seining, was owned
by a woman. She was colored. She was named Mrs.
Pinafore. And she called to Willis from the porch
on this day not to go down there and seine for them minnows.
And Evelyn stood there awkward and beautiful at fourteen.
And Evelyn was caught in between Willis and the porch.
And Evelyn wished she was on the Opry.
And Willis called Mrs. Pinafore a woman,
told her to get in her house.
He and Evelyn was going to seine some minnows.
Mrs. Pinafore got her husband, Mitch Pinafore,
and since Evelyn was all there and all awkward beautiful,
Willis left and got drunk. They went back to seine minnows
that same night. Mitch Pinafore was not at home,
and Willis had left his seining bucket at the bar,
so Willis just stood in the street and called Mrs. Pinafore a woman.
And he called her a woman and a woman again and again,
And he called her a moan. She called him a trespasser.
And when he was all done, he looked at, and she was,
all the time of his hollering,
just as awkward beautiful as she ever was.
Willis took her home.
Willis was called to appear before his good friend the judge.

Willis was called a trespasser. He was a drunk.
He was a carpenter, and he brung Evelyn
as witness. This is what he told her beforehand,
Cash crop can be fond in small lies, little gal, my pride.
For the record, Evelyn was beautiful, she testified,
We never even went down there to seine no Goddamn minnows.

Evelyn washed Willis' face, hands, arms, and feet
       every evening after that—
Evelyn, the oldest, and Dot, the second to oldest, watched on.

Evelyn and Dot

About hard things, if one of them knowed it
the other knowed it too—Evelyn, the oldest,
Dot, the second to oldest, Goddamn
the man and the man's thing hollerin'. His duck was harder'n water.
His dick was pretty as crystal, solid as pigs cryin' in the dark. Dot
and Evelyn was both dark headed. And what they held
in them dark heads was bone dark. What they held in them
dark bones was just about the same. They was Blantons
and Willis was their daddy. And Evelyn washed the day out
from Willis's face, hands, arms, and head and hound every evening
the holler dwindled into blue light. Evelyn cleaned for the flood.
Evelyn knowed, so Dot knowed it too. Evelyn knowed what Willis
was waiting for was the Goddamn spring with Uncle Dovie.
And if Willis was waiting, Goddamn, Evelyn waiting too,
and Dot was all full of hell fire and Opry music.
If one of them hated the waiting, the other one hated it harder.
Waiting for Uncle Dovie was the devil. About Uncle Dovie,
it was a flood of possum. This was true now, when the stream
of possum come, Willis and Uncle Dovie would hunt
possum all Goddamn day, take 'em down and trade
with the coloreds. When the stream of possum come
down the holler, Willis would bring them home and chase Evelyn
chasing Dot. And when one started hollerin',
the other went hollerin' too,
Goddamnit, Daddy, don't take that possum up close to Mama.
She'll mark that baby.
Willis was a Goddamn drunk with as much possum as he and
Uncle Dovie could press to fit.
He'd take that possum down to Mrs. Pinafore.
He'd take her a sack alive, half the night sweet potato breaking
necks. Goddamn, Evelyn ate. And Evelyn, the oldest, was touched
too beautiful. And Evelyn, the oldest, was too beautiful to tell
in every batch of them Goddamn possum
was at least one black-colored squirrel.
And Willis would save that squirrel for savin'

in his Liberty overalls,
And Willis would bring that squirrel back to the house.
And Willis would slam that squirrel against the screen door
hollerin', *Goddamnit, Dot, you get the head end of this squirrel*,
and she would. And then he'd holler, *Evelyn, little gal, my pride,
grab that tail, and tug and pull and yank that beast out its shell.*

The holler trespassed her skin. Evelyn, the oldest,
pulled and pulled and prayed and prayed herself
away from the holler, whispering the vice of her teeth,
Get on off devil skin, Goddamnit.

Evelyn and Me

Evelyn Louise, no longer Evelyn, the oldest, creeps in my skin
like it was a Goddamn screen. Things get caught and ripped
on the screen door. *Goddamn it,* Evelyn Louise broke pearls
from her wrist on her way in from the drive-in tonight. The holler
is a Goddamn million miles away and that makes Evelyn Louise
turn and think the screen door is solid and it ain't at the same time
the drive-in screen passes behind it—a screen through a screen.
Goddamn that. Evelyn smokes Virginia Slims
two-at-a-time and one-right-after-the-other.
Evelyn Louise holds in her head a vision of Willis and Dot—
what was they running, tugging while Evelyn Louise sold night
tickets at the drive-in. And during the day, Goddamn it,
she couldn't keep her eyes off the screen. Evelyn Louise dreamed it
big as the Opry stage. There she was—all nineteen years being
poured into a woman. During the day, every day, she watches
Robert Lee leave for C&S Oldsmobile in those God-blessed
white coveralls. He handles the cars, he winds the worlds.
When he sits down to eat, he prays,
This ain't makin' the babies no new shoes.
Evelyn Louise walks the floor of her heart day after red-dirt day—
Susan, the oldest, on her hip, and Robert Jr.
inside her, pulling her harder down. After she walks
home from the Goddamn drive-in, Evelyn Louise
can't break sleep. She sinks into her
dark head. Susan, the oldest, grabs at Robert Lee's hand through the
Alabama dark, and Evelyn Louise sees this—Goddamn beautiful.
She drives the loose hair from her face—*Goddamn Vivien Leigh,*
Evelyn Louise cries for what she can't see
coming on the far side of the screen door.
In her chair, Evelyn Louise can feel everything in the house
pushing her forward. She rocks hard against herself.
She's low singing, Evelyn Louise moaning across the room.
Her heels are Opry music never played. Evelyn Louise sees
something dark on the screen, on top of the river, a sister
in trouble—penned. Evelyn Louise needs, she reaches under

herself—there it is—what Willis gave and what he left was shotgun. Evelyn aims fire, blows the screen door wide.

Goddamn, Evelyn Louise.
There creaks rusty me.

Dot Eating Greens at Top O' the River

Evelyn, I done seen what's on the far side banks
of Jordan ain't nothin'
like going down to the lumber yard singin' pines.
Evelyn, if you are followin' me, I ain't leadin' you nowhere
worth a hill of muscle. Hurting a man's heart hurts or it don't.
Evelyn, a man will take you in his taxi and marry again.
Evelyn, he won't even tell you,
Evelyn, that little girl had a name.
I called her and she ain't come back yet.
It ain't no wonder we come from mountains.
Evelyn, we're always buryin' things we want kept alive.
I seen you with that cuttin' gun. The way you look
like cryin' down a drain. God lets it rain
all the sudden, then don't know when
to tilt his bucket back the other way.
Evelyn, what kind of man is that?
Mama took me down that hall, and I knowed
you was watchin' my shadow
fallin' into hers. That little girl—Donna,
God left with her like he's done
left with me. God gave me a boy who shot me
through the face, and I survived, Evelyn, don't forget,
like I said, it ain't no wonder we got drops
of Cherokee. Evelyn, why you look just like Mama
when she lost Willis—Fevered Scarlet
come down through the holler hollerin'
like a drunk, knockin' on the door like God
wantin' your heart. When he comes
'round here, I'm tellin' Him to sell
to someone who's buyin'. I don't even know
what that means to mean, sugar. Evelyn Louise,
if you're followin' me, I ain't movin'. Lord,
let me see Jesus before it's all over. Lord,
I got to go. The only thing I ever knowed about ridicule
was havin' it all over my hands.

RANGI McNEIL

Paterfamilias

Because *dead* isn't as cliché as *deadbeat*, I said he was
though he lives & breathes & is always almost the first
to call come Christmas or my birthday.

He swears to recall my bout of chicken pox (a legion
of lesions littering the inside of my mouth & all of my
8th-grade flesh, save the soles of my feet)

my aversion to tomatoes, affinity for *Jesus Christ Superstar*
& The Solid Gold dancers. He's kept some baby teeth
& a shoebox of Polaroids gone off-color with time & touch—

our gaping grins proof enough that once upon a time,
in a land of malt liquor, cotton fields & *Sanford & Son*, we were together—
free of the stench of steadfast disappointment.

He loves the Lakers, the Yankees & his t-bones well done.
And on more than a few lunch breaks, he pays any available crackhead
$5 to suck him off behind the gunmetal grey utility shed in the cemetery

where what remains of my mother's mother lies in an unmarked grave.

Family Reunion

Today I'm thankful for kosher hot dogs (no elbows
or assholes) & mood-regulating medication;
for rehab, gastric bypass & abortions.

Summer suits us: dark as we are & so prone to revelry.

Samson

> *I have been a Nazarite unto God from my mother's womb:*
> *if I be shaven, then my strength will go from me, and I shall*
> *become weak, and be like any other man.*
>
> — Judges 16:17

One cousin was born ashen & still, his viscera
on the outside of his body. At sixteen he died

young though much older than had been expected.
Another was run over on a sidewalk in Midtown

by a diplomat's son who sent a check
& a rose-covered cross to the funeral.

It was lupus that left my mother speckled
as a hyena, gnarled as ginger root.

Nothing betrays like the body. Nothing?
Not love? *No, not even.*

What I Tell Myself (Concerning Death) When Next I Have My Full Attention

Because it is the ultimate resolution, it cannot be unresolved.
And is less decipherable than prophesies spoken
in an oblique language lacking proper nouns, innuendo & action.

You returned to this place you are grateful to no longer
call home to help bury your youngest uncle: he who let his only

child & myriad sisters believe his chemo & radiation reached
their appropriate & resolute resolution, so that he might
pass his last days unfettered by premature grieving.

And this passes for peace: confidence in the availability
of icy refreshment come summer; of heat in bleak midwinter.

KELLY McQUAIN

Brave

From rough burlap we cut loincloths, fringed the ends,
strung cheap plastic beads into wampum belts,
sucking our thumbs when our needles drew blood
—done not so much for merit badges as for
the Kool-Aid crazed shenanigans got up to that day
in our frazzled den mother's cluttered house:
ersatz Indian finery pulled over blue uniforms
as we danced and whooped and bounced like hooligans
from La-Z-Boy recliner to afghan-covered couch.
A turkey feather fell from my paper headband
on the long walk home through kickable leaves.
Part of a pack, but where was my true tribe?
Those Cubs in their happy savagery? Boys whose hands
I sometimes longed to hold, hard, like a toy tomahawk.
I needed stealth, a new way to hide in the world:
patient as stone, elusive as water. I wanted to become
a stranger to myself, someone stronger in different skin.
I knew my bedroom slippers were not Indian moccasins
that night as I stood naked before my closet mirror—
lipstick war paint striping my cheeks, a welcome scratch
of burlap on my hairless balls (it was always
so *involved* being me). No uniform. No fear. No one to see.
I was alone and for once loving my aloneness. My body
an arrow shooting somewhere far off, its bow and quiver
triggered in this act of making the invisible visible at last.
Fringe on my loincloth tickled my thighs and knees
as I wound my wampum belt around my waist
and wondered what my new Indian name should be:
Feathered Dream-Catcher? (we had one in the kitchen)
Or *He Who Sees Shapes in the Random Patternicity of Things?*
But I was only a kid too quiet in his room;
at the sound of someone's feet on the stairs, I hid.

A turn of the doorknob and my father leaned in to ask
what the hell was I doing crawling under the bed?
He laughed as I rose, my hands hiding my bare chest,
my pale skin reddening as I stammered to explain.
I couldn't explain. What was I in his eyes? A silly boy,
his little wild thing. So I laughed, too—what else could I do
as I stood before him revealed:
                        being scared
                                    being brave.

Spirit Animal Chant

When I learn
    I'm one-eighth Cherokee,
        I resolve to claim   my spirit animal.

            I get up before first bird chirp,
    drive to the biggest forest I can find.
I get out of the car,

    step among fern and pine,   hoping
nature's solvents
    will erase me,

      give me what's mine:
        the hawk's eyes,   the turtle's tough,
        the fish's gills,   the goat's gruff.

Too long I have been waiting
    for a lid inside me
  to unhinge,   spill all my darkness,

    quench thirst for revenge,   leave kindness,
balance   love, loss, sin.   I'm a man who needs
    a spirit animal   within.

So I trail a thorny creek
    that feeds into a lake.
        I lay my clothes on a rock,

     bathe in water's ball-aching embrace.
                    I smear red clay on my face;
          my war paint bakes in the sun.

     Is this how you make   your lost tribe proud?
          My father is dead;   no one's left
                    to show me how.

I dig a hole.   I make ropes from vines.
     I carve a very bad spear.   I crouch and listen.
                    I wait ...

               Not a damn thing comes near
                         except mosquito swarms
          and stomach grumbles—

               I should have packed a lunch,
     some bug repellent,   some peyote,
          at the very least, a loincloth.

When I finally do
     find my spirit animal,   what will it be?   Wolf?
          Jaguar?   Mountain lion?

     Some monstrosity?   Will it force me   on all fours,
          teach me to howl with feral will,   or will it be
                    a nervous flying thing,

     piloting through moonlight and mist chill?
          It'll probably be some mangy bear
                    escaped from a failing circus,   de-fanged,

                still balancing on a ball,
stripped of wild purpose.
                      But it's getting colder;   it's getting later;

        my back is stiff;   my legs are sore.
I put my clothes on, drive back home. Rest itself
                  becomes a chore.

Come Monday morning,   I'm back at work
        sifting though papers   at my desk,
eight-eighths a failure,   my Indian burn

      rubbing me raw   inside my chest.

M.
★ MACK ★

Havelock Spots Inverts at the County Fair
(Their genders are classified as other.)

Young butch girls at the country fair.
Butch women at the county fair.
Men dressed like butch women at the county fair.
Cowboys named Butch at the county fair.

Later, at the County Fair

EXT. FAIR GROUNDS—NIGHT

Havelock is astute.

We observe the bull riding, the men bouncing and humping.

The cowboys up high on the fence pull the others up by their chaps.

Havelock points and asserts, "It is well known that in every herd of bulls there is nearly always one bull who is willing to lend himself to the perverted whims of his companions."

The cowboys all caught up on the fence edge. An old bull struts out to collect the others.

ED MADDEN

Among men
> *farm shop, Cowlake, Arkansas, 1974*

The rain beats insistent
against the shop's walls, the men

stand around the stove
or sit, or lean over to spit

in the plastic bucket,
the slung string of it, fragrant

and chewed, and butts fizzled
in the brown pool. One man

cuts hair, a boy stuck there
while the men talk

or don't, hands shaping the air
around his head, comb and

old scissors mincing around
his ears. He stares into the stove,

one of those with gas flames
licking the broken grates—

ornate radiants glowing
and broken, bright combs maybe

for some devil's honey.

Wrestling / Fable with shag carpet and bean bag chairs

In this corner: my brother, grinning.
In that: my young uncle, flexing.

After dinner, time for the games.

In an arena bounded by sofa
and window, by our parents

listening from the kitchen,

we mimicked moves we'd seen on TV,
standards of spandex and skin,

boys learning the throw and pin.

This was before the den's deep swank,
its shag, its fireplace, its beanbag chairs.

This was before sin.

On this side: light. On this side:
darkness. Between them

the lunge, the chokehold.

Tagged, I'd take my place in the ring,
take my stand, my stance,

assume the position.

I could never escape, pinned
and wriggling like that,

pinned to the mat.

This was before Little League football,
before the house burning down,

before *The Clue in the Embers*.

In this corner: a boy who will win.
In this corner: a boy who will lose.

Heaven
    Church party, Halloween, 1976

Barn party for the teens, that Halloween,
a sheet ghost (a wad of pillowcase choked
into a head with rope) was splayed across

a corner, corners nailed up into hands.
All afternoon an owl watched from rafters
the sweep and straighten, bales placed about,

leaving after, at dark, when the place
filled with light. Everyone had to climb
the ladder to get there, even the fat girl afraid

of heights, who made someone follow her, as if
to catch her should she fall as she ascended
to a heaven of punch and cookies and haunted

loft, costumes mostly of homemade sort—
scarecrow, hillbilly, devil, pig-tailed doll—
selves we didn't recognize. I'd made my own:

basic makeup, pink cheeks, each wrist
bound with twine to two slats twinned
for control bar—puppet on a string,

loosely noosed around my neck and dangling
down my back. All night the boys would grab it
as if to make me dance, as if they could,

choking me every time.

JEFF MANN

Blue Ridge Heating and Air

He will keep me warm, he will
cool me down, this good-looking cub
from Cambria with his local accent
so like mine, his ruddy goatee
and fine pecs and glutes I make
out despite the baggy jeans
and hoodie. He's in the attic,
in the basement, fooling with
the heat pumps, adding Freon,
calling me "buddy" the way
we mountain men do. He is
today's highwater mark,
among student poems I have
to judge, independent study essays
to read, a bibliography to type up.
So much of life is spent sifting
last year's dead and brittle leaves.
I write a check for services sadly
limited to the mechanical—
the cost of Freon has indeed
gone up. Grinning, he shakes
my hand. Wind-frenzied, pear
petals play like flurries across April's
flower beds, the hyacinths' purple
wounds, last of the species tulips.
God's alms keep us hungry:
a silver hoop in his left earlobe,
stubble on his cheek, and, left
on my desk, his business card.
Tempted as I am to call tonight,
asking if bourbon appeals,
explaining how good a man

of my experience might make him
feel once I had him stripped
and bound to a chair, I will not,
for I have some sense, after nearly
fifty years, of how mean, how
narrow, how ungenerous are
facts. What's left to learn is
how to press palm to palm
and not want more; what's left
to learn is how to be entirely
grateful for what's given,
a handsome boy from Blue Ridge
Heating and Air who made me
hunger one gray spring morning
in my salt-and-pepper forties.

Dear Pastor Dickweed,

yesterday my New Orleans buddy Neil came to visit me,
in this small conservative mountain town you and I share.
Not a mile from your Prayer Infirmary, from your precious
Sunday congregation, your indoctrinated brats, I stripped
Neil down and tied his hands behind his back, here in
my curtained living room, after good red wine and barbeque.
Were you reading the Old Testament as I spoon-fed him
homemade cheesecake ice cream, dribbled it here and there,
licked it off his chin, his big soft nipples, his belly hair, as
he grinned—what a stunning smile—and nuzzled it off
my torso, as we swapped cream from bearded mouth
to mouth? This morning, sweet souvenir, my chest hair
and goatee are still sticky-stiff. Dear Pastor Dickweed,
were you railing against morphodites, their hellish crusade,
when I knotted a camo bandana between Neil's white teeth,
led him upstairs by his cock, pushed him belly-down
on the bed, ate his ass, his beautifully furry ass, for
nigh onto an hour? Jerry Falwell is dead, Dickweed,
your vast book's the gilded guts of pulpwood trees.
Neil's butt-fur was a mythic forest, his hole a Viking
mead-cup. When he came, I rubbed his nectar into
my belly hair, into my beard. Bear Heaven would be
keeping him bound forever beside me, riding him
into the stars, never saying goodbye. You are looking
for God in the wrong direction, purblind Dickweed.
Follow my lead: earth's the place to start, not sky.

THE QUEER SOUTH

RANDALL
MANN

Complaint, Poolside

Brushing pollen off my chaise longue,
easing my feet into chlorinated water,
I knew it wasn't paradise. The Florida dust,

thick, oppressive, had yellowed the concrete,
the poplars and scrub oaks been dispossessed,
leaf by yellowed leaf—my life too had fallen

into routine: work, workout, lying out.
Across the water, the chiseled young man
(my old favorite), as always, reading a thick book—

philosophy, maybe? I would have rubbed him
with tanning oil, kissed him hard on the mouth,
but he never returned my not-so-covert stare.

It wasn't paradise. At dusk, when he was gone,
the leathery old men gone, I was the master
of empty chairs. A shock of pink, the sky

went on forever at that hour, the moon
creeping into its corner—paradise, you might say.
If Florida were such a paradise, then why

have I decided to leave? I have forgotten
my reasons, all but one: men go here to die.

The Shortened History of Florida

The white men far across the unknown ocean.
The one famous dog, named Bercerillo.
The spotted, wrinkled skin of Ponce de León.
The bones littered in Cayo Hueso.

The horses eaten at Apalachicola Bay.
The gold, like lightning: everywhere, nowhere.
The Cradle and the Grave Company.
The water lilies slowly moving toward the shore.

The scars of cannon fire, the fort's reminder.
The French, half-asleep, half-dressed.
The great Turtle Mound near Coronado.

The long-robed friars and the Indian, Peter.
The Indians, who sometimes killed a priest.
The days of lighthouses, before the weather bureau.

South

I

Yellow is the verse,
a cloudless sulphur butterfly.
Yellow are the poplar leaves,
a soldier's dead letters.

Yellow, the recitations:
the sag of sunstruck palmetto fronds
and the bright, new ties of fraternity boys.
The patch of crabgrass poisoned,

the stucco, rain-stained—
yellow the unfounded city of gold.

II

In the wet air, fronds down-turn;
the plated backs of palmetto bugs
glisten like rain.
It is late July, the sky is hot.

Cattle refuse the cattle egrets—
out of their flight I hear heaviness …
You are not the alligator below mangroves;
not the heron,

great blue general,
who slowly lifts his head.
Runaway, you should not be here.
Be somewhere north by now, asleep, asleep.

III

Too many white moths,
their shadows far too large.
And so begins the idling
of yellow buses,

the drivers stepping out to smoke
under a gray sky seceding
from the full moon as it sinks.
This is the hour of sprinklers

on the Southern windows of history
at the darkened Heritage Museum,
of the reflector strips on the heels of the shoes
of the lone runner, of the creep of the pickup truck.

IV

When the last Confederate widow
still sat at home in the damp of shadows,
Confederate jasmine crawling
over a crooked trellis;

when converted men cruised
the streets like crows;
when houses lapsed into the sleep
of history, then so might arise the arsonist,

his South a gray blaze of moonlight,
blue magnolia trees.

Social Life

Hickories. Ash. Feathery-leafed locusts.
The wide green fields lay
in the distance, the cattle

up to their knees in clover, the world
filled with scudding shadows.
Who understood the darkness of the soil

under the broad lapping leaves
of mottled tobacco?
Robins foraging in the grass

for their greedy yellowthroated chicks;
or far off, in the dirt, white-shirted,
singing ploughers following their slow

teams in the fresh furrows?
On the long porch of the weatherboard home,
the young gentlemen veiled

their evil, their doctrine—
maxima reverentia pueris debetur—
that of a language long dead.

The End of Last Summer

    The good white laundry
            dreamlike between white dogwoods;
the Spanish moss; the palm-flanked
            Baptist churches
along the small hill of Eighth Avenue—

    none of this matters.
            This landscape is just too much.
The termites are too busy,
            eating the heart
of the wood of the houses of the dead.

    —Seven years have passed
            since the red, long-faced tourists
mailed their glossy postcards home,
            regaling friends
with tales of the Gainesville student murders.

    All is as it was
            before the murders. The dead?
Names spray-painted on a wall;
            trees providing
shade for the brick, the undergraduates.

    It's time to leave now.
            The old professors have gone
on sabbatical, across
            the Atlantic
to visit their favorite fallen empires.

    The hidden tree frogs
            have begun to chirp again.
The peninsula grows dark;
            the dead stay dead.
The sea is rising ... and the world is sand.

MARY MERIAM

The Sum of Fall

Outside, surprised, you see a flare of red.
It is a fox, lit by the sun, I said.
The fox glides by. That is the sum of fall
for us, outdoors. Then you give Steve a call
about the trees to trim and dead tree wood
that he should cart away. *Is Thursday good?*

As good as fox can get, whose gliding's good,
whose tail in slanted sun turns fire-red.
*Please take the fifty-foot dead ash, for wood
to sell or burn as you see fit,* you said
to Steve. He'd check his week then give a call.
The red fox-tail, the walk we took this fall.

The ash is dead, and wind could make it fall
right on our house, with us inside. Not good
how long it took to give this guy a call.
I try to hold the image tight, fox-red
in slanted sun, the glide. Steve called and said
that Thursday still is looking good; he would

be here to chop the ash tree down for firewood.
I stand outside with Steve. *The ash will fall
safely, away from us, I'm safe,* he said,
this giant fireman. I see he's good
with ladders, ropes, and saws. He's used to red-
hot crises, used to falls, the desperate call,

but does Steve know we had no one to call
when they would burn our house like firewood?
They torched bonfires day and night, the red
flame flicking near our house, in spring and fall,

the devils tried to drive us out for good.
You don't belong with us, the sheriff said.

Get out, get lost, go back, the whole world said.
We stay inside; there's no one left to call
but Steve, who felled the dead tree, clean and good,
then sawed the trunk in chunks and took the wood
to sell or burn, as he sees fit. The fall
leaves turn, lit by the sun, turn gold and red,

but we were good, no matter what they said.
The wild geese call, we saw the red fox glide,
and creatures cry all through the wood in fall.

STEPHEN S.
MILLS

Even Drag Queens Are Christian in the South

Like the one who died a week after you fought with her
        over the use of Happy Holidays instead of Merry Christmas.
How she mocked you for your inclusive tendencies.
        We never learned what killed her, or how they fit her
Reba McEntire hair and tight sequined dress inside that coffin.

The one some Jesus-freak Gay Preacher bellowed over proclaiming
        God loves all the Children of the world, even those bent
on gender-bending. I'm sure there was an *Amen* from every Southern
        gay boy seated in that church in Tallahassee
where everyone believes in something and the Holy Ghost hangs

from the Spanish moss. Like the time you dreamt of a drag queen
        church where they spoke in tongues, wailed
on the ground, pounded fistfuls of press-on nails, and sang gospel
        music dressed in their finest attire:
hats balanced on weaves, heels six inches high and counting.

Unlike the actual gay church we attended where lesbians
        in their button-ups served communion to the old men
in wheelchairs, tubes in their noses, twinks by their sides.
        How they all tongued those wafers, drank the juice
of forgiveness. Swallow. Swallow. Later everyone huddled together

crying and swaying with the spirit. We only watched from the back,
        slowly peeling off the cross-shaped nametags they gave us.
Afterward, as we crept to our car, we saw them
        moving inside the windows like the cleaning crew:
stacking chairs, lowering the rainbow flag, erasing their very presence

from the church they rented on Sunday nights. And there, in the gravel
        parking lot, even the spirits in the big Magnolia trees
were as silent as a dead drag queen.

CAMERON
★ MITCHELL ★

Pornography for the Gods

Sometime between the years of first discovering the guilt-ridden joys of chronic masturbation and reaching the near-adult status of being able to drive, my sister Michelle polluted my mind with images of real-life demons walking the earth amongst us. It was the early Nineties, in the age before DVDs, mp3 players, and the unlimited possibilities of going online to discover what the internet had to offer. I lived in Burnsville, a simple country town hidden away in the mountains of western North Carolina. We were about forty-five minutes outside the nearest city, Asheville, and lifetimes away from anything remotely cool or interesting.

As Michelle made a sandwich on the counter near the sink, I sat at the kitchen table, barely aware she was even talking at first. She had a way of rambling on about nothing in particular, with or without an engaged audience. When she mentioned *the gays*, however, I stared up from my algebra homework, no longer able to focus on the x and y of my equation. Her strange, religious assertions had snagged my full attention. I could already feel the heat of embarrassment rising up my neck and spreading across my face. I prayed my cheeks weren't burning bright red as I knew they must have been.

"It says so in the Bible," she said, her back to me. I stared at the poofy, peroxide-tinged curls hanging down her back like orange cotton candy.

"Really?" I asked. "It says that?"

"Yes, of course," she answered with a certainty I didn't yet know how to doubt. "The Bible talks about demons walking the earth in different forms. Gay people are just one of 'em—one of the disguises they use."

Although I'd never heard of these so-called demons before, it was hard to question my sister's biblical expertise. I mean, she could have been right since I never paid attention to anything in the Bible outside the book of Revelation. Most of the rules and stories filling the rest of the holy book bored the hell out of me. But what kid wouldn't be captivated by tales of a great beast, the end of time, and all the other apocalyptic doom in Revelation?

If I'd known there was a section about demons disguising themselves as effeminate, limp-wristed men who like to shop and fornicate at wild orgies, as my sister claimed, I would have definitely sought that out. Then again, it didn't concern *me* all that much since I wasn't gay or anything. And, even though my skin had turned bright red, I certainly wasn't a demon walking the earth.

Well, I didn't think so, anyway.

Sure, over the past few months, I had engaged in rituals that might not be considered normal by folks in my mountain community—or anyone else, for that matter. These acts started with fantasies of naked men and ended with more guilt than I could stand and sacrifices to the gods above.

The images of naked men touching each other—and touching me, and me touching them, just a little—were the vexing part of the ritual that led to the need for absolution ... only after I'd climaxed, of course. As long as I didn't act on such thoughts and fantasies outside the privacy of self-pleasure, I felt safe.

Sorta.

No one in my immediate family had very strong religious beliefs. Yet, growing up in the tightened grips of North Carolina's Bible belt naturally affected everyone. We never went to church on our own. When I was about eight years old, a fat classmate's grandfather came by our house to invite us into his congregation. He lived less than a mile down the road from our modest three-bedroom home. For whatever reason, my father agreed to let us go. He'd never expressed concern about our spiritual well-being before, other than the time he told us that bad kids go to Hell, while gently stoking the fire in our woodstove. He probably just wanted us out of his hair for the day.

I wasn't terribly enthused about giving up my Sunday for church services. My fat classmate, Jonathan, was just that—a chunky boy whom I couldn't have cared less about. Each day in the lunchroom line, he skipped by the cooler with cartons of milk and waited for the cafeteria ladies with their hairnets and giant spoons full of slop to get him a glass of water. He was lactose-intolerant, something I would have found thrillingly exotic if not for the fact that he was such a dolt. Back then, I was always jealous of the kids who had glasses, braces or neat medical issues that distinguished them from everyone else. As

I got older, primarily around the onset of puberty, it's funny that I wanted nothing more than to just fit in.

Other than the fact that Jonathan couldn't drink milk, there were few things about him that would leave a lasting impression. He chewed the erasers off pencils all day long, possibly because he was constantly hungry. He drooled a lot, usually letting the rivulets of spit ooze across his bottom lip and drip down to his desk, collecting into a sticky puddle there. The janitor must have wanted him dead. Oh, and his grandfather was a preacher—a fact that meant nothing to me until the man came knocking on our door.

Apparently, Father Phillips had nothing against our family. Other religious folks had dropped by before to let us know we were living in sin. They cited my father's bootlegging career as the main source of our collective evil. They were a married couple who had recently rented a house up the road from us. Both had dark hair and looked a lot alike. In fact, I remember them bearing an unsettling resemblance to Donnie and Marie Osmond, but that could just be wishful thinking. After blocking our driveway with their junky Toyota, they shouted a lot and wouldn't leave.

Calling my father evil was fine since it seemed like an accurate description to me. But the rest of us? *Come on*, I thought. We didn't tell him what to do for a living. Besides, he performed far more "evil" tasks than illegally selling alcohol to local drunks.

My father told the screaming duo he was going to *make* them leave as he hopped inside his truck. He had just returned from a beer run, so his beat-up Datsun was still parked in the driveway right in front of our house. Normally, he parked his trucks in the second driveway, which was about thirty feet away from the first one.

Miraculously, the Bible-thumpers jumped in their own vehicle and pulled out of my father's vengeful path in just the nick of time. He was serious about making them leave and barely missed crashing into their car.

It was one of the rare decent things I can remember him doing.

Father Phillips, however, never uttered a single word of disapproval over my father's bootlegging business. After all, was it really a sin to provide our townspeople with the beer and liquor they so desperately craved? We lived in a dry county that prohibited the sale of alcohol, so my father was just meeting a need. I didn't know much about the Bible, but I was pretty sure bootlegging didn't break any of the commandments.

Also, Father Phillips, a man called upon by a higher power to preach the Good word, bought a six-pack of Budweiser before leaving our house that fateful day. In my young eyes, that gave my father's career choices the religious stamp of approval, even though witnessing a holy man purchase beer from my dad was a little troubling. Unable to pinpoint why, it just didn't feel right.

But really, who was I to judge?

Despite Father Phillips' initial efforts, we never caught the religious bug and visited his church just two or three times. After that, he dropped by our house only when he wanted to chase his Sunday sermon with a cool, refreshing six-pack of beer.

So I'm not sure why I let my sister Michelle's religious theories worry me. When she announced that gay people were demons walking the earth, I should have ignored her. Yet, I couldn't escape the possibility that she might be right. Didn't it mean something that waves of guilt washed over me each time I masturbated to the images of naked men having sex on the television set in our living room?

Well, I mostly felt excited and kind of cool that I had this sacred secret all to myself. The guilt didn't set in and take hold until after the point of ejaculation.

Acquiring the pornography in the first place was both risky and complicated. Had I not been such a crafty young man, who knows how long it might have taken me to get my hands on the forbidden good stuff? The gas stations in my hometown didn't have something as tame as *Playboy* on their magazine racks, so of course our local video huts didn't carry X-rated films. And a sex store was completely unheard of in Burnsville. This was a *dry* county, after all. If it was illegal for stores to sell alcoholic beverages, then pornography was definitely out of the question.

(Hmm, I bet my father could have made a lot of money if he'd expanded his offerings to include dirty tapes and girly magazines.)

Like many adolescent boys finding themselves more attracted to their friends in the locker room than to the girls in the hallway at school, I often turned to men's fitness magazines for … inspiration. While rummaging through one of the muscle rags at the drugstore one day, I came across an advertisement for a porn catalogue. I immediately requested it by mail—under a clever pseudonym. I used our family's last name, *Mitchell*. That would ensure the catalogue made it to our mailbox. I scribbled in the very plain and inconspicuous *John* as the first name. There actually was a John Mitchell that lived down the street. For that reason, I added an *L* in for the middle initial.

Hopefully, the postman would think *this* John Mitchell was a different John Mitchell from the one down the road. The real John Mitchell was a teenager, so I doubt he got much mail anyway. If anyone in my family happened to check the mailbox the day the catalogue arrived, I could simply play dumb, letting them think that the John Mitchell kid down the street was the real pervert, not me.

The chances of someone other than me discovering the catalogue were pretty slim. Checking the mail was one of the things I enjoyed most. I would order cassette tapes and compact discs all the time. Getting a package in the mail was almost more exciting than the merchandise itself. The smell of cardboard boxes was one of the most alluring, mesmerizing scents of my childhood.

Lo and behold, I was the one who checked the mail on that momentous day when the catalogue finally arrived.

The ads for different movies were quite tasty and served me well behind the bathroom's locked doors. Since school was out for summer in a week, I felt safe enough to put in an actual order. Although straight porn was the predominant feature in that first catalogue, there were a few "solo" male videos that piqued my interest.

After a trip to the gas station for a money order, I was good to go. I couldn't write a check for my order since I had no banking account, and I took the catalogue's warning against mailing in cash very seriously seeing as how I was so intent on making sure nothing could possibly go wrong.

"What do you need a money order for?" Mother had asked.

"CDs, Mom."

"You're actually paying for them this time?"

"Yeah, uh, it's a good deal."

Yeah right. Like I'd ever actually pay for the CDs I got from music clubs seeing as how I was such a little crook. If they were dumb enough to send them to me and all my fake names over and over again, then they deserved to be ripped off.

A couple of weeks later, after almost rubbing myself raw just thinking about what I'd soon see, our wonderful postman delivered my very first pornographic video.

It was perhaps the most amazing, erotically charged thing I'd ever seen. After what felt like years of waiting to have the house to myself, I finally had the pleasure of watching twelve different guys masturbate. With my pants around my ankles, I somehow managed to pleasure myself with one hand and fast forward the video with the other. I needed to see everything my porno had to offer before my family got back.

Each actor had his own scene, all alone. For the time, that was enough for me. One of the guys could lick his penis and even suck it some when he contorted his body in very creative and quite uncomfortable looking ways. It was so strange and earth-shatteringly exciting at the same time.

The film climaxed with Jeff Stryker giving a solo performance in a hot tub. Mr. Stryker, a porn star famous for swinging both ways on film, was even more famous for his huge penis. And man was it big! Not that it mattered all that much. He could have had a four-inch penis, and I would have enjoyed watching what he did with it all the same. After splashing my seed into some paper towels and awkwardly shoving them deep inside the garbage, I ejected the tape and put it back into its hiding place under my bed.

Later that evening, once my mother and siblings had returned, I started a ritual that would continue for months.

I quietly crept to my bedroom and shut the door. Like a spy or burglar, I tiptoed over to my bed, slowly placing one knee on the mattress. Careful not to make even the slightest squeak, I reached down into the dark crevice between the bed and wall, feeling around for the tape. As I gripped it in one hand, a sudden anger shot through my body. In one quick swoop, I jerked the tape out and shoved it down the front of my pants, not caring as much if I made any noise or not. I stood up and took a deep breath, covering the pornography with my shirt. Then, I sucked my stomach in to keep any suspicious lumps from showing and rushed out of the house, holding my breath the whole way. Once I reached the yard without anyone noticing me, I finally allowed myself to breathe again.

My walk to the manufacturing plant across the street was filled with guilt, shame, and a strong desire to purge myself of any and all dirty thoughts. I figured masturbation alone was probably wrong in the first place. Anything that felt so good just had to be wrong.

As long as the naked men touching themselves lived only in my head, I didn't have to admit that I really might be gay. And even though I didn't believe gay people were demons walking the earth like my sister would soon inform me, I still thought homosexuality was a crime against nature, pure evil, or something along those lines. Everyone around me reinforced the idea that being gay was quite possibly the most devastating thing that could ever happen. At the time, I felt sure my family and peers would be more forgiving if I murdered someone than if I admitted how much I kinda sorta liked guys. Effeminate boys in school were called fags and homos, and they were always bullied more than anyone else.

Despite my family's lack of spiritual beliefs, I believed what all the Christians said about homosexuality, that it was one of the worst sins, that you'd burn in Hell if you had sex with other guys, and it was a disease like alcoholism that you had to overcome in order to enter the glorious and eternal kingdom of heaven—amen and Praise Jesus!

The porn hidden away in my pants proved that something was wrong with me. It was physical evidence of my crime that could be used against me if ever discovered. I had to destroy it, so no one would ever know the truth.

I did not want that to be the way I felt inside and thought I could choose not to be gay. Watching the tape and masturbating to the filthy images was caving in and succumbing to my carnal weakness. I could have sex with women and raise kids one day and be normal like everyone else if I only tried harder.

So when I got to the manufacturing plant, I walked behind the long, box-like structure for privacy. My siblings and I had always gone up to there to play. As I got older, I played less and instead visited the area so I could be alone. Sometimes, I rode my bike around in circles across the wide parking lot. There was a comfort in that, in knowing what to expect as I counted each trip around the edges of the lot. It was quiet there after work hours, and I didn't have to worry about dodging cars in the street.

On that particular evening, I had a special mission to accomplish. The hard edges of the tape pressed uncomfortably against my stomach as I stared through the tree branches at the injured hillside about fifty feet away. A small gravel path started at the back corner of the parking lot and winded up to the hill; it was the site of some long-abandoned construction project. The hillside had been dug into and dramatically altered by a backhoe and other heavy equipment. Mounds of red clay had been left exposed, and a sort of cliff had been created at the top of it all. As much younger kids, my brother and sisters and I loved playing up there, climbing up the hill and then rolling back down, over and over again. The red clay stained our clothes something awful, so Mother demanded that we stop going up there right away. We didn't really listen, and she never came down on us too hard.

A part of me wanted to run up there once again and roll around in the sand and dirt, covering my body in the red clay. Then, my mother would yell at me for the offense of bringing her impossible-to-remove stains and not for the far more serious offenses that could compromise my very soul. I would take a reprimand for stains any day of the week over her finding out what I was really doing up there that day and yelling at me for that—or, worse, hearing nothing but silence from her as she looked away from me in shame.

In a full-blown rage, I pulled the porn from my pants and ripped the ribbon from its black case. I made sure this particular piece of pornography would never grant me pleasure again. While destroying the tape, I prayed.

Please God, please make me normal. I don't want to be a sinner or a sissy or a faggot. Please forgive me for this and see that I'm destroying this gay porn and that I'll never do it again. Really, I'll never do it again, especially if you take these thoughts away from me. Just take them out of my head, please. See, watch me destroy this. Watch me do it and then make me normal. I just want to be normal.

After completely tearing the long roll of crinkly ribbon out and stomping the plastic casing and frantically praying, I tried setting fire to the whole mess. I ripped the cardboard box with Jeff Stryker's image and made my own small pyre. I thought of all the words and condemnations dropped so casually into everyday conversations and wondered what my friends and family might say if they knew how sharply these things stung. I thought of the sissy boys at school, the ones who sat alone at the front of the bus, staring out the window and biding their time; I thought about how I never heard any words from them at all. My mind raced with words and phrases like *abomination* and *against God*, and I set fire to it all.

The shreds of cardboard were quickly engulfed, and the ribbon melted away easily enough, but I couldn't produce the flames I craved. And I needed that fire—to set fire to the whole mess and watch it burn. To my utter dismay, it seemed some things wouldn't turn to ash no matter how hard I tried.

So once my sister unleashed her biblical lessons for me to mull over, I started thinking that perhaps I was a demon. Maybe there were yellow eyes, crooked claws, and a forked tongue, all lurking just beneath the surface, waiting to tear through my seemingly human flesh and wreak havoc upon a small country town.

Then again, I had absolutely no desire to do the Devil's bidding or wage some kind of demonic war against the more wholesome and righteous people all around me. I just wanted to have sex with men, pure and simple. Despite my prayers, God never took those dirty thoughts away.

Two weeks after my first pornographic offering to anyone listening in that expansive blue sky above my head, I found myself going to the gas station again.

"What do you need a money order for?"

"CDs," I said. "More CDs, Mom."

Within two weeks, I had more pornography. This time, there was actual intercourse on the tape, and I managed to keep hold of it for a little longer.

For months, I did the same thing.

I got the porn.

I enjoyed the porn.

I offered the porn to the gods.

That was my ritual. Soon, college would come along and take me off the mountain. The internet would also come around, introducing me to chat rooms and all sorts of X-rated videos that I could watch instantly. Still, I think back to that year of my life and can't believe how much money I wasted on perfectly good pornography. Thank God I eventually came to my senses.

FOSTER
★NOONE★

Fostering

August:

My first national queer conference is in Louisville, Kentucky, and my nametag reads "Sarah: she/her/hers." It is 13 days before my 16th birthday. I have never heard the word "non-binary" used in the same sentence as "transgender." I sit in the back of a car with Violet as we return to our hotel. I fixate on the wings of their eyeliner, red and yellow under the streetlights. I rub my nametag back and forth across my palm while they tell me about being 15 and pan in Arkansas. We fake nonchalance in our discussions of our own genders. I'm intoxicated with them, with this city, with this new realm of Southern queer solidarity, but I also feel sick.

October:

Every night for three months I have lain awake with "nonbinary" pulsing urgently behind my eyelids. Flashbacks to junior high, flashbacks to the third grade, flashbacks to last week. I'm not a boy. I'm a not-boy. And maybe a not-girl. Neither the ceiling vent nor the bags under my eyes have answers.

February:

The heat of August congeals into the wetness of Alabama's February, and Tuscaloosa looks even sadder in the gloom. I'm representing my high school at the Southeastern LGBTQ Leadership Conference. On the first day, my name tag reads "Sarah: she/her/hers." I'm sitting in the back of a lecture by an Alabamian trans activist who now lives in DC. His workshop is about lots of things that I don't hear until he mentions a nonbinary woman he knows who has top surgery. I don't know if I'm cis, but I know what my body wants. I sit in the back, and I start crying because I don't really know what my options are, but being that woman sounds more right than anything else.

On day two of the conference, my nametag reads "Sarah, any pronouns."

March:

A friend and I create a petition to support a bill removing homophobia from state sex-ed laws. We get 100,000 signatures and are on all the local news shows. The captions read "Sarah Noone, student," and I feel like a liar. I don't know how to tell the state of Alabama that its new favorite teenage lesbian is bisexual and has too many genders to count.

April:

In my sock drawer fits my first binder, unsure of whether or not to make an appearance.

June:

I'm collecting interviews from queer kids at Huntsville Pride. I ask for their names, but I don't have one to give them in return. "Just call me 'Sir,'" I say. They giggle, but I sign my new name neatly on their consent forms, dotting the "i"s with hearts.

I march in my own Pride, pronouns ze/hir/hirs neatly printed on my cheap green tank top. I carry the only blue, white, and pink flag in Birmingham's parade. The cheering seems quieter when we march by.

July:

Summer is neon short-shorts and lipstick so bright it consumes my face. I finally find my name in a graveyard in Glens Falls, New York. The Catholic angels glare down at my sticky pink dress as I wander through the family plot in 90-degree weather. I'm here to mourn and remember, but I read the headstones like a menu. I imagine myself, hand clasped in that of a dapper-suited stranger. "Hi, I'm _____

Noone." I try to taste the syllables and imagine them on the tongues of others.

He was my great-great-uncle, and his name was a verb meaning growth, promising futures. A name filled with potential, filled with antiquated masculinity and tinged with androgyny. He went by Buck, but in that moment I realized I needed to be the one to reclaim the name he left behind.

Hi, I'm Foster Noone.

August:

A conference in Denver. I have altitude sickness, or food poisoning, or am allergic to non-Southern air. I spend two days lying in a dorm room, eating applesauce with a straw. On the third day, "Foster ze/hir/hirs" rises and presents a workshop on trans youth in schools.

November:

It's cold, and people don't know what to look for under skinny jeans and boxy suit coats. I try to avoid public restrooms. The first boy I ever dated tells me that I'm "a fucking joke," that real trans people hate me, that I should hate myself.

I apply to colleges as an openly trans student.

January:

A year-and-a-half later, Violet and I have words to talk about our identities as we sashay down the hallways of a conference of 4,000 people in Houston, still reveling in our Southernness, but having shed the skin of baby queer naiveté. The names we don't always get called at home hang haphazardly around our necks. We smirk at the cis gay boys in our scholarship programs, grateful for a space where our jaded, queer/trans teenage angst is valued.

February:

Back in Tuscaloosa. I am the closest thing to a trans 101 presenter at this college conference. In the year since my feet last touched the manicured frat lawns of Alabama's campus, I've become someone with expertise to share.

Once more back home in Pelham, I remove the name sticker from my sweater and stick it next to my mirror. My room is a mess of names, with lanyards on bedposts, stickers on the door, and lopsided certificates taped near the ceiling. I never throw any of them away. I'm drowning in documentation of my names. Or floating in the ocean of my discoveries.

THE QUEER SOUTH

JOSEPH *OSMUNDSON*

This is not My Story to Tell

Looking back at photos is a dangerous game. Nostalgia can be a caustic drug, particularly when loss is involved. Here in the New York winter, those August days in the South feel impossible, unreal, until a picture brings it all back, all of it, the good and the bad, and there were plenty of both.

This is the story of my introduction to the American South. I feel the need to introduce myself. I am a 29-year-old white faggot from the West, born and raised in a small town where most folks were loggers or farmers or worked at Boeing. My West is the poor white West, the rural West, the outsourced, economically depressed West that doesn't seem to exist in the minds of many.

This is the story of my introduction to the American South,
      but this is not a love story.

Joan Didion, a Westerner herself, claimed that she was "most comfortable [in New York] in the company of Southerners. They seemed to be in New York as [she] was." In my early years in New York, I too found myself surrounded by Southerners. Maybe it was a common magnetism that drew us all to here. New York symbolized the great queer adventure, the great queer future, to those of us growing up in the great queer elsewhere. We arrived, refugees, and we found companionship and common experience.

D-- was part of this circle that dominated my early years in New York.
      This story would not exist with him.

I love him,
      but this is not a love story.

I met D-- at a party years ago. He was short, cute. That night he was wearing frames with no lenses in them and was immensely proud of himself for it. After poking my finger through the empty space that should have held the lenses, I gave D-- nonstop shade about it. D-- gave me shade all night back. There are a lot of things that I find attractive in partners, but intelligence and wit are probably numbers one and three. I was hooked. But I was dating someone, so was he.

Two years later, I was single and D-- RSVPed to an event on my campus. We got a drink after. We talked that night about the (im)possibility of anti-white 'racism'. We kissed that night on the cheek. A week later, drunk after a happy hour, my lower lip found the space between his upper and lower lip in the tentative beauty of a first kiss with someone you could genuinely care about. His lips parted, just slightly.

A couple of months later, D-- was my boyfriend. I loved this man in the real and terrifying way you love the first person you can picture as the father of your children, the first person you can see by your side in the hospital decades later.

★ ★ ★ ★

What should I call you? I can't use your name; you're too private. You're not going to like this much, as is. It will be pretty obvious I'm talking about you. I always hate when authors use dashes to make people or places generic. But this is nonfiction, and if I'm going to be honest, I have to hide you, at least a bit. For you, and for me.

★ ★ ★ ★

I have always thought that to truly understand someone you had to know where they were from. D-- grew up in South Carolina. Because this part of the story is truly not mine to tell, I will simply say that D-- had a hard beginning to his life but was smart and survived extraordinary circumstances. He was bright, but D-- was also hard to get close to. Over our first months together, I watched D-- open up, and I saw the attributes I knew and loved become clearer. We both grew better. And that is exactly what I thought love would do to me. D-- and I were shocked, at times, by what we had in common: a twinky white scientist/educator from the West and a fierce black activist from the South.

But this is not a love story.

A friend of mine dealt with his recent breakup by posting to Facebook roughly three times a day about his workout routine. He had never been much of a gym guy before, and this performance seemed, to those of us watching, sad and unconvincing. Breakups can feel like vertigo; they can make one feel adrift, unmoored, as the minutiae of daily routine can no longer follow the same beat. We all have our ways of working through that particular brand of devastation.

D-- and I were going to move in together. But, when I needed him most, D-- told me he simply wasn't ready. The future I imagined, that I wanted, that I had built in my mind, unraveled in hours. Maybe unraveled is the wrong word. This future was demolished. I want to imply destruction. And I still see D-- sitting in the seat of the wrecking car, pulling back the massive metal ball, releasing it, and letting gravity pull it toward our collective life together.

* * * *

> Is it fair to admit that writing this is giving you up? It's probably obvious, right? I need to get over you. I mean I *am* over you. It's not that I want to get back together. I don't see you, 40 years from now, by my side in the hospital. I cannot imagine our children, anymore. But what I need to do is stop being so angry. So, I write, and try to tell the truth, and hope that the act of giving testimony frees my spirit from this particular demon, this particular hurt.

* * * *

But this isn't a break up story, either—it's a story about a place, and how I came to know it. D-- traveled a lot for work. He probably still does, but I can't currently verify this fact. When a trip in late summer took him to Atlanta for five days, we started to scheme. I had never been south of DC, and I wanted to go. We could rent a car, drive down, camping along the way, seeing the South, and end in Atlanta. On the way, we would spend a few days at his sister's place in South Carolina, and he would show me his roots. It was pure coincidence that his time in Atlanta overlapped with ATL Black Gay Pride, after which we would work our way up the coast, camping and making things up as we went.

We left in late August, driving south, inland from the coast. Jersey, Pennsylvania, Delaware, and into Virginia. Rural Virginia, where we camped our first night, was another world. The mountains looming farther to the west kept the late summer heat low, especially at night, and the foothills rolled a deep, saturated green. I had a knot in my stomach pulling into the first campsite. D-- had never camped before, and while I grew up with it, I had never camped as precisely one half of an interracial gay couple in rural Virginia. D--, the good Morehouse man that he was, presented as fairly straight, but I don't. You can smell my gay a mile off, and it is not an accident. I love being perceived as queer, even if it makes people feel uncomfortable.

That night, after the tent was pitched and we were sitting around a small campfire, neither of us was at ease. I wouldn't admit it, speak it into existence, and I know that D-- wouldn't either, but I think we were both waiting for some angry rednecks to come floating out of those woods. We went to bed late, with my arm wrapped around his frame. In the end, I think each of us thought the other one strong enough to handle whatever might come. In the end, nothing did.

The next morning, we hit the road. Driving was the best way to see the country. We moved through it slowly, and it slipped inside us almost without being perceived. I saw thousands of forgotten miles flash by in dark shades of late-summer green at 75 miles an hour. When twilight hit, we rolled down the windows and let the humid air fill the car with the smell of trees and cut grass. Country smells, Southern smells.

* * * *

After all that we went through, after all I gave, you gave, we gave, to one other, and to us. I haven't emailed you, other than to get back my shit, since we broke up. We used to email everyday. I've only texted you once, this year. On election night. Gay marriage, your campaign, passed in Maryland. Where we had spent so much time together, on your trips. I was trying to give it up, then. To stop hating you so much. That's what I am trying to do now. To give it up. To stop hating you so much. To get to the point where I can write about this and not cry. You never liked how much I cry. Even that night, when we were breaking up. You said you couldn't move in with me, then asked why I was crying.

★ ★ ★ ★

The next day we stopped for a late lunch. Virginia has a lot of country, and we were deep in it. The joint we chose was a barbecue restaurant, one of the places where you order at the counter and get your food on a tray. As we walked in, I was performing the straightest version of myself. It didn't matter. It's not that there were only white people in this establishment, but the tables with white people had only white people, and the tables with black people only had black people. Already as people who were clearly not *from* there, we probably would have attracted a certain amount of curiosity. But, as a black man and a white man, just two of us together, we were an anomaly. Perhaps we weren't great at hiding our intimacy.

D-- and I were both good at powering through. We were both from places not too different from this. And we weren't the types to walk away, walk out. We got our food. We sat and ate. There was a white woman at a booth behind us who had her neck turned 90 degrees to stare at us. She was the type of old white lady who is both so old and so white as to appear almost translucent. She sat there, head turned, for the entire time we were in the restaurant. She appeared not to eat. At a table to her right, there was a relatively young mother and her two children, a girl and a boy. The boy was rambunctious and kept getting up from the table and walking around the restaurant. He walked past our table, time and time again, and stared at us from a foot or two away. On his third lap, I realized that on the back of his t-shirt was a drawing of a Confederate flag with a growling dog in the foreground, decorated with words 'Cross the Line, Your Ass is Mine'. He wanted, this young man, us to see the shirt. And he kept making laps around the restaurant, looking at us to make sure we understood the message. As they were leaving, his sister stood by our table for a few seconds, sticking out her tongue, bright blue from a sugary drink. She stared. We sat in silence. We sat, and we ate. We did not hurry, but we were happy to get back in the car and get moving.

We landed in D--'s hometown of Columbia, South Carolina, where we camped on the floor of D--'s sister's spare room. His sister was hilarious and warm, and I loved her before I knew her for the role she had played and continued to play in D--'s life.

Columbia is the state capital where the Confederate flag still flies, where college football rivalries are the central topic of conversation, even in August, and where Chick-fil-A makes the best damn chicken sandwich you could put in your mouth. That night, relieved to not be worried about safety, we drank Miller High Life and played cards. D--'s sister went to bed, and D-- and I just relaxed and talked smack and reveled in each other's company.

D-- lived in Columbia for a while after college working on local political campaigns, and I asked him to show me a Columbia gay bar. Gay bars can tell you a lot about a place. Pulling up to the bar in South Carolina, the windows were papered over, and we had to double check the name and address. It was maybe a Tuesday night and there was a smattering of folks, a mix of gay men and women, mostly sitting at the bar, mostly alone. Nursing drinks, talking to the bartender, talking to each other. D-- and I sat and lingered over two drinks and never managed to strike up anything more than a superficial conversation. People seemed wary of anyone they didn't know, and the papered-over windows made me think they were perhaps wise for being so guarded. After our drinks, we drove home in silence. Twenty minutes later, I lay awake in my sleeping bag on the floor staring at the ceiling, my arm again finding its way around D--'s torso, but sleep wouldn't descend. I was thankful, I think, that he had survived Columbia, and I could see how this place had made him strong, and fierce, and silent, and wary.

★ ★ ★ ★

You know, I'm seeing someone now, and I love him; he is one of the reasons why I am doing this, why I am writing this, why I am trying, D--, to move on; I don't want to carry around this anger, at you, because I can't love him as honestly as he deserves. So here I sit writing and quoting Faulkner and thinking about the American South, your South, writing about the American South, your South, thinking about how it changed me, how you changed me, how home feels different, how America feels different, how love doesn't quite feel the same. I don't know if this catharsis will diminish my anger. I just know that now that I've started I feel powerless to stop.

★ ★ ★ ★

There is not, obviously, one South. After 3 hours on I-20, we landed in ATL at Bulldog's for the opening night party for Black Gay Pride. Line around the corner. Hundreds of boys and girls. Drinking in the parking lot. Kiki-ing. Folks knew each other, but tourists flocked in from all reaches of the American South and beyond.

Outside Bulldog's, the air was alive, and you could literally hear the excitement people felt for the night, the weekend to come. Gurls being loud and acting up. In this space, I couldn't help but smile, add a little extra sashay to my own step. Especially since it was a step that had been very actively avoiding a sashay in order to feel comfortable camping in rural Virginia. D-- and I were ready to drink and wile. Our drink: gin with a splash of tonic, and the grand total for 2 was $5.50. I laughed, and said that this sure isn't New York. We cheersed, and we drank. We mingled, moved, mixed, hopped outside and back in—this night we had no problem striking up conversation, laughing with strangers.

These types of spaces are healthy for my soul. I love being around queer folks, surrounded by them, speaking our language, using our non-verbal communication that was practiced for so many generations of hiding in plain sight. I feel the most myself, whatever that means. It's a space where I can just be, do, act. Dance, even, if the mood should strike. Flirt, talk. Where my language is understood without translation by either party.

D-- and I had our worst fight ever in Atlanta. It was Sunday of Pride weekend, and I was hung over. It was a beautiful day, and there was a live house music party and picnic in a park across town. A bunch of D--'s college friends were going, and it sounded dope. We showed up at the picnic, and the music was blasting from an open-air building, essentially a roof with no walls. Folks had set up tents all around the park with food and chairs. I didn't know a soul, but people were friendly and made sure I always had a plate full of food and some one to talk to. D-- was drinking and smoking and giving into his vacation mode of being. Going in. By the time we left the party, he was pretty drunk and extremely high.

Afterward, we had a chill drink at the house of a friend of mine. Let me just say that D-- was still in full Pride mode. He was too drunk/high for the situation and kept talking over folks. He asked if he could smoke up inside and then didn't offer to share. Nothing dramatic, but I was annoyed. By the time we got back to the hotel, he was so fucked up that I should have let it drop. But that's not something I'm great at. I was pissed, and he laughed in my face. Which made me lose it. I lost it. I had been babysitting the man all day, driving him around. I screamed. I wasn't pretty. I told him to take his drunk ass to bed, that he embarrassed me, that he was so fucked up he had no idea what he was doing. I told him that he didn't respect me, that I was taking the car that night and driving home, to New York, without him. I went to sleep on the couch, that night, but two hours later there I was. Back in bed. Lying next to him. After all that time I just slept better with my one arm wrapped around him, with the back of his head being bristled by my stubble.

On our way out of ATL, we spent one day in Savannah, Georgia. It is supposed to be the stereotypical South. Looking back at photos is a dangerous game. There is a picture in Savannah of a horse-drawn carriage with the words "Plantation Carriage Company" written in a pleasant gold cursive on the back. There is D--, in shades, holding a sightseeing guide in front of his face. There are my feet and D--'s on the plaque demarcating "Calhoon Square"—named after the Vice President from South Carolina and which, Google now informs me, is the site of an 18th-century slave cemetery. We had no idea that we were standing on the graves of black people, a hidden history. This seems to me to be stereotypically Southern. Next is a photo of the plaque in front of the home of Jefferson Davis, where I shot with a wide angle lens, in black and white, and tried to make the massive tree branches behind the plaque seem ominous. Finally, the reflection of a bridge in D--'s sunglasses as we got out of town. Savannah, I think, was too pretty, too picturesque, to be the site of hidden slave cemeteries and plaques commemorating the worst of our history as though it were the best. There is tension in Savannah between how things look, bright and sunny and clean and old in the charming sense, and how I felt there, confused and almost sad and very, very queer and, at once, close to home and very far from it, as though my home, itself, had become a shifting place, as though all places suddenly were jolted beneath my feet.

* * * *

Why did I want to write this in the first place, why did I think I could? An anthology on the queer South? What the fuck do I know? Maybe all this is just so that I can tell you, finally tell you, how I loved you and how bad it hurt when everything went to shit—how I miss the future we imagined together. Maybe I can't do anything else until you know. It'll make me look weak, I've been trying so hard to win the break up. But how else do I stop missing the future we were building, together, and really imagine that another future is possible, necessary?

* * * *

After Savannah we drove east, to the coast. Back to South Carolina. After the mess that was Pride, the nights out and the acting up and the hangovers, we wanted a few days on the coast, on the ocean. Just us two, our books, cards after dinner, bed early. We decided on the low country, a long series of deltas and plains extending to the ocean. My photos of the low country, on Facebook, prompted a friend to comment that they made him nostalgic for a land he had never seen. This captures, more or less, my feeling. The sky seemed massive in the low country, the colors saturated. At sunset everything appeared yellow and pink above the houses that dotted the plains, standing on stilts, water snaking underneath.

Our campsite was directly on the coast, and it was idyllic, the stuff of postcards and corny calendars, just off a long sandy beach. The first thing we saw upon pulling into the camp site was the area reserved for long term campers, mostly RVs; the first RV we saw had, of course, a giant Confederate flag planted out front. And it wasn't alone. The notion of bringing a flag, any flag at all, camping, seemed to me entirely foreign. And this particular flag felt like an omen, a threat.

D-- and I chose a campsite nestled towards the back in the woods where we could sleep in the shade until noon. We spent that first afternoon on the beach, lying in the sun, reading, enjoying each other and the relative silence, the rhythm of the waves. That night we played cards in the dark, and D-- complained about the animals, the raccoons and the deer, that rustled the nearby bushes.

After cards, we sat together on the picnic table at our site on the same bench, both facing forward, D-- leaning with his back against my chest, my arms around his shoulders. This part of the park was empty, and we felt, both of us, tired and calm. I kissed his neck, and grabbed him tighter. Within a few minutes we were fucking, there in the campsite dotted with Confederate flags, out in the open, under the stars, under the trees that occluded that wide Southern sky. I leaned back on that bench and looked up at D-- above me, and the humid air enveloped us both. We felt, at that moment, like a couple, like any couple, camping, driving, fucking, fighting, loving against our will, and against all odds, against history itself, in this place. At that moment, it didn't feel like anything complicated. It just felt like us.

* * * *

It's been two weeks since I emailed you. Now, I'm writing on an uptown 2, on my phone. It was last weekend that I saw you getting off the 2 at 14th. You bolted, and I walked 50 yards behind you on the dank, echoey passageway to the L. I know where you were headed—home. You should have waited for the L right where you always did, but you walked down to avoid meeting me. We had waited there together countless times, a year ago. Needless to say, you haven't responded. My email, unanswered. Maybe you heard that I had a moment with your best friend where I cursed you out. Maybe you know I'm dating someone. Maybe you think I'm crazy, obsessed, unbalanced. Or maybe you are haunted, too, by our past, and think it's better, safer, cleaner and more adult, to leave that shit where it belongs: in our memories. You're probably right.

* * * *

Two days later, leaving this place, D-- and I staged an act of protest. We packed the car, got every last thing ready, and stopped just inside the gates of the park. We left the car running and walked to the RV with the biggest Confederate flag. I held my camera like a gun. I pointed it back at D-- and myself. D-- and I posed in front of that flag, hugged and kissed, taking every image possible. Me kissing his cheek. Him kissing mine. Him in my arms. The two of us hugging. And finally a daring kiss on the lips, with tongue. We ran back to the car, laughing, put her in drive, and drove. We stopped later to look at the images. I am looking at them now, as I write. I see two men who loved one another putting their mark on a place, and admitting to the mark that that place left on them. And trying, really trying, to love each other in spite of it all.

I want now, looking at these photos, to deny the anger, the pain, the hurt, and the hate. To rebuke it, to claim only the love. Like one of the narrators of Faulkner's *Absalom, Absalom!* who attests, on the final page of the book, "'I dont hate [the South] ... I dont hate it. *I dont hate it ... I dont. I dont! I dont hate it! I dont hate it!*'"

There is a special blend of love and hate that we save for our immediate family, ex-lovers, and hometowns. People and places that you cannot take out of yourself, no matter how hard you try. One can, as D-- did, get rid of a Southern accent, the external signifier of place, but getting rid of the South inside you is another story.

You can love a place, a place like the one where we took the picture in front of that Confederate flag. You can love a place for forming this man and forming this country and being an inescapable part of this story, personal and collective—mine, yours, ours—love a place for its beauty and its history and the struggle that it has been to just live there; but also hate this place for the real pain it caused, the blood that was spilled, the ways in which it has failed us and the ways we have failed others; hate it because of the culture that was built in that place that continues to fail us, all of us, even now, even today.

And you can love someone, real, present-tense love, see the beauty and righteousness in them, you can know where they came from and how hard it was, at times, to survive, but also hate that same person for the hurt they caused, or the reasons they failed, or the times they came up short, especially that last, most crucial time, the only time, now, that seems to count.

* * * *

I will never be able to see the American South without seeing you; and I will never be able to love it, honestly, again; and I will never be able to avoid loving it, either; and this hate, this anger I must relinquish; and they feel, this love and this hate and this anger, all in the present tense, one and the same.

THE QUEER SOUTH

EDDIE
OUTLAW

Coming Out to Jimmy Swaggart in a Pantsuit

1.

In the summer of 1991, after almost 20 years spent working the land, my father had given up, restructured his debt, and set off to find a new way to support our family. My mom and dad had lost the farm, and I had to move out of my first apartment and get a second part-time job. I had two options: come home and work for my dad or go to college to earn a degree. The choice was easy. As I packed my things, I planned on never going back to the Mississippi Delta, save for the holidays. My mother had insisted I attend a conservative Southern Baptist college despite my logical arguments for attending a community college until I knew what to do with myself. Realizing I could now start over with real direction, I rolled head first into my new life.

Over the previous several months, I had begun to let myself consider what it meant to be openly gay. Before the bankruptcy, I figured I'd better fight to fit in and do my best to be like everyone else. After the bankruptcy, virtually on my own and faced with a new beginning, being myself didn't seem as daunting. That was the moment of inception for me. That was the jumping-off place that led me to where I am today: in a long-term relationship, co-owner of a gay-owned small business, and, hopefully, living proof that my partner and I aren't much different from the rest of the world.

That fall, I began classes at Hinds Community College, where I studied graphic design, and I met my first boyfriend. I was 19. I imagined we were going to be together forever, and nothing could change my mind. He, having been married, was still semi-closeted. When friends asked if we were a couple, I'd coyly refer that question to him.

I also began coming out to friends and classmates. It was difficult at first, but each telling of my truth became easier. I never faced judgment, which surprised me, but one friend asked, in a serious tone, "Doesn't your butt hurt?" That was the first time I realized people had ridiculous, preconceived notions about what it meant to be gay. I knew there would be those who spewed scripture and/or hate, but I never entertained having to explain that I didn't plan to be a girl, a drag queen, or a drug-addicted, alcoholic AIDS patient, as they all seemed to think.

My instructor in the graphic design program was an insufferable ass. In addition to the random, inappropriate sexual joke or the comment that verged on racist, he'd throw out a "queer joke" when least expected. Still, with all my newfound pride, I never spoke up about my truth. After all, he was in a position of authority, and I was just a student, subject to his views about good design, as well as life choices. It was enough for me to know he'd left his first wife for one of his students, and I took every opportunity to take a jab at their age difference.

My boyfriend and I ventured out to the clubs a couple of times. We'd talk about making "gay friends," but that never really happened. His being secretive about our relationship led to my becoming irrationally jealous. Everyone was a threat in my eyes, and he seemed content to live in secret. I became possessive and inconsolable when we couldn't be together all the time. The sad thing is, almost like an out-of-body experience, I could see what I was doing but seemed unable to stop.

By the following summer, I was out to everyone but my family. I decided that there was no reason to bring that shame on them and to live a double-life that kept my parents and siblings at arms-length. I figured that what they didn't know couldn't hurt them. I would never have to break my mother's heart. She would never have to beg my father not to beat my ass and throw me out. There would never be conflict between my siblings and their future spouses. I would never give them reason to suspect a thing. Sure, I would still be living a sort of lie, but some lies, I convinced myself, were worth telling.

Headstrong and naive, I went down that road, picking up souvenirs and sprinkling lies and half-truths along the way. What I didn't know was that my mother had begun to piece together a timeline of sorts. Like a private detective, she compiled a list of corners into which I'd painted myself, and she patiently waited to confront me.

The following summer, nine months into my first relationship, I was dumped. For all the reasons there were to be together, there were more that drove us apart. Two kids, each trying to figure out what it meant to be gay in a world before *Will & Grace*, had little but the token homosexual on *The Real World* to turn to for direction. When, after weeks of begging, phone calls and stalking my beloved failed, I accepted my situation and spiraled into a depression that lasted longer than I care to admit. I ran with a pack of gay acquaintances at the bars, danced my ass off—literally—and drank too much. I flirted, kissed, and "fooled around" with several guys, but I just couldn't get over my first. I dropped out of school, continued beating myself up for running him off, and ultimately tipped my mother off in a way that only happens in movies.

2.

Mother furrowed her brow and spoke in a quiet, apologetic tone, "Son, we can't figure out how to help with your tuition and your apartment." I knew what was coming next. She continued, "I know it's not ideal, but we want you to move home. You can commute to school from here."

Just like that, I lost my foothold in Jackson. To be honest, I was exhausted with my life as it was. Buying groceries with my mother's Chevron card was less than glamorous, and I'd stopped going out as often, choosing to sit in my darkened apartment and smoke, torturing myself with Celine ballads. I managed to get enrolled in school without my parents discovering I had dropped out the previous semester, but scrambling to cover up that secret was a hefty burden. Driving an hour-and-a-half for school sounded dreadful, but I decided I could do anything for a year if it helped me move on.

Less than two years after coming out, falling in love, and starting a new life, I packed up my studio apartment and limped home with my gay tail between my legs. I took a part-time job in the kitchen at the Humphreys County Country Club. There, I cooked dinner and Sunday lunch for members. While I chopped and sautéed, washed dishes and cleaned up after receptions, my mind was always on Jackson. "One day," I told myself, "I'll get out of here. I'll be successful, and someone will have me."

On occasion, I'd make the drive to town for a random Saturday at Jaded or Beer Bust at JC's, Jackson's gay bar. Always looking and ever hopeful, I longed to find "the one." Friends introduced me to other "gays," but none seemed right. During this time, I was introduced to a guy I thought was kind of cute. I had seen him on the dance floor the night of my first visit to a gay bar. He was one of the "cool gays," and I immediately deemed him "unobtainable." He turned out to be another in a string of hot messes that always seemed to be around at closing time.

One sunny summer afternoon, just when I had resolved to keep moving ahead, I ran into my first love by chance. It was an awkward exchange during which I struggled with the urge to be hateful and the overwhelming need to throw myself at his feet. In the end, I walked away with the feeling that I should be as happy as he, so I faked it.

A few days later, in a fit of stupidity, I whipped into a florist and sent him flowers. "It's nothing," I told myself. "It's a gesture—innocent! And, who knows? He might fall in love with me—again." Someone on Madison Avenue better be rolling in the dough for making floral delivery the answer to life's problems:

Lost your job? Have some flowers!
Dried up ovaries? Have some flowers!
Dick-mo-tized, unable to forget your first love, and pathetic as a cat turd? Send him flowers!

When I got back to the Delta, my mother greeted me. Quickly, I recognized the look on her face. I had seen it when I was a child. It was disappointment rolled in disgust, and she aimed it at me with ease. She sat in a chair, legs crossed without so much as a "Hello!" or "How was your day?"

This came as a shock to me—my mother was the veritable Donna Reed of the Delta. She was known throughout the Delta as one of the few who had not only the means, but also the unbridled talent to organize any social gathering required in advance or at the last-minute. No one knew, but Mother always had the essentials in the cupboard. She could throw together a catfish creole or fling a kabob on the grill. To say the least, when she set her mind to it, she only needed 15 minutes to set up a gathering. God knows how many times Mother stood up and invited the entire congregation back to our home for a mixer just after Sunday night service. In Mississippi, the "Hospitality State," she made it look easy, but at that particular moment, I did not feel welcome in my own home.

"Son, we need to talk," she said. "Have a seat."

As I sat, my mind locked on the reason for the talk, and I knew the jig was up. You see, I had given an "emergency number" in case of any trouble delivering the flowers, which were supposed to endear me to my beloved. Knowing he worked in the art department at one of Mississippi's largest grocery companies, I foolishly assumed everybody knew where that was. And, as we now know, they had "trouble" finding it.

"What's this about flowers for your friend?" she said through tightened lips, like salacious gossip.

"What?" I asked.

She tilted her head and squinted, "The flowers you sent to that boy!"

"I don't know what you're talking about."

"We're going to have a long talk with your father tonight. We'll get to the bottom of this. You mark my words."

I found myself standing in the middle of my room, unaware that I had even left her. I quickly scanned for things I couldn't live without. What I couldn't fit in my trunk, I didn't need. There was no question in my mind how this would end. I would have to tell my truth once more. My father, a peaceful man for the most part, would physically toss me out of the house. Mother, clinging to his ankle, would be dragged along the gravel driveway, yelling "Wallace! Don't hurt him! No, Wallace!" And my siblings, driven from slumber by all the commotion, would witness me "stealing" my car as dust billowed behind me on my way back to Jackson.

3.

I sat in an oversized Queen Anne chair, feet flat on the ground. My sweaty hands were crammed under my legs, helping me feel grounded—almost safe. I thought I might slip from gravity's hold and drift off into the dark Delta sky.

"If I concentrate, I can disappear into this ugly upholstery," I thought.

My father knocked on my door. "Your momma said we need to talk? Are you okay, son?" I could tell he had no idea what was going on. My mother wasn't just leading me to the slaughter, my father was along for the ride as well. In one evening, his boy would both become a queer and dead to him very soon thereafter. As I followed him downstairs, I replayed what I thought was about to happen over and over in my mind. There would be the telling, the ass whipping, and then the exile.

My father has always been a pretty levelheaded man. I've only seen him lose his temper once, when I was no more than ten years old. My aunt owned what we call a "country store" just down from our small home. A small crowd had gathered around the The Hole In The Wall. When I approached, I saw a disheveled man pushed from the doorway and down to the gravel parking lot, my father hot on his heels. The scuffle ended with the man apologizing over and over for what he'd done. The crowd dispersed, and my father stood red-faced, holding his twin sister Wilma, as she wept. I learned later that the man, drunk and belligerent, had groped my aunt and pinned her behind the counter. My father had come to her rescue, but the image of my father, filled with rage, hitting another man was burned into my brain.

Mother had taken her place on the sofa to my left, and Pop was in his recliner to my right. My father's bad back placed him in one of two places: the recliner or flat on his back on the floor with his big pillow. I sat in the middle. My mother glared at me with cold eyes. I could feel no emotion from her at all.

"Tell him," she said. "Tell your father the truth."

Pop looked from my mother to me with confusion. "Tell me what, son?" he said.

I began to sob. I felt the life slipping from me as I willed my body deeper into the chair. I knew there would be no relief in the telling, no weight lifted from my shoulders, and certainly no healing in this truth.

"I'm gay."

There was a loud clap that made my eyes spring open. My mother had produced a Bible and had begun to slap it repeatedly. She was on her feet now, and the scripture and hate were flowing from her clenched teeth, as if she were speaking in tongues. I never expected to be yelled at by my sweet mother. She was my safe haven, my protector. But then, I saw my defender transform into Jimmy Swaggart in a pantsuit.

"We didn't raise you up to become a queer!" she yelled. "THIS is not God's plan! You've got the Devil in you, and I'm NOT gonna let him have you!"

My father looked on, still confused by what I had said. Then, just as quickly as mother had turned on me, my father spoke, and I'll never forget what he said.

"SHUT UP, BONNIE!" he yelled and pointed at her.

I didn't grow up in a home that "got loud." We didn't fight or even have heated debates. There was only respectful dialogue around the dinner table. I had never even seen my parents disagree. My mother stood there, the Bible hanging by her side, her mouth agape.

"Wallace!"

"I said shut up!"

Then, in what can only be described as the most powerful moment I've had in my entire life, my father got out of his recliner. He looked at me, with the eyes of a parent, placed his oversized pillow at my feet, and lay down directly in front of me.

"Son, tell me why you think you're gay."

SETH PENNINGTON

Death-Raised

Five years old when I first stepped
from freezer to office, when I learned
what a morgue was after being
locked inside the cold by my
older brother: *Say yell*. I couldn't. He would
quiet, abandon, leave me finally
in Autopsy with its hearts in glass, and
then sixth grade—we dear
hearts given bonus for bringing
deer hearts to dissect but not
for throwing them like footballs
through ceiling tiles and into our own
faces—these things that make grade
school more memorable. When you remember
the taste of animal blood on your lip, strawberry
ice cream after being suspended, sliced
prejudicially from the slab of Neapolitan, the vanilla and
chocolate left to frostbite by Grandmother, her
loose skirts and tight Depression-era sense of *Hell,
I'm gonna use all the sugar I want.*
I would eat so much the spoon
would exhaust into a dumbbell—I swear—
until it would fall sticky onto the shag
(this before my lesbian cousin told me
carpet is for more than cleaning—this
before I knew what carpet meant).
Girl friends tell me this is why
I have no girlfriends.
Boyfriends say
this is why I have boyfriends.

EVAN J. PETERSON

Heck House

Morningstar Baptist Church is about as far to the east as you can drive down Highway 90 and still be in Tallahassee. I'm in the car with Nathan, who is one of the most widely read people I know, not to mention a former Satanist and recovering speed addict. He quit that life when it became too chaotic; close friends started ending up in jail, and his former roommate decapitated her own fiancée with a samurai sword during a bender. I'm utterly fascinated by him.

These days, Nate's merely an atheist, the occult nothing more than an academic affection. For me, it's quite different. I want to bend reality. I want to channel spirits—but I'm busy reading a book a week for grad school at Florida State and trying to find a boyfriend, so I'm not exactly a diligent occultist. Perhaps if Nathan and I were lovers, it might be different. We almost hooked up the night he introduced me to LSD.

"Why this drug went out of style, I will never understand," he said, placing the tiny gelatin squares in my mouth—but even at a higher dosage than I'd intended, sex with Nathan seemed like an initiation ritual for which I wasn't remotely prepared.

Instead, I've developed a tail-wagging attachment to Nathan due to his knowledge and his collection of rare books and films. It's not a one-sided relationship, but I'm a blithering neophyte and a bit selfish, and I know that there are days I like his library more than I like him. We bicker, we insult one another, and now that we've started an electro-punk band, we also argue about that. What keeps us together are our mutual obsessions with all the little disquieting things life has to offer: John Waters and David Cronenberg films, books written by the disturbed, fetishes no one else has heard of or wants to. This is what brings us to a church on a Saturday night, the chance to experience the particular brand of hysterical mysticism that only Southern Baptists can provide.

When a Hell House popped up in Tallahassee, we were *on it*. Hell houses originated in Texas as church-sponsored, Christian versions of haunted houses. Some congregations plan from January through October to prepare for them. The original Hell House claims to have converted thousands of people and has featured such horrifying scenes as school shootings, hospitals in which young people die of botched abortions or AIDS (just the gays), and raves that lead to drug overdoses and gang rape. The rape victims, unable to face the "consequences of their actions," commit suicide and, of course, end up in Hell.

Charming.

The pinnacle of existential horror is, of course, Hell itself. Each church that hosts a Hell House tries to make its version of Hell so scary that it will compel visitors to bend their knees right there and give their lives to Jesus. This reaction is not at all rare. For more information and the vicarious experience, you could check out George Ratliff's 2001 *Hell House* documentary.

Nathan had heard that Morningstar Baptist's version, located in one of the more liberal counties in the Bible belt, paled in comparison to the Texas shitkicker version. In fact, they don't even call it "Hell House," but rather "Judgment House." This tactic emphasizes the option of going to Heaven instead, not a bad rhetorical move at all, but it definitely takes away from the anticipation. From descriptions that our friends had given us, there would be no preaching against abortion or homosexuality and barely any violence. How disappointing. Instead of going to Baptist Hell, we're going to Heck, a place that really, really sucks but where you might still find decent conversation, like Dante's early circle where all the virtuous pagans who can't go to Heaven can nonetheless avoid being set on fire and torn apart by chainsaws or whatever.

"Maybe they're really a Satanic church, masquerading as Baptist? Lucifer is represented by the morning star," I tell Nate as we pull into the parking lot, as though he didn't know. "And the morning star is actually Venus. Maybe they're a Roman sex cult." We should be so lucky.

Nathan stretches out of the car, 6' 2", Palestinian background, and built like a bull, while I hop onto the grass all bright and bushy. In our short-lived band, Eros & Thanatos, I've conceptualized us as a fox spirit and a minotaur. Nathan's friends calls us "Ego & the Sheik."

I am not the Sheik.

John and Liam pull into the parking lot right after us. John is gay, but not metro-gay. He's more of the type, *Hi, my name is John and I design websites while listening to The Smiths. All. Day. Long.*

John looks tired. Liam, on the other hand, practically sparkles, adorable in a way that only someone unaware of his own beauty can be, like a shaved satyr covered in dew. I figure he's probably straight, but his quiet aloofness leaves just enough margin for speculation. He wears a nondescript navy blue hoodie on top of toast-colored hair. He greets Nate and me with the usual, "Hey." I want to chew his jeans off like a goat. John comes bopping up next, zonked from another sleepless streak of web development and uppers but more excited than I've seen him in weeks. He and Nathan will soon be dating.

"Allison and Mike are on their way," he informs us. "What name d'you want Saint Peter to call you?"

At some point in the performance, we will be called before Saint Peter. This is relatively standard practice for a Hell House, right before you tour Hell and Heaven. Before we go in, we have to fill out little cards so that the actor playing Saint Peter knows what to call us, an interactive *whoa!* moment as chintzy as E.T. thanking you by name on the Universal Studios theme park ride.

Though it's past Halloween, the heck house is staying open an extra weekend to save as many sinners as possible. It's cold out and getting colder as Allison and Mike arrive. They are the classic nerdy straight couple: he's short and slim with glasses and braces, and she's a plump college radio DJ with a Betty Page cut.

John decided that on this night, when Saint Peter calls him, his name will be "Tudor." Allison is "Cosette," and Mike is "Andre." I'm hoping that Nathan won't write his name down as "Oliver Clozoff" or worse. "Fisty Crisco" is not beyond him. He instead picks "Tzvetan." I choose the name "Kevin," lacking any inspiration. Liam is just "Liam."

We wait in the pews until the guides come for us. The only other people in our party are another young straight couple, a deaf woman and her boyfriend, who signs the information for her. Before the guides take us into the scenario, they inform us that in each scene, the actors will change, but the characters remain the same. The character of Kelly Parker will wear a pink shirt at all times. Her older brother Matthew Parker will be wearing a white t-shirt and camouflage hat.

Their younger brother Peter will always be wearing a green shirt.

Peter Parker. Spiderman's secret identity. I wonder if this script is intentionally geared toward kids.

A compound made up of portables and wooden walkways adjoins the church. Each portable contains a different scene, and the first few are pretty boring. The story focuses on family values rather than sensationalism (dang it all to Heck). It goes like this: Mr. and Mrs. Parker neglect their kids. Kelly, their only daughter, has recently been attending Bible study with friends and is ready to give her life to Jesus. Matthew, the oldest, thinks this is stupid. When the parents go out of town on business, Matthew throws a keg party at home. Kelly urges him not to, but Matthew won't be deterred. Meanwhile, Peter has taken up smoking cigarettes.

We don't converse amongst ourselves during the walk from scene to scene. There's a certain reverence for the location, despite the fact that we're only here to gawk. Our guides, dressed in sweaters and jeans, fill us in on what happens in between scenes. In Texas, the tour guides wear black cloaks and speak in ghoulish voices, but I keep reminding myself that we're not in Texas and that I should probably be thankful for that.

As the teens get drunk, one of Peter's cigarettes starts a fire in the house. This scene works incredibly well (we discover later that this production is staged from a starter kit available over the internet). The exterior of the house is realistic, and the lights inside mimic flames convincingly. All three of the Parker children are injured to varying degrees. The teens fleeing the house were smeared with soot, which seems like a very Hollywood affectation. Perhaps all the drama is not lost.

Before the next scene, the guides inform us that we are about to enter Kelly's hospital room. As we walk in from the cold, my stomach squirms. The actress playing Kelly has been made up to look severely burnt. The realism of the makeup is so effective that I have to look away at first. Those campy elements I had been looking forward to have been replaced by the charred face of a teenage girl. This isn't what I was expecting. No buckets of blood in the abortion clinic, no abstinent teens dressed in glow-in-the-dark rave gear. I squat on the ground and focus on the parents and the nurse character.

"I'm so sorry, Mr. and Mrs. Parker. We've done all we can for her," says the nurse, without a trace of overacting.

The parents start to wail as the nurse pulls the sheet over Kelly's raw face. At this point, I've had it. This is serious tragedy, and I do start getting teary. Nathan hears me sniffle and looks down indignantly. Allison rubs my shoulder.

"Why is this happening? First Matthew, now Kelly!" the parents bawl.

The nurse tells them, "You have to be strong now, for Peter."

From behind a curtain, another nurse pushes a wheelchair into the room, in which sweet Peter is literally *still steaming*. Did they do that with clouds of talcum powder?

"Where's Kelly? Where's my sister?" He looks so much like one of Jerry's Kids that the sheer maudlin absurdity dries my tears. I now have to pinch the bridge of my nose and chew my tongue to keep from bursting into inappropriate laughter. Now we're cooking with Hellfire.

"I don't want to die without giving my life to Jesus. I want to see Kelly again when I die, and I'm going to be a Christian, just like my sister!" the boy says.

Mercifully, we're ushered off to the next scene.

Aluminum foil coats the far wall. In the center is a podium, behind which leans a man who looks like Colonel Sanders.

"I thought Baptists didn't believe in saints," I whisper to Nathan.

"Saint Peter's an exception; you can't pray to him. He just tells you if you go to Heaven or Hell. Someone has to be the bearer of bad news."

Two characters named Peter, I think cattily. *I should write scripts for Hell Houses.*

On one end of the room, there is a portal draped with strips of silver mylar. It looks as though a drag queen will burst through at any moment and start lip-synching "Heaven Must Be Missing An Angel."

The opposite side bears a gaping black hole in the wall, outlined in jagged bricks. It's either Hell or a leather bar.

"Let me see here." Saint Peter peers down at a list. He even sounds like Colonel Sanders. "Kelly Parker, come stand and be judged."

The actress runs up to the podium, barefoot. This Kelly is chunky, and it makes me happy to see that large people go to Heaven, too. I never really doubted this, but the whole sin-of-gluttony issue makes me wonder if fat people are considered sinful. Then again, this seemed to be a relatively progressive group of Baptists. Something to google later.

"Kelly Parker, you are a sinner! But you have given your life to Jesus. For this reason, you will be welcomed into the kingdom of Heaven!"

Saint Peter slams his gavel, and I notice that rather than finding a judge's gavel or making one, Morningstar Baptist Church has provided their Saint Peter with—it can't be, but just as sure as you're born, it is—a crab mallet. That's so Florida.

Kelly joyfully runs through the mylar gates.

"Now, what have we here? Matthew Parker!"

Apparently, no one in the afterlife wears shoes. This Matthew could be a teen model. The actor's glossy black hair, tight white t-shirt, and Mediterranean face have me wondering if he's eighteen yet. I keep checking Matthew out as Saint Peter lists the sins he has committed, but then I look to Liam and return to pining for him.

"Matthew Parker, you could have saved yourself by giving your life to Jesus, but you have been stubborn and rejected your Savior!"

Matthew protests that he didn't know that the Bible was true, but of course ignorance is not a defense that stands up in this court. Two hooded figures emerge from the black hole in the wall and drag him off. I notice that the soles of his feet are very pink.

"Now, as I call your name, please step forward. Cosette. Andre. Tudor. Liam. Kevin …" I step up to join the group.

"… um … Taz-veton.…" Nathan steps up behind me.

"Kathy, and Rick." The deaf woman's boyfriend nudges her, and they join us.

"It is not your time yet. But when your time comes, will you walk through a door, or be dragged through it?"

I was raised to believe that there's a God, some mysterious higher power watching over me, and that each person has to approach this one in his or her own way. My mother, a Jew, doesn't believe in a devil, and I still can't figure out what my recovering Methodist father believes. Though secular, they're both very superstitious, and I've inherited this trait. Here, at the staged crossroads of damnation and salvation, I did start to wonder if there's an afterlife organized into punishments and rewards. What leads a person to Hell? Cruelty? Or a mere disbelief in Jesus? The Hell I imagine, one even a Buddhist could accept, is filled with nasty people who are too self-centered to surrender their souls to the afterlife. They aren't in Hell because they shoplifted or had an abortion or sat in a church pew thinking about the subtly nuanced flavor of Liam's left earlobe, they're in Hell because that's where your soul goes when you want to keep it all to yourself. It's not about getting what you deserve, but rather a continuation of a life of selfishness.

In the next room, the lights go out. *Good luck signing for Kathy now, Rick*, I think. *Wait, I take that back, that was uncalled-for.* I'm already apologizing for catty thoughts. The threat of damnation is working.

I'm standing in the middle of a relatively equilateral triangle made of corners of Nathan, John, and Liam. We hear the click of a tape begin playing. There is howling wind and the distant laughter of demons. Two voices become distinct, one of which, definitely in charge, is obviously Satan's. The other voice is that of a grumpy, high-pitched gremlin. It sounds agonizingly familiar, and though it's on the tip of my brain, I can't recall who it reminds me of.

Now that it's completely dark, I debate the pros and cons of just sticking my hand into Liam's back pocket. Not that I'm bold or arrogant enough to actually do this, but I like to think about it.

He's not going to hit me or anything. He's a totally passive guy. I could always blame it on John or Nathan.

The demons are having a predictable conversation: "My dark Lord, your drugs and violence have saturated the world! There are more damned souls than ever!"

Maybe if I get Liam stoned enough, he'll make out with me. If he makes out with me, it's carte blanche from there. I wonder if Allison and Mike have weed.

"We lost Kelly Parker's soul to Christ," says the little demon.

"No! We were so close!"

"But wait, Evil One—we got her brother's soul!"

At this point, a single orange floor lamp illuminates this scene's Matthew and the requisite tissue-paper-flames-on-a-fan. The poor guy is writhing in Hell quite believably, and the light gives his profile a flattering glow. I remind myself not to cruise the damned, especially when they're such likely jailbait.

"What am I doing here?" shouts this scene's Matthew. "I thought that Hell was just a story! Where are my friends? This isn't the way I thought it would be at all!"

Nathan leans in to whisper, "That's good. They're playing off that old adage that Hell must be full of the fun people."

The lights go out again. *Liam would never know it was me. I could sneak around by the deaf lady and come in from the opposite side. I bet his ass is really warm and soft.*

Satan is back on the speakers.

"Excellent work, demon!"

"Mission accomplished!" says the gremlin, and that's when I realize that the voice sounds like George W. Bush, and not in a this-is-my-nonfiction-story, I'm-going-to-lambast-the-former-President kind of way. The demon certainly, even intentionally, sounds like Bush. What were they thinking?

The door opens, and we file back out into the autumn chill.

"Did the demon sound like George Bush to you?" I say to Nathan, under my breath.

"'Mission accomplished?' Totally. What an odd aesthetic choice."

Having seen the torments of Hell, the only thing left to see is Heaven. I expect lots of cotton batting and cheesy white robes on cheesy white people.

The light is gold. Not yellow, but gold. The entire room, floor and ceiling, is lined with billowing white fabric blown by unseen fans.

"Oh my God, we're in a Celine Dion video," John says. We all stifle laughter, even Kathy when Rick signs to her. Try as I might, I am unable to describe in words the sign language for "Celine Dion."

The room is huge, and I wonder what purpose it serves during the other eleven months of the year. Day care? Social hall? Snake storage for weekly handling?

We walk in at one corner of the room from which, no kidding, a yellow brick road proceeds. It runs half the length of the wall, makes a ninety-degree turn into the room, and continues about five feet up to an iron gate. Beyond it dance twelve of the blondest children I've ever seen, six to each side of the path. They are draped in white, slowly rotating with their arms spread. Occasionally they change this rotation up with what appears to be low-impact Jazzercise calisthenics, and they don't look happy.

I want my angels to look happy. These angels look as though they've been slowly rotating like rotisserie chickens for two hours, and I whisper to Nate, "Child protective services would shit the bed over this."

Past the children, there is Jesus.

He actually looks pretty close to what Jesus must have looked like: curly dark hair, gathered close to his head, but still a little puffy. Sort of a short Jew-fro, but not in an annoying hipster way.

Jesus of course has a beard, but not a Jesus beard. It's neatly trimmed, very professional. He's a regular door-to-door Jesus. And, my favorite part, he's burly. Chunky, even. This immediately makes me comfortable. I *want* Jesus to be a chunky, gregarious, clean-cut guy, a thirty-three-year-old Santa Claus, and that's exactly who this guy is. I'd hook up with this Bear Jesus, but more importantly, I'd take him home to meet my parents. This Jesus has a real job and knows how to cook.

Christ lines us up single-file in Heaven. Then, he does something that makes me question my snarky, arrogant, judgmental life. He hugs each of us. Not a hard-patting, begrudging hug with the pelvis withdrawn as far as it can get from the hugee, but a full-body hug of utter kindness and acceptance. He rests his hands on my shoulders, looks into my eyes, and says, "Welcome home."

Marry me, Jesus.

As I regain my composure, we're led out of Heaven into the cold, then back into the main chapel. I start thinking about what a friend once said about cocaine: that it's like getting a hug from Jesus. I can't imagine that anything's as good as a hug from Jesus.

Later, in the car, I will tell Nathan that I think I might want to try going to the local Metropolitan Community Church, the gay one. He will roll his eyes. "Evan, you're Jewish, and you despise organized religion. Don't get hoodwinked by some backwoods horseshit."

He's mostly right. I don't want to go to some big lecture hall on my day off and listen to some woman with a sensible haircut preach about how God loves all of us unconditionally. I don't want to tithe or sing in a choir or be able to argue the context of the story of Sodom. I don't want to surround myself with a bunch of pious people who would rather read *Chicken Soup for the Queer Soul* than *Naked Lunch*.

What I want at the moment is for someone to welcome me home and hug me like Jesus hugged me, unconditionally, forever, and I don't know if that means I need Jesus or just a stable boyfriend who isn't anorexic, alcoholic, meth-scrambled, incidentally straight, or the kind of person who sits around on Adderall designing websites for thirty-six hours without blinking. But before any of that is decided, we still have to sit through one last-ditch effort on the part of the Morningstar Baptist Revue.

The final stop is a small room with four rows of chairs lined up. The chairs face a wall that bears a poorly painted mural of Noah's Ark, post-Deluge, with a rainbow in the sky and two of each animal leaving the boat—giraffes, owls, zebras, and turtles, but only one chimpanzee. The pastor starts talking about salvation or something, and all I can think about is hugging Bear Jesus and also this one chimpanzee, destined to roam the earth alone and defy evolution.

I'm brought back into the moment by Kathy, who begins cracking her knuckles. She has no idea how loud that is. *I wonder how Deaf Jeff is doing,* I think. My mind is wandering all over the place in the aftermath of Bear Jesus. I once slept with my deaf friend Jeff, and he was completely silent, even during orgasm. I had expected just the opposite. Soon I think about Bear Jesus again.

The pastor asks us if we would bow our heads as he prays for us. Not wanting to be disrespectful, I do so. He then asks who wants to be saved tonight, "because we have people right here, right now, ready to help you begin your journey to Jesus."

But I just saw Jesus. He hugged me and everything.

"Well all right, maybe some of you believe that you're already saved. Just remember, you can always come back to us."

I'm hoping that Rick or Kathy or even Liam will run up and ask to be saved. Oh well, *not Texas*.

On the way out, a woman from the church asks me, "So what did you think?"

"Well, I thought you did a bang-up job. It was more about Heaven than Hell."

"Oh yeah?"

I can't resist adding one little barb. "I do have one small criticism. Why did Saint Peter have a crab mallet for a gavel? Doesn't he deserve better?"

The woman gives me a beaming, bless-your-heart smile as my friends quicken their pace to get the fuck out. "What do you think he'll be holding when you really see him?"

"Well ma'am," I say, "I'm in no position to speculate about such things."

I'm still not.

KENNETH
★POBO★

Deep Into Georgia

Clay and I won't last. We're
too different. Brenda says having
much in common is overrated.
Dean says that the best way

to know someone
is to travel together,
so Clay and I head for Georgia
where he has business in Macon.

The soil reddens in a state
not known for Communism.
Such a bloody color
evokes many deaths,

those whose skin offends,
those whose loves offend.
Yet this soil is wise too,
like it learned firsthand

all the lessons that the sun
has to teach. Clay and I
aren't wise. We can't choose
between the Waffle House or

Cracker Barrel for dinner.
Either way, we know what
will happen if
we hold hands.

This Guy I'm Married To

well, not legally, this is Tennessee,
and I had a fight again, the usual thing,
he's a pack rat and I'm a throw-awayer.

I don't fight fair. I go mum. He says,
"You look like Richard Nixon
in that face." I bark out

something nonsensical, he raises
his voice, I remember a scene
in *Dynasty*—Crystal descends

down a long staircase,
Linda Evans' finest moment, she's ready
to ditch Blake—we have no staircase,

Nixon lacks her panache, I sit,
he sits, we chill, laugh at the cats,
nothing's resolved, but Nixon

slips back in the closet
(is Bebe Rebozo there?) and
my not-legal spouse talks softly,

like a winter aconite, small,
just blooming, another night
coming to a close.

The Factory, Knoxville

All I have to offer a horny stranger
is the smell of Newport Light 100s
on my shirt and breath. New

in Knoxville, my nerves crack—
grits, fleas, the Tennessee Vols.
Scared to talk to a stranger, I smoke

and smoke, pretend to like
the music's thump thump thump
when I'd rather be listening

to Tommy Roe's "Hooray For Hazel,"
order a martini followed by
another, don't get drunk—

I sip to make them last for 3 hours.
Many guys look hot,
either sexually or just because

September is stark muggy.
Time to walk back
to my apartment which at least

has my cat. Sunday will offer a walk
in the foothills of the Smokies,
a quiet I will climb like a mountain.

BRAD RICHARD

Carl

You landed randy in New Orleans, ca. 1983,
hustling your past to fit new needs, told me
you'd hitched a ride from Hannibal, ditching

Bible-thumping kin, told others Oregon, on the trail
of some lost high school boyfriend. "Let's get married
and move to Tokyo," you whispered on the levee

our one night, my legs over your shoulders,
the last I'd see of your flamingo tattoo, your
missing molar. Worked your way, I'd bet, around

The Loading Zone, The River Bottom, to the lap
of an uptown daddy, maybe, though that wouldn't last
as long as this memory I'm making up

to say how you finally found your way back
to your nameless upriver home, worked for your dad,
watched him and the town die, lied to your wife

about the months you spent fucking boys
into further dark, all our unimagined lives
on starlit levees, the dark river flowing.

Alex (Flamingo's Cafe, New Orleans, 1983)

Hostess for Christmas in July, he's lit, gowned
head-to-red-heeled-toe in layered twinkle lights,

silver tinsel. He stoops, *'scuse me,* to unplug
before guiding guests to tables, bends to snort

from toilet tank lids sparkly lines of crystal,
stumbles in the afterglow. Lowly busboy, I

am hooked on his twitch and sway, but queasy
because I know I like *boys,* but ... Bosses' orders,

every morning he feeds the jukebox a quarter
for Kate Smith's "God Bless America." Back home

in Poplarville, he sneaks from Mama's cabinet
Mama's hormone pills.
                      Oh Alex, first boy

I helped zip into a wedding gown, first
disturbance of my desires, free me, kneel me

at your feet, bow my head under your skirts,
fill my mouth with your holy light.

HANNAH
RIDDLE

Georgetta, Alabama

She thought I was a boy
until, in the blue glow of her stage lights
she felt me up, laughing, surprised

enough to interrupt her own number—
*you're still cute baby, we'll love you
anyway,* kissed my face,

my mouth, turned
to take another drink, kept on
lip-synching her low hum, half singing.

Later, when I wash the dark
purple from my jaw, lipstick
slipping the bowl of the hotel sink,

the bar's still open, 24/7
like a place to stay: grown men fallen
full on the long pool table,

someone sliding a hand
down the cigarette machine,
that same drag queen, her voice

deepening, dress stretching
across the barstool, knees
relaxing open.

LAURENCE
★ROSS★

A Partial Guide to Camp: How To Get Dry Again

> *They were indeed a queer-looking party that assembled on the bank—the birds with draggled feathers, the animals with their fur clinging close to them, all dripping wet, cross, and uncomfortable.*
>
> *The first question of course was, how to get dry again ...*
>
> — Lewis Carroll, from *Alice's Adventures in Wonderland*

Admittedly, New Orleans is reputed to look for solace no further than the drink in one's own hand. *It incarnates a victory of "style,"* to borrow Sontag's words from "Notes on 'Camp.'" This city is a stylized one: *Style is everything.* When Isaac finally dragged his sopping hemline away from the city, the first place many sojourned was the bar. There was no power, and would not be for days. The cigarette machines ran on generators. The neighborhood lights diminished to candle flickers and flashlights.

Once again, a hurricane struck on the weekend of Southern Decadence, one of New Orleans' largest tourist draws, known to many simply as "Gay Mardi Gras." People had flocked to New Orleans, to set up camp, and local religious leaders did not waste the opportunity of such an easy open metaphor to suggest the hurricane was God-sent, to purge the city of sin. *Thus, the Camp sensibility is one that is alive to a double sense in which some things can be taken.* So here is an alternative lens: at night in the Bywater, to look toward the East was to peer into a pitch-black void; on the other side, to the West, one could spy a verifiable, enticing beacon of light. The French Quarter shone as salvation, for *Camp is solvent of morality. It neutralizes moral indignation, sponsors playfulness.* Camp is a haven.

For the past thirteen years, the Grand Marshal of Southern Decadence has named an official theme song for the event. This year's song: Nicki Minaj's "Starships." And it was while sitting in a bar in the Quarter, with Nicki playing at the water's edge on the televisions and the song playing over the loudspeakers, that my friend M asked me, "What is this even about?" The question is a good one, and one I had not asked myself before. I typically reserve my pop-music analysis until I can pair the lyrics with the visuals of the artist's accompanying music video/film—an endeavor that does not always yield a bounty of meaning. *It is the difference, rather, between the thing as meaning something, anything, and the thing as pure artifice.*

The "Starships" video opens with four barrel-chested men clad in red loincloths and bowler hats performing a ritual-esque dance to summon Nicki from on high. She complies, carried in a spacecraft mirror-plated as a disco ball, and transmitted to earth in a beam of light. This ritual is a rain dance designed to deliver techno beats rather than water. (Of course, the last thing New Orleans needed was more rain.) The barely-clad inhabitants of the island look exhausted, despondent until Nicki emerges from the sea foam like Venus. She practically commands the spectators to have a Bud Light, Patron, to imbibe, consume as she assumes her place upon the litter that awaits her before being carried away into the depths of the crowd. She claps her hands, as if in prayer. She wears a pink headpiece, a cross between a nun's habit and Red Riding Hood's cape, a conflation of the worlds of religion and fairy tale. The aesthetic here is one of character creation/amalgamation. *Camp is the glorification of "character."* And, true to hers, she is indeed glorified, borne away on the shoulders of the very ones who summoned her as she constructs and reconstructs identities: "My name is Onika, you can call me Nicki."

And it is here where one could begin theorizing why Nicki has been so embraced by queer culture. Queer culture, and the Camp aesthetic in particular, maintains identity as one of its primary concerns—both its construction and deconstruction. The mission of emphasizing the world's inherent artifice, and therefore the constructed nature of identity itself, results in the consciousness and the freedom to make one's self and to name that self however one pleases. Nicki Minaj and her numerous, neon wig changes, suggests that any hairstyle is exactly that—a *style*, an aesthetic choice. I'm not sure I have ever seen a photograph of Nicki's "real" hair, which, from the spectator's perspective, implies that there is no "real" hair. That her hair is a signifier, that her hair is "hair," just as much of an accessory as the pink harness she adorns halfway through "Starships." And yes, the video does (as Southern Decadence did) evolve/devolve into a kaleidoscopic, epileptic, black light montage. Keith Marszalek of nola.com has described Southern Decadence as "a happening of haberdashery fit for an LSD Alice in Wonderland," but Nicki Minaj is not echoing Lewis Carroll so much as Oscar Wilde. As Lord Henry, Wilde's maxim-ushering promoter of unbridled hedonism, notes, "Being natural is simply a pose, and the most irritating pose I know."

In many ways, Minaj's song, "Beautiful Sinner," would have been a better choice for the weekend. An embrace of the hedonistic, of love in spite of social/moral connotation, of the "wicked" heart as work of art, "I didn't know that bad could look so good." "Beautiful Sinner" is more clearly a statement of identity. The notion of a beautiful sinner is, itself, if not a paradox, at the very least a challenge to the meaning of the word "sinner"—and *Camp taste turns its back on the good-bad axis of ordinary aesthetic judgment.* The lyrics of "Beautiful Sinner" end with "Maybe you're the master of disguise ... and you're really the saint"—a blatant deconstruction/subversion of the other's apparent/original identity.

The lyrics of "Starships" are, in part, so confounding because the identity of who or what is a starship is relatively obscured. The song seems entirely shallow, entirely surface and gloss. The words, however, function like Nicki's own false eyelashes—attention-worthy and distracting in their own (superficial) right, but also a device to frame the (ever-blinking/winking) eyes. Eyes that are a site of simultaneous entry and reflection, a gateway for light (illumination) with the image of the spectator reflected on the surface. *It is the difference, rather, between the thing as meaning something, anything, and the thing as pure artifice.*

Do we all become a "starship," as Nicki's use of the first-person plural ("Let's do this one more time") suggests? That would be a pleasant enough notion, an expression of simultaneous unity and self-affirmation that events such as Southern Decadence would want to at least keep afloat in the background. Southern Decadence, however, is quite distinct from Pride. The event is not foregrounded in striving for visibility (though there is certainly a lot of seeing and showing), but rather in having a gigantic, unbridled five-day party. ("But fuck who you want, and fuck who you like / Dance all ya life, there's no end in sight.")

Though despite the song's lyrics, "Starships" is a remarkably sexless video (in stark contrast to Southern Decadence itself). The most intense expressions of joy come when an individual is just that—individual. For example, the series of shirtless men who gleefully leap through sprays of colored "paint." The only thing erupting is the volcano. At the end of the day, Nicki is left (or perhaps has chosen) to fuck no one, to roll around with herself in the glitter and sand. The act *reveals self-parody, reeks of self-love*. A lone star in the sky. And perhaps this (dance) step of individual expression is the most important, the first one to make before finding your (dance) partner. As Nicki tells us, "Twinkle, twinkle." An implied "how we wonder what we are."

As Nicki says, "Let's do this one last time," and return to the question(ing) of identity. The song, the video, and Southern Decadence are all celebratory in tone. Those attending Southern Decadence were ready to party. My friend P—who drove four hours to stay in my powerless, dark, sweaty, foodless house—said with optimistic cheerfulness, "It will be just like camping!" And yes, there were certainly elements of Camp at play, but not the sort of camp that involves tents or suspending coolers from tree limbs. The weekend contained a palpable individuality ("If you want more, more / Then here I am") combined with an acknowledged unity ("Can't stop cause we're so high"). A collective "we," twinkling in the sky, a drink in every hand. (Gin and tonics, by the way, will glow beneath a black light—each plastic cup its own little celestial presence.) The dance floors of Southern Decadence were markedly more crowded than the dance floor of "Starships" and everyone seemed poised to leap on stage. While many people, like Nicki, were performing, these performed identities are not inherently false. In all likelihood, the contrary is the truth—that through performance and an embrace of artifice (an embrace for which the queer community is often harshly judged/misunderstood), we collectively exert our agency as individuals. It is through performance and artifice that the accepted notions of "normal" or "straight" can be questioned, debased.

If this reading of the weekend/song/video seems a bit overdone, overwrought, then it is merely in keeping with the aesthetic. Southern Decadence is rooted in costumed play and "decadence" carries connotations of the indulgent, the stylized (appearance of) excess. *Camp is art that proposes itself seriously, but cannot be taken altogether seriously because it is "too much."* That artifice Nicki Minaj so adores can be used as a vehicle to unveil a spectrum of dualities. The individual/whole, the love/parody, the wet/dry, the compromised liver, and the critical lens. That queer theory and the dance floor can exist in the same space. That *One can be serious about the frivolous, frivolous about the serious*. And if Nicki indulges in a few plumes of purple gas seeping from her island, I will allow a few lines of purple prose to seep from this essay.

I wore a white shirt the last night of Decadence, a shirt that most certainly did not remain white. There were sprays of pink hurricane and glitter, remnants of rub-on tattoos and eyeliner. There is no shelter on Nicki's island. You are forced to make Camp on the dance floor. The canvas of the self is mixed in with the whole. And if you happen to lose yourself or your way in the process, thankfully, after Southern Decadence/Labor Day weekend, one has the option of purchasing new whites at a significant discount.

[Lines in italics are taken from Susan Sontag's "Notes On 'Camp'"]

LIANA ROUX

Brookgreen Gardens, South Carolina

i.
Eighth-grade art class field trip,
maybe five or six of us, all girls,

best friends so strange to see
out of uniform—no tartan skirts

or white socks, shapeless green
sweatshirts with unraveled cuffs

of sleeves, no white shamrocks
over *St. Patrick Catholic School*.

ii.
Sprawling lawns and lanes
through live oaks, twisted branches
trailing Spanish moss,

perfect-bodied men and women
from all the myths we didn't know:
fat granite-winged Pegasus,

Muses rising lithe from a fountain,
Orpheus, head turned, straining
for Eurydice already lost,

a nymph carved in white, bathing,
arms folded over breasts,
soft-looking, delicate,

smooth. I stood so close
to the thin arcs of her fingernails,
reached out, secretly, to touch.

iii.
We snuck out that night
in our pajamas, bare feet on concrete,
quarters in our hands
for the hotel vending machine:

slick bags of Cool Ranch chips,
Mellow Yellow, Wintergreen gum
we shared on the balcony,
our shoulders wrapped in scratchy comforters

we stole from the beds.
Over the pool, lit water flickered
unreal aquamarine, streetlamps
washing out the stars.

In the morning, our parent-chaperones
found out—we forgot to close one door
all the way, and we could have been
murdered, kidnapped or worse,

and *I'm not angry, I'm disappointed*
and I felt so ashamed
when I remembered Madeleine
in her pajamas, long brown hair,

bundled on the balcony with me
and whispering *let's be lesbians
together*, and me laying my head
on her sweatshirt, almost

holding her hand. We went to different
high schools, never talked about it
after—night when I could feel her lungs
move in her chest, breath warm

in dark air, look up
at the pale streetlight shine
on her face.

THE QUEER SOUTH

KEVIN
SESSUMS

Skeeter Davis, Noël Coward, and Eudora Welty

"Fuck," said Frank Hains. "I knew I shouldn't have given that last bourbon to Eudora."

It had taken me almost a decade after that day of my mother's funeral, but I had finally found the only equivalent that Mississippi offered to a *What's My Line?* life. Frank—a John Daly-like presence in Jackson—was the arts editor of the state's afternoon newspaper, for which he also wrote a column called "On Stage." Eudora was writer Eudora Welty. We were at a cast party for New State Theatre's latest production, *Long Day's Journey Into Night*, starring Geraldine Fitzgerald as Mary Tyrone. Frank and Miss Welty were active members of New Stage, and he was playing host that night at Bleak House, the name given facetiously to his antebellum home by the local literati of Jackson. The Dickensian nickname derived from the house's outward appearance of haunted dilapidation where it sat, rather spookily, on a hill opposite Jackson's lone Jewish cemetery. Inside, however, past the vast front porch, Frank—also a gifted set designer—had redone his home with a lovely simplicity. Books abounded. A collection of vintage LPs filled one whole room, alphabetized and all of them encased in brown paper sleeves. Even though he had this wide selection of music, he usually only played Mabel Mercer, his favorite, or Erik Satie or Blossom Dearie. He also liked Fred Astaire—for his voice, not his dancing—which was so like Frank; he was always looking for the different angle, the way to appreciate an artist or a piece of art in his own way so that appreciation itself became a kind of art form. There was even a Leontyne Price album of pop songs arranged by André Previn he loved to listen to for some rueful smiles; especially the Mississippi diva's rendition of "Melancholy Baby" with Previn on the piano and Ray Brown on bass. On the night of that latest cast party he was playing, as a tribute, a lot of Noël Coward, who had died the night before.

Frank Hains went to New York City several times a year to review theater and opera for his newspaper and had begun to allow me to stay at Bleak House in his absence. He also subscribed to *After Dark* magazine, and I would peruse the pages of the slender and sleekly photographed issues when I visited him for their overt appeal to the kind of eroticism I had begun to seek out anyplace I could find it. Frank would stand over my shoulder when a new *After Dark* arrived in the mail and point out his latest favorite photograph by Roy Blakey or Kenn Duncan and regale me with stories about Angela Lansbury, who was often featured in the pages, or Rudolph Nureyev, whom he insisted I resembled in some sort of Slavic/Southern sleight-of-hand. "I should be more supportive of the ballet," he said once, staring at the latest photo of Nureyev that *After Dark* was running. "I'm much more at home in literature and drama and musical comedy and opera. Satie is just about the only thing I can stomach that doesn't have a lyric. That, and Bach, but there's a mathematical genius to old J.B. I find fascinating. I once had a crush on a mathematician when I was, like you, a college sophomore. I know—can you picture me a sophomore? Hmmm ... why Bach and Satie? *There's a column in there somewhere,*" he said, using one of his favorite phrases as he pushed his black-framed reading glasses atop his thin-haired head, a habit of his when a concept for a column occurred to him, as if he were helping his brain to see the idea floating about his skull back there around his bald spot.

Frank's kitchen in Bleak House was as big as most homes. Theatrical posters—along with several of the photographs that Miss Welty had taken of innately elegant dirt-poor Mississippians when she worked as a publicist for the Works Project Administration during the Depression—hung along the walls of the house's "dogtrot," the open hallway that runs through the center of so many Southern homes of the antebellum period. A couple of years earlier, Miss Welty had collected many of the photos of her Depression-era travels in a volume titled *One Time, One Place*. She always preferred to refer to them as "snapshots," however, and recalled fondly the little Rolleiflex camera she toted around with her upon her return from her year in business school up at Columbia University, her eyes readjusting, expertly so, to the reasons that had drawn her back home.

I had first met Frank and Miss Welty when I was still in high school. A mutual friend from Forest had taken me to a book party Frank had thrown for Miss Welty at Bleak House. Although I was only sixteen at the time, I had immediately been accepted into their fold. No eye masks were needed, I discovered, but there were other requirements. A liberal political bent helped. A sense of one's own sensuality. Discernment certainly. And, most important, enough knowledge to know when to join a heady conversation or, better yet, simply to listen while others carried on one around you. I learned more sitting at Frank's big round kitchen table than I ever did in any classroom as he and Miss Welty—who would wander over the few blocks it took to drive her blue Ford Fairlane from Pinehurst Street—went off on Richard Nixon or Vladimir Nabokov, but practically swooned over the poetic justness to be found in Jane Austen and somebody "just about the best" named Henry Green. They liked jazz, too—Miss Welty had done a lot of club-hopping in Harlem—and taught me that bourbon was never to be augmented by anything other than maybe an added ice cube if one *simply must* when yet another Mississippi August demanded such a dilution, and sipping at a slightly watered-down potation was the only reasonable exertion that such heat and humidity humanly allowed. Their refilled glasses—it was my honor to administer the respective cubes—fueled their conversation until they drifted sometimes, not often, from cerebral musings to those of the heart.

They were mostly circumspect when discussing their lost loves. Frank would often allude to his "dusky endeavors," as they had come to refer politely to his interest in young African Americans, some of whom had touched him deeply with their aspirations and narratives of maternal love. Miss Welty welcomed these stories of nuanced carnality, as Frank was careful not to tell her the details. One especially hot night under the glow of the big light that hung over his kitchen table, Miss Welty, her upper lip damp, did hint at the feelings she had for one young man long, long ago. Frank had tears in his eyes as she lyrically, elliptically, without ever admitting the depths of her own emotions but not denying them either, told us of a young poet who could obviously still summon a profound sadness within her all these years after he had moved away from Mississippi, from her, and taken up residence in San Francisco and Italy, places more "welcoming to his kind, to yours," she told us as her voice came to a halt and she perhaps heard only his now lost one in the sudden comfort of her silence. She finished neither the carefully diluted story nor the freshly diluted bourbon in front of her, both making it too dangerous that night, she seemed to reason in her reverie, for her to drive back home to a house forever musty with familial love alone.

Years later, my little brother Kim—a Mississippi obstetrician/gynecologist who has also become a sculptor of some renown—presented to Miss Welty a bronze bust of herself. It was the last year of her life and she had taken up residence in the downstairs parlor of the house on Pinehurst. She was in ill health by then and no longer able to make it upstairs to the bedroom where she had written her short stories and novels, putting their freshly typed pages on her old bed, then cutting them up with a pair of sewing scissors before pinning the paragraphs and sentences back together as if literature of the highest order were indeed the piecework of her life.

Many of her favorite books had been moved downstairs also and were scattered everywhere about her—lined on shelves, stacked on the floor, overflowing a loveseat. An autographed photo of President Bill Clinton sat framed on her mantel. Kim lifted her fragile body from her daybed and gently placed her in her motorized lounger. Her head fell back onto the chair's giant pillow. "How can one accomplish this kind of work and practice the art of medicine at the same time?" she weakly asked him, her teeth slightly bucked as she began to smile in the exact smile-ready expression displayed in bronze before her.

"I kept the bust in my clinic and worked on it between Pap smears," Kim told her.

A twinkle came to Miss Welty's eye. "We should call it *Between Paps* then," she said, always good at titles, even in her weakened state. Kim, relieved by her success at levity, attempted, with the bedside manner he had developed in his medical practice, to engage her in more conversation but words no longer issued from her with the ease they once had. She could remember incidents from years past, according to Kim, but had trouble with the flow of raillery that was a generational marker for a certain sort of gentlewoman of the South, of which she was one of the last and finest exemplars. He finally commented on her collection of short stories, *The Golden Apples*. The mention of that particular title sparked something deep within her. Miss Welty raised her head suddenly from her pillow. Her voice grew strong, assured. "Isn't that lovely?" she asked him. "I stole that from William Butler Yeats," she said and, without hesitation, recited the final stanza of Yeats's 'The Song of Wandering Aengus":

> "Though I am old with wandering
> Through hollow lands and hilly lands,
> I will find out where she has gone,
> And kiss her lips and take her hands;
> And walk among long dappled grass,
> And pluck till time and times are done
> The silver apples of the moon,
> The golden apples of the sun."

She placed her head back on its pillow. She sighed, satisfied with this last rendition of her beloved Yeats she would ever get right. Kim compared his bronzed handiwork to what lay before him: her ancient brow, her white wisps of hair, flesh's feeble decay. Reverie was all that was left of her now. Were the words of that other beloved poet in her life haunting her still in the comfort of an even deeper silence? Was it he who had led her to Yeats in the first place? She turned toward the bronze for one last look. She stared into her own eyes.

I had been discovered at an earlier party for *A Midsummer Night's Dream* at Bleak House by New Stage's artistic director, Ivan Rider, and cast in a subsequent production at the theater, which enabled me to be even more securely ensconced in the only cosmopolitan bohemia that Jackson, Mississippi, offered. I was at the height of my surly, shaggy-haired teenage beauty back then—more punk than Puck— which was exactly the type the director was looking for to play the role of the deaf-mute Toby in Gian Carlo Menotti's one-act opera *The Medium*. The production was a local sensation and enabled me to gain a drama scholarship to Millsaps College, the Methodist-supported school right up the hill from Bleak House. Frank not only designed the sets for New Stage, but also taught stage design at Millsaps and oversaw all scenic aspects for the productions of the Millsaps Players. He was even a lighting director, and Bleak House was scrupulously lit so that any guest looked lovelier in its environs. "Well, at least less haggard," he once remarked when I pointed this out to him.

Our friendship—though he was almost thirty years older than I—deepened during the two years we got to know each other. He cast me as the newspaper boy with whom Blanche Dubois desperately flirts in a production of *A Streetcar Named Desire* he directed at the Vicksburg Little Theatre. We would talk and talk in his Pontiac LeMans on those ninety-minute round-trips from Jackson to Vicksburg during the six weeks we rehearsed and performed the play. We became so close, in fact, he sprung an odd request on me while we were listening on the LeMans's radio to a bare-bones country station. At first we had tuned in to the twangy numbers and corny, locally produced commercials as a sophisticated lark, but we discovered the longer we listened to that station, the less frequently our laughter came, and we had actually started to sing along with the weary reverence the now familiar lyrics called for. Frank got his start as a disc jockey over in Vicksburg and had a lifelong respect for the discipline and musical knowledge the job required as well as "the way a d.j. of any stripe must harness the mayhem of station life to soothe the listener into believing the lovely lie that there is order in this world." He sometimes confessed that he was at his happiest spinning records all alone in his little glassed-in cubicle, way back in 1956, the very year of my birth, as I liked to point out to him.

"I have something I really must ask of you," he had said that night on our drive back to Jackson, already blushing before the request could be made, his voice meekly skimming the surface of Skeeter Davis's toughened alto singing a James Taylor song, which was barely audible now from the radio Frank had turned way down. "I have an old trunk locked up in my closet. It contains … well … it contains what some might consider …" He gripped the wheel tighter. "Itcontainswhatsomemightconsider*pornography*," he said, all the words rushing from him in a jumble and tumbling over that very last one. "There—I said it." I turned my head and smiled out the window at the passing pines, an exit sign or two, some roadkill that looked like another opossum too slow to make it across both lanes of the interstate. "Promise me, Kevin, that you will dispose of that trunk if anything ever happens to me. Promise me. My West Virginia family cannot find it upon my demise; they simply *cannot*," he said.

"Of course, Frank," I assured him. Though he did not mean for such a request to be regarded as funny by me, it was certainly seeming that way at the moment. I tried not to, but I could not help myself: I started to giggle.

Frank flipped up the volume of the radio just as Skeeter was going after her toughest James Taylor note. "Don't you dare laugh at me," he said. "Don't you dare." It was the only time I can remember his ever being curt as far as I was concerned. "I'm being quite serious. I've never been *more* serious. This is our secret. No, it is more than that. This, dear boy, is a *confidence*," he said, imbuing the word with all the meaning he could muster as he launched into that haughty Mabel Mercer mode that could overtake him from time to time, one that seemed rather out of place in the presence of Skeeter. "I thought about asking Eudora, but there are limits to her empathy. I've watched you closely this past year or so since we've gotten to know each other. Don't ask me why, but I trust you completely. You are remarkably free of judgment and yet you are preternaturally wary. It's a nice combination. You seem to be spying right there out in the open all the time, right there in our midst," he said, nailing me. "It's quite disarming. Eudora even commented on it when she first met you. I asked her what she thought of you—I would not have included you in our sphere without her approval—and she said, 'That child is so ripe with private assessments I'm surprised the skin hasn't begun to bruise. Does he *read*?'"

"Yeah, I read," I said. "I read her fucking short stories. She's no Flannery O'Connor."

"Thank God," said Frank. "There's all that Roman flimflam in Flannery. Eudora is more welcoming. You'll see, dear boy. One reaches a certain age and all one longs for is to feel welcomed." I turned and looked at Frank. Really looked at him. Skeeter was singing the Taylor lyric, "All those lonely times when I could not find a friend," and I knew in that moment I had found my first true one. I felt—there is no other word for it—such tenderness toward him as I noticed there were tears beginning to fill his eyes. But he held them back. He did not let them fall. He had too much dignity for that. Too much grace. Those are the two main characteristics that Frank Hains so effortlessly possessed, and to this day, when I am lucky enough to summon one or both of them at the most unexpected of moments, I am certain that it is he—ever ephemeral, ever Frank—who is present and enabling me to conjure such characteristics in my own less dignified, less graceful life. Just as I feel his hand still on my shoulder in those moments, I put my hand on his in that one. "I'll get rid of that trunk if it means that much to you," I told him. "Say no more." And we never did. We never mentioned it again.

By the time of that bourbon-drenched New Stage cast party for *Long Day's Journey into Night,* I had decided to rent Bleak House's front bedroom from Frank for the upcoming summer while I earned some much-needed money working at a Jeans West store in a local mall. I had recently auditioned for the Julliard School of Drama, at Frank's encouraging insistence, and been accepted for the next term. Manhattan—and an even grander *What's My Line?* life—beckoned. But first I would have to get through the upcoming Mississippi months, which would prove, even with my tragic past, to be among the most difficult days of my life. As I look back on it now, that cast party for *Long Day's Journey* rivaled my first locker room visit with my father for its happy allure. The rooms were echoing with the sound of laughter and music and glasses being constantly filled. I knew Frank was certainly having a ball, for he loved playing host. "I'm the hostess with the most-ess," he would sing under his breath, breezing through the place and making sure everyone was having a good time.

Back in the record library, Geraldine Fitzgerald had just finished singing an Irish ballad, one of the numbers she was preparing for a cabaret show in New York called *Street Songs.* Miss Welty, taking the cue, attempted to perform her own little musical ditty for a few of her friends surrounding her on Frank's low-slung, circa-1969 sofa: Jane Reid Petty, a beautiful petite blonde who was New Stage's resident diva (her performance as Edna Earle in Frank's stage adaptation of Miss Welty's *The Ponder Heart* endeared her to local audiences much less sophisticated than she); Charlotte Capers, Miss Welty's lifelong best friend, who was the head of the Mississippi Department of History and Archives; Miss Capers's protégée at the Archives, a smart-as-a-whip, willowy blonde named Patti Carr Black; and Karen Gilfoy, a mannish Rosalind Russell manqué who decided to be a lawyer while learning most of Cole Porter's catalogue.

"When Eudora gets a little drunk like this, she always likes to show off," Frank whispered to me as we admired Jackson's reigning doyennes assembled before us. "Big Char there can really loosen her up," he said. Miss Capers, in this crowd, was lovingly referred to as "Big Charlotte." She hovered around six feet tall and loved—humorously, intellectually, socially—to throw her weight around. Frank and I were standing sofa-side at the stereo, which gave us a lay-of-the-party view. "Too much bourbon can literally bring out the Bea Lillie in Eudora," he whispered.

"Who's Bea Lillie?" I asked. Frank rolled his eyes at me. Miss Welty's unsteady warble—she was certainly in no Yeats-spouting mood that night—tried secretly to amuse her pals. "Wait a minute," I said, suddenly discomfited, a detail from an awful memory darting to the surface before submerging itself once more. "Is Bea Lillie Mrs. Meers?"

"I have no idea what you're talking about," said Frank. "Mrs. Meers? Bea Lillie—a.k.a *Lady Peel*, not Mrs. Meers—is a great comic genius. Eudora says her recent autobiography has one of the best titles ever—*Every Other Inch a Lady*. Eudora loved that title so much I didn't have the heart to tell her Lady Peel stole it, paraphrasing a remark Rebecca West once made about some *gentleman* she could not abide. Lillie's voice was once described as that of a bunch of drunken fairies—quite apt for this room tonight—who have been hit over the head with a golden hammer. Shhh … listen … Eudora does a great Lady Peel."

I looked over and was shocked to see Miss Welty, winking up at us, lower the strap on her dress. Vamping now, she exposed a bit of the flesh on her gibbous shoulder and continued her rhythmic high-pitched patter to her friends' muffled laughter:

> Yesterday night—
> I went to a *MAAAAAHVELOUS* party
> With Nunu and Nada and Nell …

Frank held up the album he had just taken off his turntable. "Noël Coward," he said, pointing to its cover. "Eudora's doing Bea Lillie doing Noël Coward." He put on some Mabel Mercer. "I met him once—Noël Coward. It was on a New York trip. We were all in the same room as Cardinal Spellman. Would you mind taking Eudora home tonight, dear boy? She's in no condition to drive herself and I have to stay around to tend to my guests. This party does not seem to be petering out. Perhaps I'll get out my *Noël Coward in Las Vegas* record and play that last cut on it, 'The Party's Over Now,' *very loudly*. Wait here. I'll convince Eudora it's time to go. Oh, God, she's starting in on 'I'm a Camp-Fire Girl.'"

"But I want to stay, I'm having fun," I whispered back at Frank while I kept staring at the dashingly handsome blond-haired thirty-five-year-old advertising executive, a New Stage stalwart, who was playing the older son, Jamie, in *Long Day's Journey*. His name was Carl Davis, and he had made it very clear that he had a crush on me. I was ready to make it very clear that such a crush was a credible emotion. "Can't someone else take Miss Welty home?" I asked. "I think Carl's ready to make a pass."

Frank placed an avuncular hand on my cheek and softly patted it. He sweetly, knowingly smiled. "Do as I say," he said. "Take Eudora home. Trust me—you'll write about it one day."

After Miss Welty wavered a bit on a "Camp-Fire Girl" lyric, Frank helped me escort her to the front porch. Behind us, the frivolity continued. "Kevin can take it from here, Eudora," he said, kissing her on both cheeks. "Talk to you both tomorrow. Have to get back to my guests."

"You're such a sweet boy to be carting me home," Miss Welty said, and allowed me to take her arm. My white Mercury Comet was parked on the little hill that led down to the Jewish cemetery. It had rained all day and we had to be careful not to slip as we traversed the treacherously slick blades of grass. I led her to the passenger side of the front seat and opened the door for her. "I'm fine now," she said. I let go of her arm and hurried around to the driver's side. When I opened the door I discovered what Miss Welty just had: I'd forgotten to clean off my front seat after I worked out that afternoon and my dirty gym clothes were still strewn where I had thrown them on her side of the car. She held my jockstrap pinched between her index finger and her thumb and was carefully placing it on the backseat. Her large rheumy eyes focused on my guilty face.

"Sorry, Miss Welty," I said as she wiped her fingers on her lap, the very same fingers—Fuck, I wanted to say aloud—with which every one of her stories had been typed on her old Underwood, upstairs in her bedroom over on Pinehurst.

She smiled at my embarrassment, then looked out her window at the neighboring grave sites. "Oh, I just thought that thing was a little Jewish ghost," she said, now waving her hand dismissively. "We've all got our ghosts to tend to." She looked back at me. She reached over and tapped my steering wheel with her story-telling fingers. "Now let's get goin'," she said.

DEL
SHORES

The Story Teller
from *Del Shores: My Sordid Life*

When I was growing up in Winters, Texas, I was a big fat liar. A storyteller. My daddy was a Southern Baptist preacher. Mama was the high school drama teacher. And I am really fucked up. My dad's side of the family was Southern Baptist. Good Christians. Boring. My mom's side of the family were also Southern Baptist. But they were the back-slidin' Baptists. The honky-tonkers. The fornicators. The ones who had to walk down the aisle and rededicate their lives to the Lord Jesus Christ. I gravitated towards the sinners. When I was a little boy, I'd come home with big whoppin' lies. "Daddy, guess what I did today? I rode over the mountain with Nana on a wild turkey! And when we got to the other side, me and Nana and my doll Susie Q had a tea party with Jesus and the disciples!" And my Daddy would say, "Son, don't tell stories." But my mom and her side of the family would ask, "What else happened?" And I believe that's why I became a writer. A storyteller. Because I was encouraged to lie. And honestly, I'm really not a writer at all. I'm a thief.

Okay, the real story of how I came out to my mother. I was working on a show called *Ned & Stacey*. It was Debra Messing's first show. She went on to become "Grace" on *Will & Grace*. It also starred Thomas Haden Church. I was the father of two little girls, and my marriage of nine and a half years had fallen apart—because for the first time in my life, I was being honest with myself. I was gay. So one day at work, I was reading *Variety*, and there was an ad—"Coming Out Day—October 11." In the ad was a quote from Dan Butler, the openly gay actor who at the time played "Bulldog" on *Frasier*. What Dan basically said was that if you are gay and working in the industry and are not out, that you are saying that you can't do your job and be gay. Well, that hit me hard—because I really wanted to come out. But I was petrified. You know, all that Baptist damage. So in one of my many therapy sessions, my therapist gave me some wonderful advice. Come out to one person at a time and start with someone that you

KNOW will be okay with it. So I called Leslie Jordan. And he said, "Oh honey, we are going to have so much fun." And we have. So I told more friends, and I felt that it was time to come out to my family. BUT, by the time I made this decision, I looked at the calendar, and it was October 18—my parents' anniversary. Now I don't know what you give a couple on their fortieth anniversary, but I'm pretty sure it's not a gay son. So, I decided to write a letter to my Mom and Dad—and brother—who is also a Southern Baptist preacher. And I mailed the letter *on* my parent's anniversary, so they would get it a few days *after* their anniversary.

That Friday, after shooting *Ned & Stacey*, I got home about one in the morning. We always shot really late. And my phone rang. "Del this is your mother." My mother always started every conversation the same way because otherwise, I wouldn't know. And my heart started beating. She had gotten the letter. But, she just started talking, "How're the girls? It's been so hot for October. Oh, you know what I did for your Daddy on our anniversary? I took him to Wal-Mart and showed him the card I would have bought for him, since he just throws them away anyway. And you know what he got me? Another romantic kitchen appliance. A toaster!" So, I relaxed. I guess she hadn't gotten the letter. Now it wasn't unusual for my mother to call this late because she suffered from severe rheumatoid arthritis and couldn't sleep because of the pain. So after about ten minutes of her just rambling, she said, "Well, we got your letter today. It's been quite a day in Palestine, Texas."

Oh shit! Deep breath. I finally asked, "Are you okay?"

And she said, "Baby, I've been waiting for this your entire life."

"Then why didn't you help me?"

"Well, I didn't want you to be that way."

Then I asked how Dad took it. She told me that he read it, then went into his study and didn't come out for about two hours. She finally went in to check on him, and he said, "I feel like someone has died." My Dad never stopped loving me, my daughters and I were always welcome in his home, but he never wanted to talk about it. But my mother ... that was another story. She wanted to talk about it a little too much. She went on a journey. A quest. She wanted to understand her gay son. And yes, just like "Latrelle" did in *Sordid Lives*, my mother did blame it on Dr. McCreight for giving her "those estrogen pills to keep me from miscarrying you." That was her first step of accepting, not blaming me, *knowing* this was not my choice.

My mom started doing research on my behalf. I wish other parents who are entrenched in the church would do research on our behalf instead of holding on to five scriptures in the Bible while eating shrimp, pork and wearing polyester—which Biblical or not, is just not right. When my mother died, I found a filing cabinet full of her research. She had discovered the internet. And *Sally Jesse Raphael*.

That Christmas I went home, and one night, Mom came into my room and asked, "What exactly do you do?"

"What?"

"You know, when you're gay?"

"Mother, you are NOT asking me about my sex life?"

"Well, if I'm going to have a gay son, then I need to know about gay sex."

"No, mother, no. I don't ask you what happens in the privacy of your own bedroom!"

"I'll tell you exactly what happens. Nothing!"

So, unlike "Ty" in *Sordid Lives*, I decided to be a big boy. So, I sat on the bed and looked down. No way I could look her at her face.

"Well, there's oral sex and blah, blah, blah, blah, blah."

"Oh, I see. Uh-huh. Yes. Saw some of that on *Sally Jesse Raphael*."

"Then there's anal sex, which involves lube and blah, blah, blah. And there's mutual masturbation." I skipped rimming. I didn't think she could handle that. I barely could. So I finished my gay sex tutorial, and yes, her final question was, "Are you the woman or the man?"

But my mother continued to try to understand. A few weeks later, I got this phone call. "Del, this is your mother. I have had a revelation! I have figured out a way to accept you completely and unconditionally as my gay son.

"Mother, that's great! What happened?"

"Well, do you remember Ethel Struble?"

"No—"

"Oh yes you do. Ethel Struble. The organist at the church. She has that paraplegic daughter who was in that awful car wreck because she was running with the wrong crowd. Had been drinking."

"Oh yes, of course, Ethel Struble."

"Well, the other day, I was in Sunday School class, and I looked over at Ethel and her paraplegic daughter—you know, she just carts that girl everywhere she goes. And that girl was droolin'. And Ethel reached in her handbag and pulled out a tissue and wiped that girl's drool off with so much love. And I thought to myself. If Ethel Struble can love her paraplegic daughter unconditionally, then who am I not to love my gay son!"

"Oh, so now you're comparing me to the drooling paraplegic!"

"I knew you'd take it wrong!" And CLICK. She hung up on me.

My mother's been gone now for many years, but I think of her often and appreciate her quest, her journey, her desire to understand her gay son. She was my high school drama teacher and is the single biggest influence on my life and my career. My friend Leslie Jordan once said, "Del, we have to give them time. They are doing the very best with what they have been given." Well, my Mom's best was the best. The very best.

ERIN ELIZABETH
SMITH

Singing Blue

There are nights
when the stars
hang like loose barbwire,
and all I can do
is pull shut
the shades, try not
to tell you about the times
I have lost myself
in produce sections,
flicking melons, rolling
gala apples in my hands
searching for brown.
How absent between the green
pepper and Romaine,
I think of you, cross-legged
on emaciated college mattresses,
telling me that Civil War cities
are like does in fog lights.
That everything sketched here
would smear and wane,
and we would not notice
in this cave of university.

But there is nothing to say,
except I still see you,
hair askew from Virginia
autumns, reading Aristotle
aloud over the light
of muted television. Except
every time I see you
I mean to tell you
that even outside

of the meandering
of grocery stores,
I mislay moments thinking
of that afternoon when I walked
past the bathroom door
to hear you singing "Blue"
through the battle
of showerhead and tile.
How I knew then
I would never
capture your hummingbird
hands, even
by accident.

Considering the Variants

> *Even in this*
> *one lifetime*
> *you will have to choose.*
>
> — Jane Hirschfield, from "Tree"

I. The Man

It's strange how quickly the fall can turn—
the blue corn parched to its husky bones.

Still there are robins in the trees,
though the clouds hang like wet clothes on a line,

though his hands bury themselves in pockets,
making them difficult to mine. The last summer

bloom pales to a thin, yellow varnish. It seems
this place knows more than we do about us.

II. The Woman

The seasons here, she says, are exact and to the point.
They change like night watchmen abandoning a shift.

She wipes the sweat from her glass,
her finger balancing the drop, then flicking it away.

Her right hand on the table is all that I can see,
thumb hemmed in like the bud of something

pink—impatiens, maybe, or milkweed—
something waiting for the season to break it free.

WILL STOCKTON

Pat Conroy, Godlike

For a week in the summer my family rents a house on Fripp Island, South Carolina—gentrified Gullah country where Pat Conroy owns a house. We share a beach access. When we swim in Conroy's dark and shimmery saltwater of love and abuse and memory

I do not tell Conroy my secret: that I masturbated to *The Lords of Discipline*, to the account of Hell Night at the Citadel. *Tighter. Tighter. Stick your dick into the knob in front of you.* I tell no one this, not even myself. I masturbated on a crab dock.

I masturbated with Tyler who looked the other way because it wasn't like that. Only it was like that when we did it again on the balcony, when what Mother called God's nightlight shown on the saltwater and lit Tyler's bare chest.

Revolution

In PoliSci 542: Theories of Revolution, I watch the bare feet of a brown boy turn circles on the tile floor of a building designed by a Founding Father freedom fighter who owned slaves and opposed slavery. After class we watch *Designing Women*. When I kiss him, the boy says, *You turn me on.*

Where are you from? comes later, after turning around each other's bodies, when I wonder whether the dark shine of the boy's taint stains my nose. When the boy answers *Palestine by way of DC*, I almost ask if Palestine's still a place, my knowledge of the Middle East now like my desire: overturned.

I have never met anyone opposed to the existence of Israel. *Not to the Jews,* the boy assures me, finger mapping lines on my forehead, *but to the state.* My parents support Israel. There is a controversy about settlements. The Allied Powers founded Israel after World War II. This is all I know.

There are things you should also know about me, the boy says, turning to sit up. And I am ready to learn. Here is where reconstruction begins. *I don't do anal. I'm a kleptomaniac. And I like to blow things up. Whatever. Small things. The biggest was a small bridge. I'm a stereotype.*

I turn a smile, but in two weeks' time the boy turns out no differently than he warned, and this is not what I want. We are not boyfriends. We may not even be good at being gay, an idea as foreign as Zion. Lying in bed, pushing aside the stolen forks and Skittles bags, we agree: *This isn't turning into anything, but let's keep fucking.*

Best Little Boy in the World

I am a lazy best little boy in the world.
One who won't learn the difference between *there*,
their, and *they're*, or place, possession, and plurality,

but who slips his tenth-grade American History
report on The Ku Klux Klan (1868-1872)
into the red plastic spine of the OfficeMax report cover

because he knows that to be taken seriously
as a writer one must present well but not so well
that readers comment on his fashion sense.

At my request, Mother buys me craft books:
The MLA Handbook and *The Chicago Manual of Style*.
Every sentence I source to books found

at the public library—my school library too small
to develop holdings on the Klan, their pranks,
played sometimes on black people.

A Klansman rides up to black man.
Requests a drink of water and says,
This is the best drink of water

I have tasted since the Battle of Gettysburg,
where I was shot to death.
The black man runs screaming.

I receive a hundred from my baby-faced, black,
tall-drink teacher one year out of Auburn.
In red ink on the title page, the only page marked:

This is the best paper turned into me this quarter—
before he runs from teaching.

DAN STONE

Emancipation

It was a migration
inevitable as any swallow's,
this flight to escape the foul heat.
It took only one finger held up to the wind,
one deliberate breath and persuaded nod.
Summer's stay in the South
can go on longer than Faulkner,
its crush crossing every threshold,
numbing all but the most
impervious crickets, stubborn
as the red clay baking in Virginia.

It was no place for unorthodox things.
There were no tolerant currents to cushion
first steps in the air,
nothing worth the labored inhale,
no welcoming floor for a dance.
There was only the outgrown nest,
clenched like a preacher's fist in its dogwood pulpit,
only the tyranny of tobacco, and the lazy eyelids
and humid stares and the Piedmont sun passing
judgment.

Plenty of reasons to escape into the clouds,
into the cold comfort of a Lake Erie snow.
I ascended into a shifting jet stream
like a slave running barefoot toward freedom,
single-minded as the sweat beading up
on the black shield of his back,
gulping the truth about going home again,
wondering what Spring in the North would be like,
calmed by the thunder of wings
beating close by.

CHRISTINE STROUD

Accidental Passing

At the Lowe's Food Store
I pick out a bouquet of daisies
for Aunt Laura.

Standing in line I clutch
the limp, white flowers and pull
crumpled dollars from my pocket.

My girlfriend's oversized navy sweatshirt
swallows me whole, my body swims
in the thinning cotton. I'm shapeless.

The cashier, a woman in her mid-40s
asks the bagger—
I wonder what he did to get in trouble?
She nods and winks
        at me.

I offer my best tight-lip, high cheek bone smile,
shrug my shoulders, palms up and she
laughs. She flushes.

I hope she wants to introduce me to her daughter,
but I know she wants to take me for herself,
run her fingers through my short, black hair
or over the sharp ridge
of my jawline. She wants to rest her hands
on my imagined flat chest.

She drops the coins into my hand one
by one, counting softly. I nod, but
do not speak, do not say thank you
as I was raised.

Farmville High

It was afterschool.
There were two boys.
One at each end of the hall.
Even before they yelled
dyke, you understood.

It was the varsity soccer
captain who grabbed
your navy Jansport
and slung you to the freckled
linoleum floor.
The boy who kicked
you first, in the face,
didn't speak, but you
knew his name. You attended
the same Sunday school
at Mount Calvary Baptist.

They took turns. One
to kick, one to guard.
They shattered you
under long fluorescent
bulbs running parallel
to the cobalt blue lockers.
Those lights always
too clear, too white.

      Underneath this light you can not
      keep secrets. Your queerness

was there, smudging those boys'
decency, like the dark gray circles
on the standardized test sheets.

In silence, the doctors
rearranged you, wrenching bones,
wiring your mouth shut.

You gazed out the window
to brown grass flatlands
and on down Jefferson Street.

While under the same light,
overbearing and transparent, your mother
and father discussed *the accident*.

BILLIE TADROS

interstate:

I like to know so sometimes I look
up the weather where you are—

                         inter- inter- interrupt me—

I know the time is not the time

       was not   I was awake

it was three a.m. and you were alive

somewhere along I-10   or I wasn't

     too young but I was   to be awake

the time was not when I woke
      again at four and you weren't

anymore   the way that grieving is

like when I accidentally write that date

     the break in the years like the break-in

the earth where the ground was not quite

frozen anymore and they said *good you're doing
so good* when they closed the hole the sound

    of *sutures susurrus* the thawed ice
    giving way for the weight   the box

the physics of lowering

a body the way that grieving is

intercourse:

I keep seeing I keep seething seeping
pine and I saw Pine Street when her mouth
engulfed me

I saw her drowning in the doors
of the café by the gulf

I was in the water I was in
the café and her watercolor

was on the wall I was in
her watercolor and pining

I was in her like water

interact:

I live in a new place now with firework stands at the end

December when it smells like warm and sulfur
and rain—

      coulee   coolly   the water—

I was holding the Roman candles and pointing the hold

      you were a whole country away from me by then

she was a hole and when I placed the shell in the mortar

      I thought of her body the base I thought

      of the fuse her fingers at the back of her

throat on the bathroom floor

gagging   the sound of your gun

interstices:

You don't need space   you need

      stitches

          slit   slight   slice

      and the spaces between her

fingers where I fit myself suggested

a gorge:

the dirty words—   they need to come

back up

TC TOLBERT

Speaking in Tongues: How we cannot see the fire by which we've been touched

> *We have to endure the discordance between imagination and fact. It is better to say, "I am suffering," than to say, "This landscape is ugly."*
>
> — Simone Weil

> *Now there are varieties of gifts, but the same Spirit; and there are varieties of service, but the same Lord; and there are varieties of activities, but it is the same God who empowers them all in everyone.*
>
> — I Corinthians 12:4-6

> *We have no reason to mistrust our world, for it is not against us. Has it terrors, they are our terrors; has it abysses, those abysses belong to us.*
>
> — Rainer Maria Rilke

■

The last time I spoke with the Holy Spirit (a.k.a. Holy Ghost) I was a 20-year-old Southern girl—long brown hair, nose ring, and a penchant for all things hemp. I was engaged to be married to a nice Catholic guy. I was both terrified and tempted by poetry. I wasn't a lesbian, and I certainly wasn't an out genderqueer or trans guy yet. The nondenominational charismatic church I'd recently joined in Rossville, Georgia, had a full-on rock band—electric guitar, keyboard, drums, even a tambourine. Running up and down the aisles was common, and the metal folding chairs were spaced accordingly. There was clapping and dancing, sometimes for hours. If you were just to watch us from the outside, worship would seem to alternate between winning a big game and being possessed. I grew up Pentecostal, so I'm not entirely shaken by charisma. In fact, I'm bored by most poetry readings. I often feel like I should take notes so that I can pass (I never pass) the discussion portion of the test.

A woman was visiting church that Sunday night. She was a traveling preacher, beehive and long skirt. The men of the church would stand behind anyone she talked to so as to catch them when they fell out. All she had to do was blow on you—she had the power of the Holy Ghost in her breath. I fell out when she blew on me. I came to quickly next to my friend Steve, and he and I were giggling ridiculously, writhing on the floor, chattering, speaking a language neither of us could comprehend. I didn't believe it fully until I was lying there. I was lost as in Rebecca Solnit's sense of lost: *the world had become larger than my knowledge of it. Either way, there is a loss of control.* It was pleasurable—an almost giddy mixture of joy and surprise.

In *Queer Space*, Aaron Betsky says, *we make and are made by our spaces*. In the South I was made by, we had secrets and we had stories. We put our hands on each other. We talked with our mouths full. We wandered. We were disowned and, then, we were smothered. We were women. We spoke in tongues. We paid for things with our good looks. We hit one another. We hit hard. We healed the people we loved. When we needed to, we would dance and we would sing.

"Glossolalia" is another word for speaking in tongues. For Pentecostals, it is considered one of several gifts of the Holy Spirit: the grace of no longer being burdened by linearity, a momentary relief from the expectations (persuasion, explication, or sense making) of everyday speech. Before my enjoyable, albeit startling, experience with glossolalia, all of my previous encounters had been a bit terrifying, even if I couldn't look away. In the church I grew up in, Sister Hazel's body regularly rose from the pew like a snake—her right hand trembling in the air above her head, her voice a song of strange, while the rest of her body buckled and jumped as though she'd been hit. There was a lot of crying back then. I thought my queerness was a devil. I wanted it out of me, but then again, I didn't. Krista Tippett says most churches think of *the body as an entry point for danger*. I didn't disagree with them. Let me say it plain.

For most of my life I've felt broken, not just tarnished. There has long been a kind of geographic darkness, a landscape of violence in me that I have feared (and that feels, to me, particularly Southern and religious) and of which I am deeply ashamed. This is less about being angry that someone did something awful to me as a kid (although they did, and god did not protect me from it) and more about being afraid that I deserved the awful and that awful is what I create. As Adam Phillips points out in an essay on agoraphobia, *James' open space is full of potential predators, but in Freud's open space a person may turn into a predator*. The open space is always writing. Always the body. Always other bodies. Always the voice. Always the page.

As a protection from this fear and this pain, I've spent plenty of time contemplating suicide—sometimes more actively than others, but the gist is this: I've always held onto it as an option. There was something about knowing I could leave this body if I needed to that made me feel safe. Thus, much of my writing (and my living) employs, enacts, or encourages erasure. Or at least hide-and-seek. It is slippery. It enjoys white space. On some level, no doubt, transitioning was a way of killing my most vulnerable, marked self and an attempt to make peace with men—a group of people I've long considered the enemy. I'm trying. Indeed, as my embodiment changed so rapidly (I suddenly really was "the man"), I was frozen by a multifaceted terror that, at its heart, was simple. I was afraid of becoming the thing I longed to be, needed to be, hated to be, and asked to be so named.

The cadence of a good Pentecostal preacher denies contradiction. There is a surety there, a solidity that exists in absolute tension with the logical ambivalence of so much in the Bible. The uncertainty of a miraculously confounding world is resisted primarily through the rhythm—a driving—where the full bore of language becomes a comfort. I saw my Papaw have hands laid down on him and be healed of cancer. Tongues, healing, prophecy. If there is poetry in that, let it rain.

■

My friend Sydney is one-and-a-half years old. She doesn't really know how to whisper yet. We've had to stop swearing around her because she just repeats every little thing that she hears. And that's different from every little thing that we know. And that's different from every little thing that's been said. I recently went to church on Sunday morning—a first for me in the 11 years since I've been living in Tucson—and I can't stop thinking about how language takes shape inside the body. Sometimes words embarrass me more than my feelings. Even though I always thought my Pentecostal upbringing was deeply anti-intellectual, and even though I was at a Presbyterian church and not a Pentecostal one, hearing the female pastor do a close (and very queer) reading of the Bible shifted the way that I understand my love of literature. Perhaps church (of any denomination) is really just book club. Perhaps my Papaw, with his 8th grade education, 15 different Bibles, and 50+ years of actively studying the same text, is the most literate man I know.

■

The more I think about what interests me in poetry, the more I realize I'm just trying to get back to church. CAConrad says: "My religion is poetry." I like that; it's close. According to Cicero, the word *religion* is derived from *relegere*, "go through again" (in reading or in thought), from *re-* "again" + *legere* "to read." My twist on CA's statement is: My poetry (all poetry?) is religious in that it requires re-reading (which is to say it requires attention). (Simone Weil: "Attention is the rarest and purest form of generosity." I always want to be surrounded by people who pay attention.) Also, reading and re-reading should be embodied (Judith Butler: "Speech itself is a bodily act"), and in this way it is a danger (as Gilles Deluze riffs on Spinoza, "we do not even know what a body can do"). Reading, re-reading, religion is a danger to what we think we already know.

■

The truth is, I'm in over my head here. What I'm trying to explain is my experience. That's absurd. And antithetical to the poem (which is my life). How about this map of my brain:

speaking in tongues ≈ nonlinearity ≈ vulnerability ≈ terrifying/blessed body ≈ queerness ≈ violence/love ≈ delight/fear ≈ wonder/constraint ≈ poetry ≈ surrender ≈ god ≈ body + bodies + space

I always want to be surrounded by readers. Which is to say, I always want to be surrounded by queers.

■

I'm still a mess of influences, accents, inflections. If I believe in god, it's because there are moments when I'm actually able to sit still inside my body and feel both solid and permeable. I want language both untamable and untranslatable—benevolent and terrifying—a poetry that is. If I'm lucky, I'll get to speak in a tongue that both is and is not my tongue again.

DAN
★VERA★

Balinesia in Virginia

Praise Kokoe, born Bruce,
who every week bought an orchid for his cell
between the elevator and the boardroom
who misted them meticulous
and thus transformed Virginia into Balinesia.

Everyone knew Bruce for the ways
he broke forth from blandness
with the spotted cowls of phalaenopsis
cymbidium's striped fingers
and the purple mouths of dendrobium
all of them pouring over the cubicles of work.

Praise what resided in Kokoe to know
what could love a light fluorescent
and make the stale air bloom with hue.

Gay Mythology: How the rivers first flowed

One July day Zeus did spy
from mighty Mount Olympus
a shimmering copper form below
at work on a pickup in a driveway.

That sinuous body with pelt of gold
turned wrench and driver in his hands,
making the Daddy of all Gods wonder
if Vulcan supplied the iron in those arms,

Or how Apollo's sun did kiss
so red upon that muscled flesh,
to bring forth Neptune's salt
that dripped heavy on the pavement.

These questions stirred him so,
and lost in thought did cause
the mouth of the Daddy of all Gods
to salivate beyond all reason or limit.

And this is how the waters of the Nile,
the Amazon, and the Mississippi rivers first flowed.

Lucifer

In the older story he's the first lover
who gets upset when God tells him
he "just wants to see other people."

Then God invites them all over
and Lucifer is creeped out at how *young* these kids are,
fumes when God commands him to serve *them,*
when all he ever wanted was to spend the rest
of his existence with his one true love.

Lucifer gets spiteful.
Starts burning the breakfast.
Forgets to bring in the newspaper.
Purposely leaves the lid up on the toilet seat.

Who wouldn't get snarly with such a radical change in the relationship?

But there are no celestial marriage counselors.
As if God would ever consent to take counsel.

Finally God rents a new pad for his new lovers
and tells Lucifer to pack his dishes and move out.
Tells him he never wants to see him again.

Lucifer smolders in some dark pad and begins to conspire.

ANNIE VIRGINIA

At DOMA's Deathbed

This Old North State has brass knuckles
on its no. Here, they still hang rebel flags
from their crumbling front porches.
Here, I am rapeable, and small,
and there is nothing equal about me.
There are no muskets in my jaw,
though they are back a couple pages
in my family history, I know.
But I am the cotton and quilts
and misleading quiet of the wives
who stayed at home and bled into the rivers.
(This is why there is fury in the rivers.)
And there is fury in my hope that we can
bend the Bible Belt, melt its metal
into a statue of liberty.

We soak tobacco into dirty gums and break
the wrists of words to utter the sickest names.
We pour chicken guts down our throats
just to smell like our fathers, but
we will not let our sons fold to bed
with our neighbors' sons. We will not
let our daughters remove the dresses
from our neighbors' daughters, though
they stitched them together.
Our Christ is white, his eyes antifreeze blue,
we find his blonde hairs on our daughters'
pillows. We imagine the blood of the gentle
under his fingernails.

But this is the fleshy thread of the flags
he has been tearing from his own name.

Maybe we have bled the color from his skin and eyes
with the shotgun shells we've been shooting
into his scripture. You would call
your brother faggot for holding the hand
of another man, so what would you call
your Christ, who came to Lazarus in his death bed?
I have found my holiest moments
in the arms of a woman who has loved me
without rhetoric. The day this country
decides to honor its god and let me love her,
I will marry her on earth where my great-grandmother
and a thousand slaves bled.
I will believe the greatest gift is love.

VALERIE
WETLAUFER

Southern Comfort

How difficult it is to say goodbye
to a place so nearly-loved. To friends
who should've become sisters, but
remain poky-faced aunts, disapproving
of your cocktail salad and pigtails.

The Most Revered One bids "Keep
In Touch," kissing the air beside
both cheeks. Her boyfriend fondles
you beneath your napkin.

You do not mourn the silverfish
who tease your spines in the night,
the tree frogs ringing your patio
lamp, the way the rain reminds you
of Africa.

It is not the Italian whose kiss you
mistake, nor his young Greek friend,
but the long hot gaze of a Louisiana
native whose perfume stains your hair,
whose absence sticks in your craw.

Your friends are getting pregnant
as you drive away, divorced.
Away from the place that has held
you captive, the women who drove
you, like a fortunate son, to gin.

She recalls the drinks shared, outfits worn,
but never the promises she let slip
from her tongue like sugar flowers,

melting easily into the humid morning.
This is a town you journeyed toward
and never found, error twisting your
bowels as the roads wind around each
tree to avoid the uprooting.

C.T. WHITLEY

Finding My Southern Roots

Just before my 30th birthday, my best friend and I were seated in a coffee shop in my hometown, a former 1800s coal-mining community located on the front range of Colorado. As usual, we were discussing our families—the complexities of these relationships and the impact of divorce, alcoholism, and mental health challenges on these dynamics. I was concerned with turning 30, feeling as though I didn't really know who I was or who I wanted to be. I craved a sense of clarity.

"I thought I would have my life figured out by now. You know … I expected to be established and successful," I lamented, knowing she felt the same. Another friend had informed me that my tri-decade crisis was due to the return of Saturn, which moves into the same position it was in during your birth every 28 to 29 years. This return correlates with uneasiness, confusion, and insecurity. He said it was nothing to worry about; I disagreed. At the time, I was a graduate student working on my doctoral degree. I had given up a well-paying position at an economic development group in New York City to be a poor college student again, making less than 25% of my previous income. Just that had been a shock; I was unhappy in New York, but at least I could afford to travel—I have always loved to wander—and then, on this particular day, the thought of escaping to a different location seemed inviting, but out of my financial reach.

It was a cloudy day, rain pouring outside, a perfect time for tea. We sat in silence, making swift statements and meditating on their meanings. As we watched the water collect on the windowsill, my friend looked at me and told me, "I think you have to figure out where you came from before you know where you are going." With my chin resting in my hand, I considered what this would mean for me, a transgender man, and how I might identify where I came from, or, more importantly, where those who had come before me had been. She continued by explaining that we rarely consider how the past experiences of our ancestors, those who we may or may not have met, impact how we engage the world on a daily basis.

"We just assume we are the way we are because of our individual experiences, and we neglect to realize that the intricate connections we carry with us are passed down from generation to generation." In a curious way, she was right. As academics, we talk about internalized homophobia and racism, but we neglect other dimensions of socialization that may be generationally multifaceted. Being a living vessel of the past, we carry our ancestral memories, like ghosts in our logic, cloudy illusions passed down through the psychology of our interactions. As I get older, this becomes more apparent. I often rattle-off statements or employ practices that I have little awareness of. Sometimes I connect them back to behavior my parents modeled, but other times these moments are so obscure and unique that their path into my being seems impossible to track.

What became abundantly clear in this coffee house conversation was that my focus for the past 25 years had been entirely on my transition. I was born in a female body with a male identity. In the interest of achieving the mind and body I so desired, I had neglected to consider how researching my ancestors could help me understand myself. With this conversation playing in the back of my mind, I embarked on a journey to explore my ancestral past as part of my present, a change in perspective that has altered every aspect of my life. While I had been familiar with my maternal ancestry, I had little knowledge of my father's Southern roots; now it was time to discover them.

Southern Rejection

As a child, I remember thinking that my father spoke differently than most of the people around me. His unique dialect, which linguists have traced to Cabarrus County in North Carolina, was not seen as unique in the Mountain West. He was Southern. I had no basis for understanding the vernacular differences between my mother and father, but to me there was a warmness in my father's speech, a friendly politeness as he responded, "Yes sir," when we were in public, or referred to a woman using "Miss" in front of her first name, as in "Don't forget to say hi to Miss Julie." When I started school, however, I quickly learned that not everyone found comfort in this accent. Instead, I had an unfortunate education on the widespread prejudice against the South and Southerners more specifically, an aversion I would come to internalize as a social survival mechanism.

In my early school years, classmates harassed me for my accent, which featured a Southern intonation they felt could not have been cultivated in the Rocky Mountain West. They were both correct and entirely wrong. I wasn't born in the South, nor was I raised there, but my accent carried the ancestral history of my father, a man born in rural North Carolina. I was mortified by the harassment, so I began mentally to document words that I would not recite in public, words that I still resist using as an adult.

Years later, I was taunted with questions about whether my family had ties to slavery. They do not; though my father was born in the South, he was born into poverty, a fact that is worse to some than a legacy of slave ownership. To many in the West, there were two types of Southerners: those who possessed old money with a history of plantation ownership and slave acquisition, and those who lived in the rural South—uneducated Appalachian Mountain folk with thick accents and missing teeth. This might sound simplistically dramatic, but these stereotypes were alive and well and sadly persist today.

Lost Father and Lost Southern Roots

I considered my father and me to be close. I looked up to him. To me, he was a tall and proud man, an intelligent war hero (he was drafted into the Korean War) who could build or fix anything. To say that I was devastated when my father passed away would be an understatement. He had suffered kidney failure six years earlier, prostate cancer two years before, and ultimately succumbed to a ruptured brain aneurysm. Even with his erratic health history, his death came as a surprise. With all that he had been through, I often considered my father to be invincible, but I guess this is often how the world looks when you are only twelve.

I had little contact with my father's Southern family after he passed. The contact I did have was in the form of an occasional holiday card or an infrequent phone call. My mother never made an attempt to visit his family, and they never visited us. There are numerous factors I can point to, but much of this disconnect was due to the 1200 miles separating the West from the South and the perilous financial situation my mom and I were left in after he, our family's sole breadwinner, passed. He was also the youngest of nine, and all of his siblings were well into their 60s or beyond when he died, not to mention that communication in the early 90s was not what it is today. We did not have e-mail, Skype, or cell phones, and long-distance calls were expensive. In these lost years, I missed out on the opportunity to grow with my cousins, to see my aunts and uncles, and to reflect on my ancestral past. It would be years before I would reconnect with any form of my Southern roots, and at first this did not involve my family but happened instead through service work trips.

Becoming a Better Ally

My first trip to the South was during my freshman year of college as a member of an ecumenical multi-faith organization. This was not a mission trip as typical of some religious groups, but rather a collective engagement activity designed to be both beneficial to the community and us. As a multi-faith group we respected all religious and spiritual paths and were interested in building connections among faith communities, not identifying which path was "right." Our leader was an out lesbian born and raised in a rural community near Lexington, Kentucky, and my colleagues were a collection of young college students, mostly queer oriented with radical hairstyles, piercings, and tattoos. Few of us had been to the South, so we decided to assist in the repair and construction of homes in Kentucky's Appalachian Mountains. At the time, I knew little about the South except that I considered it to be largely conservative, racist, and homophobic. I could not imagine being queer or coming out as a transgender man in the South. I expected this trip would challenge my perceptions.

We chose to take the train, a multi-day experience from Denver to Lexington. Not only were we able to take our tools with us, but we were also able to form bonds while trying to sleep upright in black and red railcar chairs. When we arrived, my initial interactions with those in the region did not dispel my myths of the South. Within minutes of getting off the train, we were instructed not to buy flowers from a black man and to stay on the "right side of the tracks" as we traveled around. I had seen racism in various forms, watching my black friends be followed in department stores or hearing the occasional derogatory comment, a fact that was made more prominent as I typically dated people who were not white, but I had never seen racism like this.

I prided myself in being an ally; however, most of the racism I had encountered had been hidden and institutionalized. I quickly learned that being an ally in the face of blatant and overt racism is different, much different. I remember crying that night, astounded by the unabashed racism that seemed to be so prevalent. More importantly, I felt horrible that I had kept silent in my first interaction, largely because I was caught off-guard, not knowing how to challenge an individual in a seemingly meaningless conversation. I had been taught "silence is compliance" and in not speaking-up about being uncomfortable with his directions, I was silently agreeing with him and reinforcing the notion that he was being helpful. Talking with my colleagues, I fully realized that allyship is not always comfortable or easy, and that people, even if approached in a respectful manner, are not always receptive to constructive criticism or dialogue, especially around sensitive issues like racism, heterosexism, sexism, etc. I often remember this trip as a significant developmental point in my life, the moment when I really began to assess the multiple layers of privilege I was ascribed at birth and the privilege I would experience as a fully transitioned man.

Beyond confronting my sense of privilege, the work we did challenged my ignorant perceptions of the rural South, specifically of those living in the Appalachian Mountains. Each morning, we took vans into the mountains to begin our work. In the midst of shrubbery, small shacks lined the canyon, and from these shacks hands waved at our arrival. Before beginning our journey, we had studied the (mis) perceptions of the Appalachian folk, who have often been ridiculed and mocked for living in poverty. In our ten days in the mountains, we shared meals, conversations, and spiritual meetings with those with whom we worked. With little money or food, our hosts showered us with anything they could provide and welcomed our presence in ways that we did not feel welcomed in Lexington. Collectively, we seemed to accept each other as we worked side-by-side. Perhaps, it was our mutual understanding of stigma, albeit different forms in class and sexual orientation or gender identity. Many of us were out about our sexual orientation (non-straight identities) or gender identities (gender creative expressions) in our communities, which seemed to be received warmly by our hosts, even if not fully understood.

I should mention that this was before I made any physical transition from female to male. At the time I had short spiky hair and wore baggy men's clothing. I was often read as a lesbian. While working on a roofing project, I explained to one man (about my age) that I was attracted to women. He had asked me some questions about my hair and clothing, and I thought I should answer his questions accordingly. I told him about being a transgender man. He nodded, taking in each word that I said. Unlike many people whom I have encountered, he was polite in his response, steering away from sex or body related questions and focusing most on my family's perceptions of my transition. We left the rural South as we had arrived. Interestingly, the trip made me feel closer to my father. It was as if I finally understood a piece of his past. It would be four more years before I would head South again.

Hurricane Katrina Relief Work

Hurricane Katrina made landfall in late August of 2005. A year later, I was living in the Virgin Islands working as an HIV/AIDS prevention and education specialist. My wife (then girlfriend) was in Colorado trying to finish her undergraduate courses. The same ecumenical group that participated in the Appalachian Mountain project answered a call for Hurricane Katrina relief workers. Although I was no longer a direct member of the community, I flew into Louisiana to meet my girlfriend and provide assistance to the team. Unbeknownst to my girlfriend, I brought a diamond ring with me. I planned to propose to her, as we had met a year earlier on a similar trip. It seemed to be the perfect opportunity as we both have a passion for helping others, volunteering, and community outreach.

I decided to propose on the last day of our trip. In the meantime, we donned HAZMAT suits to remove sludge and mold from houses, working ten-hour days. On most homes, we could see the water breach, a debris littered waterline far above our heads, more than two times my height. All of the houses had large orange *x*'s with numbers in each section. As many will remember, this was how survivors and fatalities were counted, a chilling reminder of the magnitude of the disaster.

We shared work and meals with the community, reflecting on stories of heroism and survival. Again, we were confronted with the realities of race relations and poverty and the widespread government disaster mismanagement in a largely black area, things that could not be considered coincidental. Once again, our communities accepted us as we accepted them. Together we worked for a common goal, the rebuilding of a community. Our individual differences were inconsequential to our goal, but not dismissed. As before, we were not there to save anyone. We were there to provide additional hands to make light of the work that needed to be done. We let our communities guide and direct us, knowing that they gave us way more than we could ever give them. At our final dinner in New Orleans I proposed to my girlfriend. She was in complete shock. Even seven years later it is the only secret I have kept from her. In front of a collection of friends, she said yes.

Southern Family Rejection

Although I had known that I was "different" from an early age, I did not formally come out as a transgender man to my mother's side of the family until I was in college. Overall, my mother's side of the family reacted quite well. Although having a transgender family member can be difficult, learning to use a new name and different pronoun, it can also be a point of clarity and for many of my family members it was just that. My mother was devastated at first, but she quickly realized that the fundamental core of my identity was not changing. As I told family members I repeatedly found that they had assumed I was different, likely that I was gay. While they may not have fully understood what I meant by identifying as a transgender man, they could recognize that I had never really been a girl. On my wedding day, my great aunt, a woman in her 80s, informed me that, "I would've liked you more if you had been born a boy.... You always seemed more like a boy." It may sound like a backhanded compliment, but knowing her I took it as a beautiful sentiment. Since I came out, I have felt more accepted in my family, more like I belong than ever before.

I considered coming out to my dad's family many times, but I was afraid of full rejection, especially with my perceptions of the South as largely conservative and anti-gay, which in my mind equated to anti-trans. My mom had described my aunts and uncles as properly Southern. For years I continued to receive cards with my birth name, a name I no longer recognized as mine. Each time a card arrived, a conversation between my mother and me would ensue. She wanted to protect me, but I wanted to connect with my father's family. Nearly ten years after I came out to my mother's family, I decided to come out to my dad's family. My mother wrote a letter, similar to what she had done initially with her family. She sent the letter to my dad's youngest sister, the matriarch of the family. I patiently waited for a return letter, a response that would indicate that things were going to be ok.

After two weeks, a letter arrived. My aunt had always written long letters to us about her family, how the weather was, and her pending travels with her husband. I grabbed the letter from the box and ran over to my mother. Inside was a tiny card with a butterfly on the front. I opened the card and read it.

"Whatever you need to do, you need to do."

That was it. She did sign it with "love," as if that would make up for the lack of words on the page. I read the letter over and over again, not sure of what it meant. Over the next year, my mother would receive a few letters, but only for holidays and her birthday. My name was absent from them all. It was a heavy blow, each letter a jab to the stomach. She did not say that she was rejecting me, but her blatant dismissal of my life was heart-wrenching.

Finding My Southern Roots

Although I no longer received communication from my father's family, I wrestled with the decision formally to cut ties. I needed closure. As a last ditch effort to make a connection, my wife and I sent Christmas cards to my father's two remaining sisters. In the cards, we wrote about our wedding, worldly travels, doctoral programs, and plans for the future. We enclosed a picture of us on our wedding day, a warm May afternoon in Boulder, Colorado. I did not discuss my transgender status. I figured that this was not a coming out letter, but rather an update, a chance for my family to get to know me outside of the "transgender" label.

My father's youngest sister did not respond. I was not surprised. However, my father's oldest sister Gertrude did respond. Actually, her daughter Caroline called my mother's house as soon as the letter arrived. Gertrude was unable to call because of her arthritic hands, but Caroline communicated to me that they were both delighted that I had reached out and contacted them. On our initial conversation, Caroline and I chatted for nearly two hours. As long-lost cousins, we compared our upbringings, parents, and personalities, finding we had much in common. I asked about Gertrude. She is well into her 90s, still living alone in a modest home just down the road from the rural farmhouse she grew-up in. I had fond memories of her from when she visited my parents and me in Colorado. I remember her warm spirit and her creativity. She was always crafting something. She brought me a hand sewn Pound Puppy quilt and other stuffed animals.

In the couple of days she spent with us, she taught me how to sew and how to knit, two things that I still remember today. I shared these memories with Caroline. She seemed delighted that, after 20 years, I still remembered her mother. In parallel, she shared her memories of my father, a man she also looked up to. To her, he had been a cool, laidback uncle, adventurous, smart, and determined. At the end of our conversation, Caroline invited my wife and me to visit North Carolina and to stay with her and her husband—a warm welcome after 20 years of separation and disconnect from my father's family. My wife and I debated visiting. Although my transgender status had not come up, I was nervous that it might. I had no idea where my father had grown up or what I might uncover should I choose to dig deeper into his past. However, the potential benefits seemed to outweigh the costs. I have always been interested in family history, and this was a perfect opportunity to make some connections and identify the missing piece of paternal ancestry.

Visiting My Southern Roots

The timing could not have been more perfect. Nearing the 20th anniversary of my father's death, I was finally able to visit the place where he grew-up and meet some of my cousins. My wife and I made the twelve-hour drive from Michigan to North Carolina, my stomach in butterflies the entire time. We scheduled our trip for a three-night stay. It seemed to be the perfect amount of time to make some connections and not wear out our welcome. As we got closer, I felt more and more connected to the landscape. The same ridges, distribution of trees, and old farmhouses I was seeing for the first time, my father had grown up with.

We arrived in the late evening, pulling up to a rather large house tucked back off of a rural country road a few yards from a smaller home I presumed was Gertrude's. Caroline and her husband, a retired marine, welcomed us in. When I saw Caroline, I could not help but smile. She shared my skin tone, blue eyes, and hair color. Our facial features were also similar. She immediately thrust our arms together comparing the two pale, freckled limbs and exclaimed, "Look at that, you are my kin."

I could barely sleep the first night. At breakfast, conversation flowed as if we had known each other for years. We picked up Gertrude at her house; she was overjoyed I was visiting. Even at 90+, she was the same woman I remembered, a kind and gentle spirit. We spent the day touring the local area. Our first stop was the house that my father was born in. My grandfather had built the home, a two-story farmhouse. Although not college educated, he was a schoolteacher and farmer, raising nine children who all learned to read before entering school. The family lost the house in the Great Depression, and my grandfather passed away when my father was only five years old, leaving my grandmother with nine children. The older kids worked to support the home. Then, in a tragic construction accident, one of my dad's brothers was killed, leaving the family with a reasonable settlement to buy a new home where my father and his remaining siblings would be raised. My family history highlighted the importance of education, determination, and perseverance.

We toured graveyards in our quest to find distant grandparents. Unlike the West, most graveyards are attached to churches in the rural South. When a member of the church dies, they are buried in the church plot. This location of the deceased gives a rich history of the community. By identifying the church of burial, we can assess what the individual's life may have been like. Often churches keep detailed records of membership, so we were also able to identify related characteristics. In a matter of days, Caroline and I fueled our passion to understand our family lineage. She had pieces passed down through oral histories, and I had the research background to locate historical documents and relevant information.

On the final day of our trip, Caroline invited my father's youngest sister over, the one who had rejected me because of my transgender status. I did not expect her to come, but she did. She stayed a few hours with her son, another cousin whom I had never met. I asked her questions about my father and their childhood, and, for the most part, she answered them willingly. She was very polite, but not overly friendly. Some of the stories she told about my father were good, while others were not. Tales of alcoholism and photos of his first wife I could have done without, but overall I was honored to have her present.

Finding Peace

I arrived in North Carolina feeling disjointed in my identity, as if the two sides of my family were incompatible because of my transgender status. I had long distanced myself from my father's Southern side, concerned that I would experience rejection—my own prejudice about the South. In doing so, I had denied a large part of myself. As my best friend suggested, I needed to see where I had come from to determine where I was going. Since traveling to North Carolina, I have continued to work on my family history, now very much proud of my Southern roots. My connection to my father's side of the family has given me a sense of peace and closure in his death. I have often wondered how he would have reacted to my being a transgender man. He supported my gender creativity as a child and humored me as he pretended to shave my face on a daily basis, but would he have accepted his daughter becoming his son? Remembering my interactions with my father and re-meeting his family, I am confident that he would have accepted my transgender status, even if it were not easy. Because of my identity as a transgender man and my connection to the South, I have continued to assess my role as an ally and my privilege more generally. I have gained a wife, participated in disaster relief work, and reconnected with my father's family. While perhaps not a traditional queer South narrative, my life and outlook has been disrupted, challenged, and altered by queer subjectivity—in my transgender status—interconnected with my Southern roots.

SCOTT
★WIGGERMAN★

Postcard from West Texas

Freckles on his shoulders,
a wolf tattoo that peeks out
from torn-off shirt sleeves,
his hair long and red.

I say nothing to this stranger,
just watch the setting sun
glow in the motel courtyard,
his nimble fingers unpeeling
one longneck label after another.
Those rough nails, that tough glue.

It must be hours.
The sun tucks behind
the mountains, and the moon
appears all lost and sappy.

We must be drunk.
He howls when he stands.
My grin shines like a prayer.

CRISTAN WILLIAMS

Alpha Male

There is a small town stuck between Houston and Galveston, Texas. It is one of the many settlements south of Houston that seems to cling to the freeway for life. This particular berg is famous for three things:

1) A large topless joint that beckons men to exit the freeway, so they can have their heart broken by at least 162 women;

2) An old Spanish-style church whose 15-foot adobe Christ is designed to inspire the unsuspecting sinner to make a mad dash for the confessional lest they be judged on the spot by its two rather large, menacing eyes; and,

3) The local water tower which is prized for its pealing façade immortalizing the high school football team of 1977.

I had the honor of calling this town my home for a few years. In fact, it's where I did a lot of my transitioning.

I'd experienced some trouble with my car's transmission, so I pulled into a local garage to have them take a look at it. As I navigated my car around used tires and oil slicks, I caught a glimpse of what seemed to be a rather large yeti attempting to till the grime under his fingernails with the edge of a screwdriver. While I had not yet transitioned, I was very close to moving forward with it. This meant that I was living in a strange twilight state whereby I was hyper-conscious of every nuance manhood demanded of me. I had to consciously carry out each action as if I had the lead part in some weird and sweaty play. Each gradation of expression that drew me away from my innate personhood exacted a psychological toll that was becoming too high.

Since I had obviously parked my car in the middle of alpha-male central, I felt it best to present this greased Neanderthal with my very best impersonation of a male. I exited my car. I tried to calm my heart palpitations by reciting my man-mantra: "manly-man, manly-man, manly-man." As I closed my car door, the mechanic squinted his eyes and stepped over to my car.

He told me that he was on his break and explained to me that every goddamned time he went on break, some asshole would pull up whining about his car. With that greeting, it was established that he, not I, was the alpha-male.

I apologized for interrupting him and asked if he would like me to come back later. He told me that he'd take his break later and went on to explain that the "asshole" in his introduction wasn't me and that he was just talking about assholes in general. I gave him a nervous tic, and he asked me, "Just what the hell's your problem anyway?" I explained that my car's automatic transmission wasn't shifting properly. After checking the transmission fluid, he shook his head and laughed at me. It was clear then that I was trapped in some type of dominance ritual males are apparently expected to engage in.

The mechanic told me to walk to the front of my car. An icy panic settled into the pit of my stomach. I told myself to make sure that I walked with the same swagger the mechanic displayed when he approached my car. "That's it. Take big steps. Big steps ... No! OMG! What are you doing?!? Are you trying to show off your swishy hips?!? Big steps ... That's right. Walk like you've just crapped your pants. Yep, that looks real good." While I was feeling fairly confident about my approach at the time, the mechanic almost dropped the dipstick he was holding as he watched my machismo in action.

He told me that the transmission fluid was low and that I needed to put some in. I desperately scanned the engine looking for a cap or sticker that read, **"PUT TRANSMISSION FLUID HERE"** but there was nothing like that to be found. Since he obviously knew, I asked him where I needed to put the fluid. He looked at me as if I had politely asked him to wear my underwear on his head.

"How much are you gonna pay me to show you?" he asked. As he looked me up and down, he added, "I've got a wife and kids to feed." Why was he telling me about his family issues? Did he expect me to express some sympathy for his plight? Was he attempting to show me how virile he was? I told him that I had about a dollar-fifty in cash when he slapped my back—hard—and began to laugh. Did I miss something? Apparently, we had somehow bonded since he'd suddenly seemed happy to show me where and how to put the transmission fluid into my car.

About six months later, I returned to the same garage to put some air into my tires. By then, I had transitioned. The same mechanic was on duty as I pulled up and instead of grimacing at me, he stopped what he was doing and bounded across the parking lot in the direction of my car. As I got out to walk towards the air-hose, he instructed me to get back into the car while he volunteered to check each tire and top them off. He also asked me if I wanted him to check the fluids under the hood. After he was done, I asked him how much I owed him. "Nuttin …" he said, "but a smile." He flashed a head full of mangled teeth at me. I couldn't help but notice that a bottom tooth resembled the dirty end of the spark plug he was fidgeting with. I automatically frowned, and he stopped showing me his tooth. It occurred to me that I'd perhaps broken some sort of rule; his disappointment was written all over his face. Worse, the disappointment was quickly becoming a display of offended neutrality. I realized that I'd just been classified and filed away under the *bitch* category in his brain. I tipped him five bucks, thanked him for his help and drove off watching him in my rearview mirror look from the back of my head to the tip in his hand.

L. LAMAR
WILSON

Times Like These: Marianna, Florida

One woe is past; &, behold, there come two woes more hereafter.

   – Revelation 9:12

In one field, husks, muscadine vines & a sugarcane graveyard furrow acres aching for the devil to beat his wife. In another, a skein of maggots & mayflies, musk thick & resolute, jockey for the cow's afterbirth. Down Old U.S. Road, weevils wheeze & chafed bales of hay settle for the wind's sneezes. *Wait for a sign*, the couple says & sets their table with damask, fresh-pressed for a feast of sardines & cornbread. Train their child in the way he should babble. From dusk till dusk, they lull the boy with tales of a faraway sea, buckets of oysters to shuck. *OurFatherwhichartinheavenhallowedbethynamethykingdomcomethy willbedoneonearthasitisinheaven*. Still no rain. From dusk till dusk, they till dust. They reach for the locks of hair & black-eyed peas, stowed away for times like these.

Resurrection Sunday

A man holds his penis in his mouth.
Sprawled on a cheap sofa like the one
that holds my bare backside, he stares blankly

through the lens at the director for his cues,
through me reaching for his gaze. I'm twentysomething
& home alone. I'm so there. I'm so not there

or here alone. See the boy in overalls: cross-legged
& wedged in the corner between two walls
of books. He stares as Claude Neal's limp tongue

holds his own limpness on the fading page
of one dusty tome, Claude's sockets fixed
on some constellation the boy wishes

he could decipher. Claude's body—chiseled
& mangled—hangs in an oak by a rope. There is nothing
in this body we can desire, & we want.

We want a body, not mangled like ours,
we can love without shame. The boy feels
so small in his body, its scars that beckon

stares & gasps. I am he, doubled in size
& solemnity. I churn. I am an ocean
of want. This video's hustler must do.

His left pec brandishes a lion's paw
& skull-&-bones. A broken heart heaves outside
his right. With each kiss, our heads swell.

He'll make $250 for this trick, $150 more
than he'd earn trading others in parked cars
on a street corner where no trees will grow,

all these miles from us. This director promises
he's stardust, has the blow to get him to the edge
& may actually finish him. He tells him,

tells me, what to do next, moans *Big.*
Black. Cock. I obey. I swell more still
& remember I should be studying

what Nietzsche says God isn't. I am
at a black university. God always
enters the classroom here,

& my professor, a newly converted
agnostic, will prove her theories. But
this video's lessons will pay off sooner

& take me & this boy closer than when
he stared at Claude, hanging, in *The Anatomy*
of a Lynching on that long ride home from the library,

squinting but unable to see Claude's pupils, see
if peace eclipsed terror before he died. *Child,*
they came from everywhere & all you could do was pray

you weren't the nigger they picked for the picnic
on the courthouse lawn, our grandmother says.
In the picture, Claude is alone, but as she speaks,

kids blur into the sepia background, ape
the grins on their parents' faces, await
their turn to prod his charred flesh.

The boy asks if Claude was a good student
like him, if she was the one who would not give
the NAACP her name when 50-cent postcards,

news of Claude's fingers & toes for sale
reached stands. *I told that boy to leave*
that white gal alone: the only words

breaking the silence of the rest of that ride,
the only words her brother says at home.
I told that boy to leave that white gal alone:

their script a shroud over faces suddenly
childlike, each crease around their eyes
a dog-eared page the boy can never read.

The boy wants to ask where the family
of Lola, Claude's slain lover, lives, where
his pickled prick must collect dust

on some shelf. He wants to say *I want
to study it.* He wants to see how he'd hang,
loosed to rove in a bottle. But he is a boy.

He does not know how to speak
the unspeakable yet. I
heave. It is almost dawn now.

The courthouse towers there,
in the center of that town, & that oak,
mostly limbless, looms.   Still.

Soon, its flaccid branches will shade
more brown boys, guilty or not, waiting
to learn what their next move will be. It's hard

to get anywhere without passing it, passing them,
bowed, not meeting our gaze. The hustler moans.
I gasp. I cannot take this boy, this fallen porn star

or his unseen master's plan where I'm bound.
I turn off the TV. I am not afraid to raise
this dead flesh, for all & no one to see, alone,

like that other hanged man the boy followed
so slavishly, to ask him what no man,
not even Daddy, can show me: Jesus,

if a man is black & his manhood is forced
into his own mouth by another man
who's as afraid of the power he holds

but is pale enough to hold the camera
or the noose, how much of a man isn't he?
Like you, O Lord, I rise with all power

in my hand, but I do not want to cross
this tempest alone. I am not that boy
anymore. I am not afraid to say

I am a man, searching for a man
whose flesh will rise, only for me,
without force, without fear. Come,

lie with me & be redeemed. See
my yoke, this flesh, broken
for you? Find here

a different kind of holy, a sacrilegion,
a sacrament for our sanctifunked
souls. Dark & darker.　　　Still.

Substantia Nigra

I pay a man to touch me now. In halogen he comes
to give what no other has. He bows at my bidding. He knows

where the burning leads, back to that thatched box, Florida,
one Saturday morn, not unlike the one that breached me

into song, to prayer without surcease, soundtracked by
that substantia nigra, that alluvial wealth whose terror deepens

with time welled in a phallic home of too many branches
of water & not enough swamps, home of broken

Spanish, moss, broken ballot boxes submerged
in swamps & locked in church halls, license to shoot

anything you fear or hate or fathom you own, if
you're light enough. It's the law of this No Man's Land,

licked dry by an unhinged ex-lover. Some call him Sun.
I call him enemy now. Now, I like it dark. I ran across

the border to clay, said here, take & eat, damned God
for a bald, shiny head. Repent. Repeat. Said he'll do

till you come home. Said he hawks black art. I won't
be a hard sell. Just need a devotional ohm for my

objectification. He'll sit through my musings,
then surprise me with his intellect, punctuating

my sentences with his lisp. He'll savor my run-
on monologues. His genteel tongue will glide over

my fears. I'll swallow his sincerity. I'll pass it on.
He touched me & made me new that Saturday morn

I could not wait for you. I pay this soothsayer now
to quiet my Cerberus, anoint my fearsome heads with oil.

I moan to silence his snarls, hum him to sleep. Ah,
this gray-scale world. Intractable. Tartarus for perpetuity. O

Florida, O Panhandle, you penal colony, you haven
of anonymous alms & arms, welcomed in pitch, home

of the men who made me wish for the womb that made me
& the ones who made me wish I had one, had the heft

to bear the weight of this needling head, this water breaking,
this grazing with the ones who gaze East daily for the first,

the man who will never be the only one, whose pining primes
our quest. I pay my medicine man, that doubting Thomas,

that one with archangel name & face, to limn what keeps us alive
& welled but not spilling, not black or white or blue enough.

These wise men say I must tell you here, again & always,
I'm sick, I'm saved by their hands. Otherwise, other men

will lock me in a steel box. A man, a white one, did once.
T'was dark in there. I escaped doing what he forebade.

Screamed *I am a man, I am* ... I refuse his bitter pills. Still.
O Doctor Jesus, part this endless sea of doctors, of men's sin-

sick vision of these scars. O mirror of my mind, here, now &
forevermore, I am not pocked. These marks, not beast stings.

These broken bones are broken bones, do not portend or pretend.
Black men not mannish among black men know how to be solvent,

Sister, Sugar, Mama, Chula, Rahab, saint, wring the taint out, where
to tuck the bleach, how to cover blotches, slice edges, cinch waste

in translucent bags. I left mine on Mama & Daddy's front porch.
The dust mites won't touch it. The might-bes can't. Ah,

I've lied. I never left you, Marianna. I am that boy, that man
in this mirror, more than enough to touch what no man can. I am

that woe man, too. I ring an other. In halogen he comes. We sing
Negro spirituals. It's a black woe man thing. *I told Jesus, be all right*

if he changed my name. Too many deaths, too infinitesimal to many,
though I'll never stop counting. Tonight, I take this ringed man.

He leaves me wanting you wanting me. Who knows the way
to Canaan? Got my ticket in my hand. I ain't got time to die.

"**Resurrection Sunday**": According to James R. McGovern's account of Claude Neal's murder in his 1982 book, *Anatomy of a Lynching*, on October 19, 1934, Neal, 23, an illiterate black man, was arrested for the murder of Lola Cannady, 20, a white fellow resident of Greenwood, Florida, who was his childhood playmate and presumed lover. Neal was coerced into marking his X on a confession letter after his mother's and aunt's joint arrest. He was taken to jails in nearby towns, reportedly to protect him. But, on October 26, a lynch mob that included Cannady's kindred (and allegedly members of Jackson County law enforcement) was allowed to take him from the Brewton, Alabama, jail back to Greenwood, where he was tortured for half a day, forced to eat his penis and testicles, and further mutilated to the point of death. What was left of Neal was dragged several dozen miles to the Jackson County Courthouse in Marianna, Florida. Along the way, his body was shot, stabbed, and run over. Having read about what was to transpire in newspapers far and wide, including in *The New York Times*, several thousand men, women, and children from across the country gathered for what was called a "picnic," whites' code name for "picking a nigger" to lynch. Fingers, toes, and pictures of Neal's mutilated body were sold for sport. Neal's corpse was left for a spectacle until the morning after his torture, a Saturday, when his body was cut down from a tree that remains in the town square today. Blacks were infuriated by what had occurred and fought back until Governor David Sholtz called in the National Guard to suppress what was deemed a "riot." No one was or has been arrested for Neal's brutal murder.

The **substantia nigra** is the largest nucleus in the midbrain and is an important player in its function, in particular, in eye movement, motor planning, reward-seeking, learning, and addiction.

CONTRIBUTOR
BIOGRAPHIES

Dorothy Allison is the bestselling author of several novels including *Bastard Out of Carolina*, *Cavedweller*, and *Two Or Three Things I Know For Sure*. The recipient of numerous awards, she has been the subject of many profiles and a short documentary film of her life, *Two or Three Things but Nothing For Sure*.

Shane Allison has had poems published in *New Delta Review*, *Mississippi Review*, *Spork*, *West Wind Review*, and many others. He edits gay erotic anthologies for Cleis Press. His debut poetry collection, *Slut Machine*, is out from Rebel Satori Press, and his poem/memoir, *I Remember*, is out from Future Tense. His debut novel, *You're The One That I Want*, is forthcoming from Simon and Schuster.

John Andrews' work has appeared in *Columbia Poetry Review*, *Short Fast and Deadly*, *Eunoia*, and others. He holds an M.F.A. from Texas State University where he served as managing editor of *Front Porch Journal*. He is currently working on his Ph.D. in English at Oklahoma State University.

Derrick Austin is an M.F.A. candidate in poetry at the University of Michigan. His work has appeared or is forthcoming in *Image: A Journal of Arts and Religion*, *New England Review*, *Crab Orchard Review*, *Memorious*, *Unsplendid*, and other journals.

Jeffery Berg grew up in Six Mile, South Carolina, and Lynchburg, Virginia. He received an M.F.A. from New York University. His poems have appeared in *Court Green*, *The Gay & Lesbian Review*, *Map Literary*, *Assaracus*, and *Harpur Palate*. He has written reviews for *The Poetry Project Newsletter* and *Lambda Literary*. A Virginia Center of the Creative Arts fellow, Jeffery lives in New York and blogs at jdbrecords.blogspot.com.

Richard Blanco was chosen as the fifth U.S. inaugural poet in 2013. He is the author of three collections of poems, including *Directions to the Beach of the Dead* (University of Arizona Press, 2005), winner of the PEN / American Beyond Margins Award, and *Looking for The Gulf Motel* (University of Pittsburgh Press, 2012), winner of the Paterson Prize. His poems have appeared in numerous publications, including *Best American Prose Poems* and *Ploughshares*. Blanco continues to write and perform for audiences worldwide.

Perry Brass, from Savannah, Georgia, has published 18 books. He has been a Lambda-Literary-Award finalist six times, a finalist for the Ferro-Grumley Fiction Award, has won four "Ippy" Awards, and has appeared in 30 anthologies of poetry, fiction, and essays. He has been involved in the LGBT movement since 1969, when he co-edited *Come Out!*, the world's first gay liberation newspaper. In 1972, he co-founded the Gay Men's Health Project Clinic, the first clinic for gay men on the East Coast, which is still operating as New York's Callen-Lorde Clinic. perrybrass.com

Dustin Brookshire is an activist, poet, and Dolly Parton fanatic enjoying life in Atlanta, Georgia. His poetry has earned him a Pushcart Prize nomination and has been published or is forthcoming in *SubtleTea, Ocho, Oranges & Sardines, Ouroboros, Qarrtsiluni, Whiskey Island, Blue Fifth Review, Shape of a Box, Assaracus,* and other publications. He has been anthologized in *Divining Divas: 100 Gay Men on their Muses* (Lethe Press, 2012). Dustin's debut chapbook is titled *To The One Who Raped Me* (Sibling Rivalry Press, 2012). He is currently working on finishing his first full-length poetry collection.

Jericho Brown is the recipient of fellowships from the Radcliffe Institute for Advanced Study at Harvard University and the National Endowment for the Arts. His poems have appeared or are forthcoming in journals and anthologies including *Callaloo, The Nation, The New Yorker, Oxford American, The New Republic, 100 Best African American Poems, Ascent of Angles,* and *The Best American Poetry*. His first book, *Please* (New Issues, 2008), won the American Book Award, and his second book, *The New Testament*, is forthcoming from Copper Canyon Press. Brown is currently an Assistant Professor at Emory University.

Joey Connelly earned his M.F.A. from Ashland University in 2010. He is Assistant Professor of English at Kentucky Wesleyan College. His poetry has appeared in *Louisville Review, PANK, Splinter Generation, New Plains Review, St. Sebastian Review, Southern Humanities Review,* and other publications.

Will Cordeiro is completing his Ph.D. in English from Cornell University. Currently, he teaches at Pima Community College and The University of Arizona Poetry Center in Tucson, Arizona. He has recent or forthcoming work in publications such as *Copper Nickel, Crab Orchard Review, Drunken Boat, Fourteen Hills, Phoebe, Sentence,* and *South Dakota Review*.

C. Cleo Creech is a farm-raised Southerner of old Scotch-Irish stock. His family raised tobacco in North Carolina before it was even a state. They founded a few churches, thumped a lot of Bibles, but probably kept a few white hoods in the closet as well. Somewhere along the line, Cleo "turned funny." Maybe it was all that 60's TV or maybe the farm-chemicals his dad sold in the family's local feed-n-seed. Cleo is now living in exile in Atlanta, working as a marketing project manager and writing poetry and such. He lives with his soon-to-be husband and live-in therapist, Michael. Cleo's work has been in many journals and anthologies; he's edited several art book/poetry anthologies; and he's even had a piece turned into a major choral work.

James M. Croteau lives in Kalamazoo, Michigan, with his partner of 28 years. He is a professor of Counseling Psychology at Western Michigan University. In the last few years, he has become a poet. He has had poems published in *New Verse News*, *Hoot: a Postcard review of {mini} poetry and prose*, and *Right Hand Pointing*. A series of his poems appears in the July 2014 *Assaracus: A Journal of Gay Poetry*. He blogs sometimes at talkingdogsholymen.blogspot.com.

J.K. Daniels's poems have appeared or are forthcoming in *Best New Poets, 2011*(UVA Press, 2011); *Beltway Poetry Quarterly*; *Calyx*; *ILK*; *New Orleans Review* online; and others. She holds an M.A. in Literature and an M.F.A. in Creative Writing-Poetry from George Mason University, where she edited *So to Speak: a feminist journal of language and art*. She teaches creative writing and American literature at Northern Virginia Community College and reads for *The Northern Virginia Review*.

Nicholas Dephtereos has contributed to the *Watertown Daily Times* and *Artemis* literary journal. Originally from Upstate New York, he earned his B.F.A. in writing from Savannah College of Art and Design in May 2013. He has lived in Savannah, Georgia, for four years.

David Eye earned a midlife M.F.A. from Syracuse University in 2008. His poems have appeared or are forthcoming in *Bloom*, *Cider Press Review*, *Consequence Magazine*, *Lambda Literary*, *The Louisville Review*, *Puerto del Sol*, *Stone Canoe*, and other journals and anthologies. He has taught at Syracuse University, St. John's University, Manhattan College, and (currently) Cazenovia College. His chapbook, *Rain Leaping Up When a Cab Goes Past*, was released in 2013 by Seven Kitchens Press.

Jason K. Friedman is the author of *Fire Year* (Sarabande, 2013), a collection of stories, and the children's books *Phantom Trucker* and *Haunted Houses*. He earned a B.A. from Yale and an M.A. from the Johns Hopkins Writing Seminars. His work has appeared in *The New York Times, Best American Gay Fiction*, and the cultural-studies reader *Goth*. He lives in San Francisco with his husband, filmmaker Jeffrey Friedman.

D. Gilson is a Ph.D. student in American Literature & Culture at The George Washington University. His work has appeared in *Beloit Poetry Journal, The Indiana Review,* and *The Rumpus*. D. is the author of two chapbooks—*Catch & Release* (Seven Kitchens, 2012), winner of the Robin Becker Prize, and *Brit Lit* (Sibling Rivalry Press, 2013)—and the book *Crush* (Punctum Books, 2014), with Will Stockton. Find D. at dgilson.com.

Ellen Goldstein was born in Charlottesville, Virginia. Her work has appeared in journals such as *Poetry Southeast, StorySouth, Measure, The Common,* and *Post Road;* and in the anthologies *Rough Places Plain: Poems for Mountains* (Salt Marsh Pottery Press, 2005), *Not Quite What I Was Planning* (HarperCollins, 2006), *Letters to the World* (Red Hen Press, 2008), and *Bloomsbury Anthology of Contemporary Jewish American Poetry* (Bloomsbury, 2013).

Miriam Bird Greenberg is the author of two eerie chapbooks: *All night in the new country* (Sixteen Rivers Press, 2013) and *Pact-Blood, Fever Grass* (Ricochet Editions, 2014). She's held fellowships from the Provincetown Fine Arts Work Center, the Poetry Foundation, the NEA, and was a Wallace Stegner Fellow in Poetry yet still cannot raise the dead.

Elizabeth Gross landed again, on her feet this time, in New Orleans. Her dreams are still peopled by friends in New York, though, and she left part of her spine in Prague. Her poems have recently appeared in *Tuba, LEVELER, Painted Bride Quarterly, B O D Y,* and the anthology *This assignment is so gay: LGBTIQ Poets On the Art of Teaching*. She currently teaches literature and writing for Bard Early College in New Orleans.

Johnathan Harper was born and raised in Oklahoma City before moving to Myrtle Beach, South Carolina, where he studied poetry under Daniel Albergotti for a year. He now lives in Syracuse, New York, and plans on enrolling the university's M.F.A. program next year.

Scott Hightower is the award-winning author of four books of poetry and *Hontanares,* a bi-lingual (Spanish-English) collection (Devenir, Madrid, 2012). In 2008, Hightower's work garnered a prestigious Barnstone Translation Prize. He is a reviewer for *Fogged Clarity,* a contributing editor to *The Journal,* and the editor of the bi-lingual anthology *Women Rowing: Mujeres A Los Remos* (Mantis Editores, 2012). Hightower, a native of central Texas, lives and works in New York and sojourns in Spain.

Matthew Hittinger is the author of two poetry collections, *Skin Shift* (Sibling Rivalry Press, 2012) and *The Erotic Postulate* (Sibling Rivalry Press, 2014), and three chapbooks, *Platos de Sal* (Seven Kitchens Press, 2009), *Narcissus Resists* (GOSS183, 2009), and *Pear Slip* (Spire Press, 2007). He holds an M.F.A. from The University of Michigan where he won a Hopwood Award for Poetry. Matthew lives and works in New York City. Visit him at matthewhittinger.com.

Darrel Alejandro Holnes is one of the authors of *PRIME* (Sibling Rivalry Press, 2014), a collection of poems and conversations with members of The Phantastique 5, introduced by Jericho Brown. His poems have been featured in *Lambda Literary, The Caribbean Writer, Phantom Limb, Kweli, Callaloo, The Paris American,* and elsewhere. He teaches creative writing at Rutgers University and now lives in New York, New York. Find him online.

Rex Leonowicz is an intersectional trans poet from Queens, New York. His work can be found in *Gertrude Journal, Shampoo, Them: A Trans Literary Journal,* the Lambda Literary Foundation's *Poetry Spotlight, Dude Magazine,* and *Testimony: a Multimedia Exhibit of LGBTQ Art and Writing,* among others. He lives and works in Oakland, California.

Sassafras Lowrey is the editor of the two-time American Library Association honored & Lambda Literary Finalist *Kicked Out* anthology (Homofactus Press, 2010) and *Leather Ever After* (Ravenous Romance, 2013). Hir debut novel *Roving Pack* (PoMo Freakshow, 2012) was honored by the American Library Association. Sassafras is the 2013 winner of the Lambda Literary Foundation's Berzon Emerging Writer Award. Ze lives and writes in Brooklyn with hir partner, two dogs of dramatically different sizes, two bossy cats, and a kitten. sassafraslowrey.com

Tyler Lynn is in the process of publishing a memoir entitled *There's No Road Map for this Journey,* which chronicles his life as a transgender child in the South. His essay, "Scars," was published in the literary journal *Saltwater Quarterly.* He holds a B.A. from Sarah Lawrence College, where he was a contributing writer to the school newspaper *The Phoenix* and led writing workshops in nearby Valhalla State Prison. He is now in medical school.

Bo McGuire hails from Hokes Bluff, Alabama. He watches people talking on the phone and studies Dolly Parton. He writes poems and hammers out motion pictures, and is currently studying in NYU's graduate film program, where he was selected by Spike Lee to receive The Sandra Ifraimova Production Award for *Shitbird*, a serialized drama he is writing and developing for television.

Rangi McNeil is author of *The Missing* (The Sheep Meadow Press, 2003), a poetry collection. An Emerge-Surface-Be Fellow at The Poetry Project at St. Marks Church, he holds an M.F.A. from Columbia University School of the Arts and teaches at Borough of Manhattan Community College.

Kelly McQuain is the author of *Velvet Rodeo* (Bloom Books, 2014), winner of *BLOOM*'s chapbook poetry prize. His most recent work can be found in *Painted Bride Quarterly*, *Kestrel*, *The Pinch*, *Assaracus* and the anthologies *Drawn to Marvel: Poems from the Comic Books* (Minor Arcana, 2014) and *Between: New Gay Poetry* (Chelsea Station Editions, 2013). His short stories have appeared in *The Harrington Gay Men's Fiction Quarterly* and numerous anthologies. His book reviews and writing on city life have appeared in *The Philadelphia Inquirer*. Learn more at kellymcquain.wordpress.com.

M. Mack is a genderqueer poet and editor in Virginia. Ze holds an M.F.A. from George Mason University and is former managing editor of *So to Speak: a feminist journal of language and art*. Mack's work has appeared recently in *Adrienne*, *APARTMENT Poetry Quarterly*, *Gargoyle*, *Wicked Alice*, and elsewhere. Ze is founding co-editor of Gazing Grain Press, an explicitly inclusive feminist chapbook press.

Ed Madden is the author of three books of poetry: *Signals* (University of South Carolina Press, 2008), *Prodigal: Variations* (Lethe, 2011), and *Nest* (Salmon, 2014). His poems also appear in *Best New Poets 2007* (University of Virginia, 2007), *The Book of Irish American Poetry* (Notre Dame, 2007), and elsewhere. Born and raised in rural Arkansas, Madden is an associate professor of English at the University of South Carolina.

Jeff Mann's most recent books include the poetry collections *Ash: Poems from Norse Mythology* (Rebel Satori Press, 2011) and *A Romantic Mann* (Lethe Press, 2013); an essay collection, *Binding the God: Ursine Essays from the Mountain South* (Bear Bones Books, 2010); and three novels, *Fog: A Novel of Desire and Reprisal* (Bear Bones Books, 2011), *Purgatory: A Novel of the Civil War* (Bear Bones Books, 2012), and *Cub* (Bear Bones Books, 2014). He teaches creative writing at Virginia Tech.

Randall Mann is the author of three poetry collections, most recently *Straight Razor* (Persea Books, 2013). He lives in San Francisco.

Mary Meriam is the editor of *Lavender Review*. Her poems, essays, reviews, and interviews have appeared in *Literary Imagination, The New York Times, Ms. Magazine, The Gay & Lesbian Review, American Life in Poetry,* and ten anthologies, including *Vincent Van Go-Gogh: A Collection of Art and Writing* (Writers Among Artists, 2013). She is the author of *Conjuring My Leafy Muse* (Headmistress Press, 2013) and the editor of *Irresistible Sonnets* (Headmistress Press, 2014).

Stephen S. Mills is the author of the Lambda-Award-winning book *He Do the Gay Man in Different Voices* (Sibling Rivalry Press, 2012). His work has appeared in *The Antioch Review, PANK, The New York Quarterly, The Los Angeles Review, Knockout, Assaracus, The Rumpus,* and others. He is also the winner of the 2008 Gival Press Oscar Wilde Poetry Award. His second poetry collection, *A History of the Unmarried*, is available from Sibling Rivalry Press. He lives in New York City. stephensmills.com

Cameron L. Mitchell grew up in a small town in the mountains of North Carolina. He earned a B.A. in Journalism at the University of North Carolina at Chapel Hill and has been published in various literary magazines and anthologies. He currently resides in New York City, where he works at Columbia University's medical school library. Find him on Twitter: @CameronLMitchel

Foster Noone is a student and queer community organizer from Pelham, Alabama. Ze will be starting at Tulane University in the fall of 2014. "Fostering" is hir first published work.

Joseph Osmundson is a writer, educator, and scientist based in New York City. His writing has appeared in *The Rumpus*, on Gawker.com, and in *The Feminist Wire*, where he is an Associate Editor. He completed graduate studies in Molecular Biophysics at The Rockefeller University and is currently a post-doctoral fellow at New York University. Follow him on Twitter at @reluctantlyjoe.

Eddie Outlaw is a Mississippi native and lives in Jackson, Mississippi, where he and his husband own William Wallace Salon and Fondren Barber Shop. The couple are the subjects of "A Mississippi Love Story," a documentary short produced by Fisher Productions. Eddie is a columnist for *Jackson Free Press* and blogs about being gay in the South.

Seth Pennington publishes Sibling Rivalry Press with his husband, Bryan Borland, from their home in Little Rock, Arkansas. Recent work has appeared in the anthology *Out of Sequence: The Sonnets Remixed* (Parlor Press, 2014), *The Toadsuck Review*, *The Good Men Project*, and *Wingbeats II: Exercises and Practice in Poetry* (Dos Gatos Press, 2014). sethpennington.tumblr.com

Evan J. Peterson is author of *Skin Job* (Minor Arcana Press, 2012) and *The Midnight Channel* (Babel/Salvage Press, 2013) and volume editor of *Gay City 5: Ghosts in Gaslight, Monsters in Steam* (Gay City Health Project, 2013). His poetry, fiction, journalism, and criticism have appeared in *Weird Tales*, *The Stranger*, *The Rumpus*, *Assaracus*, *Nailed*, *Court Green*, and *Aim for the Head: An Anthology of Zombie Poetry*, from which his poetry was excerpted in *The New York Times*. evanjpeterson.com.

Kenneth Pobo has a new book of poems forthcoming from Blue Light Press called *Bend Of Quiet*. In 2013 Eastern Point Press published a chapbook of his poetry called *Placemats*. His work has appeared in: *Indiana Review*, *Nimrod*, *Mudfish*, *Hawaii Review*, and elsewhere. He teaches creative writing and English at Widener University.

Brad Richard is author of *Habitations* (Portals Press, 2000); *Motion Studies* (The Word Works, 2011), winner of the 2010 Washington Prize and finalist for the Publishing Triangle's Thom Gunn Poetry Award; and *Butcher's Sugar* (Sibling Rivalry Press, 2012). Winner of the 2002 Poets & Writers, Inc., Writers Exchange Award in poetry and recipient of fellowships from the Surdna Foundation and the Louisiana Division of the Arts, he chairs the creative writing program at Lusher Charter School in New Orleans.

Hannah Riddle is a native of North Carolina and a graduate of the Creative Writing program at UNC-Chapel Hill. She is the recipient of the Suzanne Bolch prize and the Ann Williams Burrus/Academy of American Poets prize. Her poems have appeared in *Cellar Door* and *Inch*.

Laurence Ross received his M.F.A. from the University of Alabama, where he served as the Creative Nonfiction Editor for *Black Warrior Review*. In addition to publishing his writing in literary journals and the *Huffington Post*, he is a frequent contributor to *Pelican Bomb*, a regional publication dedicated to the Louisiana arts community. Laurence Ross lives in New

Orleans, where he is at work on a book-length project concerning the lives and deaths of our cultural spectacles/specters.

Liana Roux teaches high school English in North Carolina. She has a B.A. in English and anthropology and an M.A.T. from UNC-Chapel Hill, where she received the Blanche Armfield Prize for Poetry. Her work has appeared in *Cellar Door*.

Kevin Sessums is Editor-in-Chief of *FourTwoNine* magazine and the Editorial Director of dot429.com. He has served as executive editor of *Interview* and as a contributing editor of *Vanity Fair*, *Allure*, and *Parade*. His work has also appeared in *Travel+Leisure*, *Elle*, *Out*, *Marie Claire*, and *Playboy*. A native of Forest, Mississippi, he is author of *Mississippi Sissy*, a *New York Times* bestseller and Lambda Literary Award winner. Its sequel, *I Left It on the Mountain*, is forthcoming from St. Martin's Press.

Del Shores is a film director and producer, television writer and producer, playwright, and actor. He wrote and directed the film *Sordid Lives* in 1999. Eight years later, he produced 12 episodes of *Sordid Lives: The Series* for the LGBT-interest cable channel Logo. Other credits include his play and film *Southern Baptist Sissies* and *Blues for Willadean*, the film adaptation of his play *The Trials and Tribulations of a Trailer Trash Housewife*.

Erin Elizabeth Smith is the Creative Director at the Sundress Academy for the Arts and author of two full-length collections, *The Fear of Being Found* (Three Candles, 2008) and *The Naming of Strays* (Gold Wake, 2011). Her poems have appeared in numerous journals, including *Mid-American*, *32 Poems*, *Zone 3*, *Tusculum Review*, and *Crab Orchard*. She teaches in the English Department at the University of Tennessee and serves as the managing editor of Sundress Publications and *Stirring*.

Will Stockton is Associate Professor of English at Clemson University. With D. Gilson, he is the author of *Crush* (Punctum Books, 2014) and *Gay Boys Write Straight Porn* (Sibling Rivalry Press, 2014). His poems have appeared in journals including *Assaracus*, *Bloom*, *PANK*, and *Weave*.

Dan Stone is the author of *The Rest of Our Lives*, (Lethe Press, 2009), *Tricky Serum: An Elixir of Poems* (Lethe Press, 2011), and *Coming To: A Collection of Erotic and Other Epiphanies*, published under the pen name, Lukas Hand (Lethe Press, 2012). A two-time finalist for a Lambda Literary Award, Dan lives in Denver, Colorado, and can be reached via his website: firstadream.com.

Christine Stroud is originally from eastern North Carolina, but currently lives in Pittsburgh and works as the Associate Editor for Autumn House Press. She has an M.F.A. in Creative Writing from Chatham University. Her chapbook, *The Buried Return*, is being released by Finishing Line Press in March of 2014. For more information: christinestroud.com.

Billie R. Tadros is the author of a chapbook, *Containers* (Dancing Girl Press, 2014). She is a doctoral student in English at the University of Louisiana at Lafayette and a graduate of the M.F.A. program in Poetry at Sarah Lawrence College.

TC Tolbert is a genderqueer, feminist poet and teacher. S/he is Assistant Director of Casa Libre, faculty in the low residency MFA program at OSU-Cascades, and adjunct faculty at University of Arizona. S/he spends his summers leading wilderness trips for Outward Bound. S/he is the author of the poetry collections *Gephyromania*, *I: Not He: Not I*, *spirare*, and *territories of folding*. S/he is co-editor, along with Tim Trace Peterson, of *Troubling the Line: Trans and Genderqueer Poetry and Poetics*. Gloria Anzaldúa said, *Voyager, there are no bridges, one builds them as one walks*. John Cage said, *it's lighter than you think*. tctolbert.com.

Dan Vera is the author of *Speaking Wiri Wiri* (Red Hen, 2013), inaugural winner of the Letras Latinas/Red Hen Poetry Prize, and *The Space Between Our Danger and Delight* (Beothuk Books, 2008). His poetry appears in various journals and anthologies. LatinoStories.com named him a 2014 Top Ten "New" Latino Author to Watch (and Read). He lives in Washington, D.C., where he edits the gay culture journal *White Crane* and chairs the board of Split This Rock Poetry. More at danvera.com.

Annie Virginia is a Southern runaway with her B.A. from Sarah Lawrence College. Her intention is to spend the next year or two teaching, roaming the wilderness, or writing a book before moving onto graduate school for an M.F.A. in poetry. Her work may be found in *The Dead Mule School of Southern Literature*, *The Literary Bohemian*, *The Sarah Lawrence Review*, and *Broad!* magazine.

Valerie Wetlaufer is the author of *Mysterious Acts by My People* (Sibling Rivalry Press, 2014) and editor of *Adrienne: A Poetry Journal of Queer Women*. She is also the author of three chapbooks. A Lambda Literary Fellow, she holds a Ph.D. from the University of Utah, an M.F.A. from Florida State University, and an M.A. in Teaching from Bennington College. Valerie lives in Iowa. Visit her at valeriewetlaufer.com.

C.T. Whitley is the co-editor of *Trans-Kin: A Guide for Family and Friends of Transgender People* (Boulder Press, 2013), which won a 2013 International Book Award. His work has also been featured in such publications as *Manning Up* (Transgress Press, 2014), *Letters for My Brothers* (Wilgefortis Press, 2011), and *Gender Outlaws* (Seal Press, 2010). He holds an M.A. from Michigan State University and is working on completing a Ph.D. in Sociology. Visit him at ctwhitley.com.

Scott Wiggerman is the author of two poetry books, *Presence* (Pecan Grove, 2011) and *Vegetables and Other Relationships* (Plain View, 2000), and the editor of several volumes, including the best-selling *Wingbeats: Exercises & Practice in Poetry* (Dos Gatos, 2011). With three Pushcart nominations, he is chief editor for Dos Gatos Press in Austin, Texas, publisher of the *Texas Poetry Calendar*. Recent gay publications include *Wilde Magazine, Floating Bridge Review, Off the Rocks* and the anthologies *This assignment is so gay* (Sibling Rivalry Press, 2013), *Between: New Gay Poetry* (Chelsea Station, 2013), and *Among the Leaves* (Squares & Rebels, 2012).

Cristan Williams is a trans historian and trans advocate. She founded the Houston Transgender Archive and pioneered trans homeless, affordable health care, and HIV services for trans people. Cristan is the editor of the social justice site TransAdvocate.com.

L. Lamar Wilson is author of *Sacrilegion* (2013), Lee Ann Brown's selection for the Carolina Wren Press Poetry Series and a Thom Gunn Award for Gay Poetry finalist, and *Prime* (Sibling Rivalry Press, 2014), a collection of poems and interviews with the Phantasique Five. Wilson, a Cave Canem and *Callaloo* Fellow, holds an M.F.A. from Virginia Polytechnic Institute and State University and is a completing a doctorate in African American and multiethnic American poetics at the University of North Carolina at Chapel Hill.

PUBLICATION ACKNOWLEDGMENTS

This project began in the summer of 2012 around July 4th, and it's drawing to a close near July 4th two years later. Each time I read through these poems and essays, I learn something new about the queer experience in the region of the country I've lived my entire life. That's the beauty of an anthology, which summons an abundance of voices: the variety of perspectives offer insight into a still(ish) point. Those perspectives invite even those of us who feel so close to something to see with empathetic eyes as we experience others' language. Put simply, these 63 authors deserve thanks not just for contributing something wonderful to this chorus of voices, they deserve thanks for clarifying how we can see and think about a place so rich, so fraught as the American South.

Long, sometimes tedious, sometimes frustrating projects are not usually successful without the person quarterbacking having a winning team with which to work and a supportive environment within which to work. I am fortunate to live and work at Indian Springs School, a place where I am valued as a member of the community and as a teacher-writer. I'd like to thank, especially, my colleague and fellow poet, Jessica Smith, for her support, conversation, and always spot-on insight. Furthermore, my students are the absolute best, and they were in many ways the inspiration for assembling this anthology. Among the authors here, one, Foster Noone, is a former student. Another former student, Seth Perlman, painstakingly read through this manuscript, making corrections, giving suggestions, and looking for consistency. To these two students, and also to my students in The Writers' Workshop over the past years and Queer Literature and Theory in Spring 2014, I am proud of you all and am pleased to have gotten to share the making of this book with you.

Sometimes the right publisher of a particular work seems obvious, and this is one of those projects. Sibling Rivalry Press has been perfect home for this book, and Bryan Borland and Seth Pennington have been great champions of this anthology from conception to execution, vision to revisions. It has been a pleasure to shepherd this book along with them. I am grateful for their confidence in me as an editor and curator; I am grateful for their love of great writers and great writing. Sibling Rivalry Press will continue to grow and impress, and I am thrilled to be a part of the family.

Finally, I'd like to thank my family and the many friends who have supported me throughout the crafting of this book: Aaron Alford, Laura Bishop, Sam Bonner, Michelle Chan Brown, Phillip Cezayirli, John Comforto, Emma Dinsmore, Matthew Hittinger, Charles Jensen, Ali Khan, Felix Kishinevsky, Sawyer Klein, Laura Kate Lindsay, Demi Lorant, Beth Mulvey, Will Nisbet, David Noone, Anna Olson, Gunnar Olson, Ankur Patel, Jessica Smith, Jack Sweeney, Gareth Vaughan, and Cameron Westbrook. I am grateful, and I am fortunate.

PUBLICATION
★CREDITS★

Dorothy Allison. "This Is Our World," first published in *Doubletake Magazine*. 1998. Reprinted by permission of the author.

Richard Blanco. "Abuelo in a Western," "Love as if Love," "Maybe," "Thicker Than Country," © 2012. First published in *Looking for the Gulf Motel*. Used by permission of the author and the University of Pittsburgh Press.

Richard Blanco. "Making a Man Out of Me," © Richard Blanco 2012. Used by permission of the author.

Jericho Brown. "Another Angel," and "Big, Fine," first published in *Weber*; "Fairy Tale," first published in *American Poetry Review*; "The Ten Commandments," first published in *New Madrid*; "On Daniel Minter's *High John the Conqueror*," first published in *The Journal*. Reprinted by permission of the author.

Matthew Hittinger. "The Light, the Idea of Light, Repeats Itself at South Beach," first published in *MiPOesias*, December 2008. Reprinted by permission of the author.

Ed Madden. "Among Men" and "Wrestling," first published in *Nest*. Salmon Poetry, 2014. Reprinted by permission of the author.

Randall Mann. "Complaint, Poolside," "The Shortened History of Florida," "South," "Social Life," "The End of Last Summer," first published in *Complaint in the Garden*. Zoo Press, 2004. Reprinted by permission of the author.

Laurence Ross. "A Partial Guide To Camp: How To Get Dry Again," first published in *Pelican Bomb*, October 5, 2012. Reprinted by permission of the author.

Kevin Sessums. "Skeeter Davis, Noël Coward, and Eudora Welty," first published in *Mississippi Sissy* © 2007 Kevin Sessums. Reprinted by permission of St. Martin's Press. All rights reserved.

Del Shores. "The Story Teller," from *Del Shores: My Sordid Lives*. Reprinted by permission of the author.

L. Lamar Wilson. "Times Like These: Marianna, Florida," "Resurrection Sunday," "Substantia Nigra," first published in *Sacrilegion*. Carolina Wren Press, 2013. Reprinted by permission of the author.

ABOUT THE
EDITOR

Douglas Ray was born in Jackson, Mississippi, in 1985. He is author of *He Will Laugh* (Lethe Press, 2012), a collection of poems. He received his B.A. in classics and English and M.F.A. in creative writing from The University of Mississippi, where he edited *The Yalobusha Review*. His poetry has appeared in *Assaracus, The Country Dog Review, Gertrude, The Iron Horse Literary Review*, as well as the anthologies *Divining Divas* and *This assignment is so gay*. His prose has been published in *The Advocate, Independent School Magazine, The Lambda Literary Review, The Los Angeles Review of Books,* and *The Gay and Lesbian Review Worldwide*. He has received fellowships from the Lambda Literary Foundation; the Squaw Valley Community of Writers; The University of Mississippi; and The Klingenstein Center, Teachers College, Columbia University. He is Poet-in-Residence and Instructor of Latin and English at Indian Springs School, an independent boarding and day school in Birmingham, Alabama.

sdouglasray.com

ABOUT THE
★PRESS★

Sibling Rivalry Press is an independent publishing house based in Little Rock, Arkansas. Our mission is to publish work that disturbs and enraptures. On behalf of SRP, Bryan Borland and Seth Pennington dedicate the publication of *The Queer South* to the memory of their respective grandmothers, Sally Lucille Borland and Nellie Mae Price, two women who were everything wonderful about the American South.

siblingrivalrypress.com

www.ingramcontent.com/pod-product-compliance
Lightning Source LLC
Chambersburg PA
CBHW031759220426
43662CB00007B/467